APAD

Association Euro-Africaine pour l'Anthropologie
du Changement Social et du Développement

Euro-African Association for the Anthropology of Social Change and Development

Inventer et mobiliser le local

Inventing and Mobilising the Local

Sten Hagberg (*ed.*)

• BULLETIN N°31-32

Décembre 2009

Cover photo: The School Saga 4, Niger, by Gabriella Körling

www.association-apad.org

Bibliographic information published by the Deutsche Nationalbibliothek
The Deutsche Nationalbibliothek lists this publication in the Deutsche Nationalbibliografie; detailed bibliographic data are available in the Internet at http://dnb.d-nb.de.

ISBN 978-3-643-10535-6

A catalogue record for this book is available from the British Library

Fresnostr. 2 D-48159 Münster
Tel. +49 (0) 2 51-620 320 Fax +49 (0) 2 51-922 60 99
e-Mail: lit@lit-verlag.de http://www.lit-verlag.de

Distribution:
In Germany: LIT Verlag Fresnostr. 2, D-48159 Münster
Tel. +49 (0) 2 51-620 32 22, Fax +49 (0) 2 51-922 60 99, e-Mail: vertrieb@lit-verlag.de

In Austria: Medienlogistik Pichler-ÖBZ GmbH & Co KG
IZ-NÖ, Süd, Straße 1, Objekt 34, A-2355 Wiener Neudorf
Tel. +43 (0) 22 36-63 53 52 90, Fax +43 (0) 22 36-63 53 52 43, e-Mail: mlo@medien-logistik.at

In Switzerland: B + M Buch- und Medienvertriebs AG
Hochstr. 357, CH-8200 Schaffhausen
Tel. +41 (0) 52-643 54 30, Fax +41 (0) 52-643 54 35, e-Mail: order@buch-medien.ch

In the UK by: Global Book Marketing, 99B Wallis Rd, London, E9 5LN
Phone: +44 (0) 20 8533 5800 – Fax: +44 (0) 1600 775 663
http://www.centralbooks.co.uk/html

In North America by:

Transaction Publishers
New Brunswick (U.S.A.) and London (U.K.)

Transaction Publishers
Rutgers University
35 Berrue Circle
Piscataway, NJ 08854

Phone: +1 (732) 445 - 2280
Fax: + 1 (732) 445 - 3138
for orders (U. S. only):
toll free (888) 999 - 6778
e-mail: orders@transactionpub.com

Bulletin N°31-32 – Décembre 2009

Sommaire/*contents*

Inventing and Mobilising the Local / Inventer et mobiliser le local

Sten Hagberg (ed.)

Editorial 1
Sten Hagberg

THEMES

Inventing and Mobilising the Local:
Decentralisation and Citizen Participation in West Africa 3
Sten Hagberg

De-Scaling without Democratic Substance:
Water Provisioning in Peripheral Kano, Nigeria 35
Gunilla Andrae

"They Have Left Us in a Hole":
Democratisation and Political Power in a West African Village 65
Lars Rudebeck

Foncier, pouvoirs locaux et décentralisation dans le département
de Dakoro (Niger) 105
Abdoulaye Mohamadou

The mobilization of the local in a public primary school in
peri-urban Niamey, Niger 137
Gabriella Körling

APAD KEY NOTE ADDRESS IN DECEMBER 2007 / CONFÉRENCE PLENIÈRE DE L'APAD EN DÉCEMBRE 2007

Anthropologie et développement :
Historiciser et localiser les approches 161
Thomas Bierschenk

APPENDICES / ANNEXES

List of Contributors / Liste des auteurs 195
The APAD Board / Le bureau de l'APAD 196
Join the APAD – Adhérer à l'APAD 197
Summary of back issues / Sommaire des numéros precedents 199

Éditorial / Editorial

Editorial

Sten Hagberg

When considering the task to edit an APAD-Bulletin on decentralisation and citizen participation, I initially hesitated. What new could be said about decentralisation after the series of APAD-publications touching on the issue over the last 10-15 years? Yet after some further thought, I soon realised that it could be both timely and appropriate to take a fresh look at decentralisation practices carried out across West Africa. The main reason is that initial attempts to decentralise and sometimes also to obstruct policy implementation starting in the 1990s have now given way to years of everyday decentralisation practices, that is, a series of political, economic and cultural practices carried out 'in the name of' decentralisation. Another reason to revisit decentralisation would be to include scholars of various disciplines (political science, human geography and anthropology) to address the issues at stake.

The articles of this APAD-Bulletin revisit decentralisation and citizen participation, so as to explore processes currently at work in West Africa, but, as we shall see, differently articulated in various countries, sectors and contexts. All authors are concerned with how the local is mobilised when decentralisation is appropriated by local actors. By doing this these authors also touch upon the invention of the local; in order to be decentralised the local must be invented in the first place! The theme of *Inventing and mobilising the local* highlights the core stakes and fundamental contradictions of decentralisation practices in West Africa by exploring party politics, water provision, schooling, territorial division, and cultural understanding. The detailed historical contextualisation of current practices runs through all articles, thereby providing thick descriptions of continuity and change. In addition to the five thematic articles presented in this APAD-Bulletin, the French version of Thomas Bierschenk's Key Note Address to the APAD Conference 13-15 December 2007 on *Development, Liberalism, and Modernity: Trajectories of an Anthropology of Social Change* in Tervuren/Brussels and Louvain-la-Neuve, Belgium, is also included. Bierschenk offers a very insightful and far-reaching overview of anthropology and development, and calls for the historicising and localising of approaches.

The editorial process has been greatly facilitated by the Department of Cultural Anthropology & Ethnology at Uppsala University. The language correction was done by Eren Zink (English) and Florence Naud (French), which is gratefully acknowledged.

Inventing and mobilising the local

Decentralisation and citizen participation in West Africa

Sten Hagberg[1]

In this introductory article I address decentralisation as a series of political, economic and cultural practices currently at work in West African local arenas. I develop a conceptual reflection of how the local is invented and mobilised through the mundane daily decentralisation practices. The very definition of the local is problematic and subject to different interpretations and meanings, and I argue that we need to simultaneously study political, economic and cultural dimensions to understand decentralisation. To focus on the invention and mobilisation of the local allows us to grasp how specific social categories (e.g. 'women' or 'the poor') may be discursively included, while being practically excluded. In conclusion, I argue for the integration of a cultural analysis – not a culturalist one – of decentralisation and citizen participation in order to understand the heat and intensity of public debate, and the strong emotions related to what at first glance may seem to be marginal political and economic issues.

Dans cet article introductif j'aborde la décentralisation comme une série de pratiques politiques, économiques et culturelles actuellement en cours dans les arènes locales en Afrique de l'Ouest. Je développe ici une réflexion conceptuelle sur comment le local est inventé et mobilisé à travers les pratiques quotidiennes de décentralisation. La définition même du local est problématique et chargée de différentes interprétations et sens, et je propose que nous étudions simultanément les dimensions politiques, économiques et culturelles de la décentralisation. Cibler l'invention et la mobilisation du local nous permet de saisir comment certaines catégories sociales (par ex: 'les femmes' ou 'les pauvres') peuvent être inclues selon les discours officiels, mais pratiquement exclues comme acteurs politiques. En conclusion, je propose l'intégration d'une analyse culturelle – mais pas culturaliste – de la décentralisation et de la participation citoyenne pour comprendre l'intensité du débat public et les fortes émotions liées à ce qui, à première vue, semblerait être des questions économiques et politiques plutôt marginales.

In the wake of democratisation and the demand for national conferences in African countries in the late 1980s, African governments and international agencies manifested a renewed interest in decentralisation. Decentralisation

[1] Associate Professor in Cultural Anthropology at Uppsala University: sten.hagberg@antro.uu.se

was seen as a means by which the over-centralisation of political decisions at the top of the state could be altered. Civil society actors and political opponents supported decentralisation for its potentials to favour the devolution of central power to local institutions and structures. Decentralisation became one central element of democratisation processes, making some refer to current policies as 'democratic decentralisation' (Crook & Manor 1998). Others see decentralisation as a legal technique of territorial administration, and as a political mode of sharing powers between central and local authorities in a country (Mback 2003:31-2). The last decade has seen a growing literature on decentralisation policies and their political and economic implications (Bierschenk & Olivier de Sardan 2003; Blundo & Olivier de Sardan 2006; Crook & Manor 1998; Dahou 2003; Fay et al. 2006; Kassibo 1997; Laurent et al. 2004; Mback 2003; Sawadogo 2001; Seely 2001; Totté et al. 2003). With years of experience of decentralising West African States, it is time to focus on everyday practices. Instead of describing how decentralisation *should be*, *ought to be*, or, once problems arise, *should have been*, I propose that we look at the wide range of activities that are carried out 'in the name' of decentralisation. Hence, I address decentralisation as a series of political, economic and cultural practices currently at work in local arenas across West Africa. Although these practices are neither coherent nor uniform, they are commonly invoked to justify various claims made by political actors.

The collection of essays assembled in this *APAD-Bulletin* revisits decentralisation and citizen participation in local arenas. All articles concern decentralisation as part of political and cultural processes at work everywhere in West Africa and, yet, differently articulated depending *inter alia* on country, context and sector. In some cases we see a 'decentralisation by default' (Andrae) in the sense that the withdrawal or disengagement (Körling) – or absence – of the state opens up for non-state actors. In others we listen to the voices of voters who have been abandoned by political parties and still continuously vote for the majority party (Rudebeck). We see how pastoralists losing out in decentralisation adopt a strategy of territorialisation of land (Mohamadou). We also look at decentralisation in various societal sectors, such as water provision (Andrae), education (Körling), party politics (Rudebeck) and state administration (Mohamadou). In addition, all articles deal, in one way or another, with citizen participation through different local actors' struggles over political, economic and cultural resources. Decentralisation practices concern the ways in which citizens are appropriating politics and making sense of state policies, as well as the means to solve daily problems for making ends meet. Meanwhile, these practices also articulate processes of exclusion and inclusion of different social categories.[2]

In this article I attempt to develop some general remarks on decentralisation practices, leading to a conceptual reflection of how the local is currently invented and mobilised.[3] The purpose is to understand the mundane everyday practices of decentralisation in West Africa by reflecting upon the different ways in which the local is transformed. In addition to conclusions from the in-depth case-studies presented in the four articles concerning Guinea-Bissau, Niger and Nigeria, I also develop my argument by drawing upon long-term fieldwork conducted in Burkina Faso and a recent short-term fieldwork in Mali.

Across West Africa we may identify three transformative processes favoured by current decentralisation practices. First, decentralisation has changed the politico-administrative stakes in local arenas across West Africa. Whereas decentralisation has historically been associated with the creation of urban communes, current practices seek to create rural communes far away from urban centres (Bierschenk & Olivier de Sardan 2003; Fay et al. 2006; Hahonou 2006; Koné 1997; Laurent et al. 2004; Sawadogo 2001; Olivier de Sardan 2003). Today rural districts are involved in, and affected by, municipal elections. Second, the primacy of urbanity and modern education are recast in present-day decentralisation. The fact that citizens now have the possibility to elect mayors with little or no formal educa-

[2] In addition to the five articles constituting the thematic issue of this APAD-Bulletin I am very happy to include the French version of Thomas Bierschenk's important key note address introducing the 2007 APAD Conference in December 2007.

[3] The ideas developed in this article were first formulated in a key note to the international workshop on *Decentralisation in Practice* in May 2004. The workshop papers were published as *Decentralisation in Practice: Power, Livelihoods and Cultural Meaning in West Africa*, International Workshop Highlights, Uppsala, Sweden, May 4-6, 2004, International Institute for Environment and Development (IIED), London & Dept. of Cultural Anthropology and Ethnology, Uppsala University, Uppsala (brochure + CD-ROM). I acknowledge inspiring comments on earlier versions from many people, notably Gunilla Andrae, Ced Hesse, Gabriella Körling, Roch Mongbo, and Lars Rudebeck.

tion is hotly debated in many West African countries. It is frequently held that mayors without skills of budgeting and bookkeeping are exposed to all forms of manipulation and dependency. And, still, most locally legitimate political actors are not necessarily those who have been to school (Camara 2006; Hagberg 2002). Third, decentralisation attempts to marry legality and legitimacy, and has often been interpreted as the return of traditional chieftaincy. While such interpretations are not unambiguously accepted and supported by all political actors, it is a political fact that discourses of autochthony, whereby family decent and ethnic belonging are made criteria for defining legitimate political actors, are increasingly ventured in local political arenas (Buur & Kyed 2007; Geschiere & Gugler 1998; Geschiere & Nyamnjoh 2000; Kassibo 1997). The reigns of the city must, so it is often argued, be held by a son of the locality (cf. Hagberg 2006a). Common to these three transformative processes is that they demonstrate how seemingly unproblematic categories – 'rural', 'local' and 'home' – are filled with new meanings.

Beyond these transformative processes, the very definition of the local and its boundaries is highly problematic, and subject to a wide range of interpretations and meanings. Discourses of the local are a central feature of political culture in West Africa (and certainly elsewhere) in the era of decentralisation and, yet, ambiguously referred to by political actors. On the one hand, the local is positively referred to in elections. The necessity to bring 'local development' and work for 'local people' is a recurrent theme. Politicians often seek to mobilise 'the local electoral constituency' by invoking their status as sons or daughters of the village or the district. It is not rare that politicians represent a village where they trace ancestry but in which they have never lived. The local also represents tradition and belonging. In village rituals and cultural manifestations, the local is associated with origin and authenticity. Only persons who have undergone initiation may attend many village rituals, such as agrarian rites in the sacred grove. On the other hand, the local is simultaneously attributed negative connotations by political actors when they represent the village as backward, static and inward-looking. Being 'the local representative' of a political party or a state service is fraught with ambiguities as it may stand for dynamic brokerage and conservative backwardness at the same time. The negative connotations of the local have for a long time been reproduced within state administration.

In Burkina Faso local government officials are often labelled *fonctionnaires de brousse* by their peers higher up in the hierarchy (Hagberg 2005). In addition to these ambiguities it is important to remember that not all social actors fit into the category of the local. Fulbe pastoralists are often excluded as they are perceived as strangers, foreigners and those coming from far away (Hagberg 2000). Other social categories often marginalised in official decision-making processes are 'migrants' and 'women'. Therefore it is necessary to explore the ambiguous notions of the local that prevail in the era of decentralisation.

For political actors, there is a need to invent the local in order to be able to mobilise it. In such processes of *inventing and mobilising the local*, decentralisation practices have reshaped the fundamental relations between citizens and the State. From a top-down and highly authoritarian State with its colonial legacy we see a process that at least holds promises of a possible change because, despite manipulations, frauds and deviations, democracy provides the framework for present-day local politics in West Africa. Even when national politics experiences back-lash, e.g. the personalisation of presidential power, local democratic processes tend to prevail. Inventing and mobilising the local furthermore opens up for the possibility of recasting the distinction between educated and urban-based salaried actors, and 'the illiterate' and 'the ignorant'[4] ones in rural areas, or perhaps better, the divide of citizens and subjects in the bifurcated legacy of the colonial State (Mamdani 1996). In this vein, practices of decentralisation present new ways in which the postcolonial state is re-appropriated, while strengthening the agenda of certain categories of political actors.

This introductory article in which I develop an argument on how the local is invented and mobilised by political actors is organised as follows. Firstly, I make an overview of decentralisation policies so as to situate current practice in the colonial and postcolonial history. Secondly, I discuss the invention and mobilisation to explore actors' ambiguous stance towards the local.

[4] For the sake of clarity let us accept, in Mark Hobart's phrasing, that ignorance "is not a simple antithesis of knowledge", but is "a state which people attribute to others and is laden with moral judgment" (Hobart 1993:1).

Thirdly, I propose that we need to simultaneously study political, economic and cultural dimensions if we are to understand current decentralisation practices. Fourthly, I develop some examples of how specific social categories (here exemplified with 'women') may be discursively included while being practically excluded. Fifthly, I introduce the four case-studies contributing to this thematic issue of the APAD-Bulletin as to highlight everyday decentralisation and development across West Africa. In conclusion, I argue that we need to seriously integrate a cultural analysis of decentralisation and citizen participation in order to understand the heat and intensity of public debate and the strong emotions related to what at first glance may seem to be marginal political and economic issues.

Contextualising Decentralisation in West Africa

Much hope has been invested in decentralisation policies since the early 1990s when decentralisation was presented as something new, a radical breach with past authoritarian regimes. Yet various attempts to decentralise, that is, the deliberate and planned transfer of authority and resources away from the central state institutions to peripheral institutions, have for a long time been the subject of experimentation. And, locally elected government bodies in urban areas are not a new phenomenon in West Africa. The *Quatre Communes* were erected in Senegal by the French colonial administration in the 19th century: St. Louis and Gorée in 1872, and Rufisque in 1880, and Dakar in 1887. Residents of these communes became French citizens whereas the rest of the population of the territory remained African subjects (cf. Mamdai 1996). In other words, the creation of communes required the distinction between citizens and subjects. In the first half of the 20th century urban communes were created elsewhere in Africa. The communes of Ouagadougou and Bobo-Dioulasso were, for example, erected to mixed communes of 1st degree in 1926 (Sawadogo 2001). An administrative mayor governed these communes with the assistance of a municipal commission. The commission was composed of three different categories of members: first, there were nominated members; second, there were elected members with a limited electoral base; and, third, there were elected members by universal suffrage (Sawadogo 2001:207; Fourchard 2001). The salient feature of these early attempts to decentralise was that they involved urban communes with a high degree of French residents. Hence, decentralisation was partial, and concerned only a small share of the population.

A word of caution is needed here. Decentralisation as a mode of governing tends to focus on the colonial and postcolonial State and, consequently, disregarding more or less traditional modes of rule. Yet it is important to keep in mind that decentralisation articulates state-society relations not only related to the postcolony, but also to traditional socio-political structures. For instance, although a hierarchical kingdom is more likely to find locally legitimate political structures in the context of decentralisation, what have been called stateless or segmentary societies are likely to appropriate decentralisation quite differently (Amselle & M'Bokolo 1985; Hagberg 1998, 2004b; Laurent 1995; Laurent et al. 2004; Lentz 2000; Savonnet-Guyot 1986).

Bamidele Olowu locates the first phase of decentralisation, at that time labelled as a system of local government, from the World War II until the early 1960s. During this phase decolonisation was on the agenda due to a variety of reasons: reward for the colonised peoples' participation in the war, agitation by the growing elite from the colonies, and the rise of social liberal parties in Britain and France (Olowu 2001:6). The development of an efficient and democratic local government was seen as a key to success in African administration. Yet, the decentralised focus was abandoned with national independence. In the 1960s the newly independent African states subscribed to central planning and consolidation of the nation-state via the single party mechanism. Local administrations were essentially instruments of control, and the relationship between the centre and the periphery was strongly hierarchical. When the economic crisis of the 1970s emerged most African states responded by adopting structural adjustment programmes. Decentralisation then presented itself as a mechanism for cutting back central government expenditures (Olowu 2001:8), and was more economically than politically motivated. Yet despite these policy responses, the structural adjustment policies incited what has been termed 'decentralisation by default', that is, "a situation in which a variety of non-state organisations filled the void left by the absence of state institutions in the production of goods and services" (Olowu 2001:11).

Since the early 1990s, however, several West African countries have undertaken reforms to devolve political and administrative power to elected local government bodies in rural areas, such as communes and regions. In contrast to previous decentralisation efforts these attempts were conceived of in the context of political liberalisation and democratisation, and the policies have sometimes been referred to as 'democratic decentralisation' (Crook & Manor 1998). The models adopted in the 1990s differ considerably with respect to the composition of local government institutions and to the powers and resources that they should control. But, decentralisation policies have been differently implemented in various countries. Whereas in Senegal rural communes have been in place for more than thirty years, they are relatively recent in Mali (Fay et al. 2006; Kassibo 1997). Niger held its first local elections in July 2004 (Hahonou 2006; Olivier de Sardan 2006). In Burkina Faso decentralisation has been under way for a decade (Hagberg 1998; Laurent et al. 2004; Sawadogo 2001), and the communalisation was completed with local elections in April 2006. And, yet, Ghana has been involved in a decentralisation process since the early 1980s (Amanor & Annan 1999; Ayee 1996; Crook & Manor 1998). The federation of Nigeria is a different case, even though the relationship between the federal government and the different states is much debated with respect to the adoption of the *shari'a* as civil law by several states (Olowu 2001).

This overview demonstrates the necessity to reflect upon the concept of decentralisation itself. It is indeed relevant to question whether one can use this concept to cover all these different policy propositions mentioned so far. Is it useful to see the creation of the *Quatre Communes* in Senegal in the 19th century as decentralisation? By doing this we may run the risk of being trapped into a purely legalistic perspective intimately associated with the colonial and postcolonial State, overlooking segmentary socio-political structures outside the modern state in, for instance, northern Ghana and southern Burkina Faso (Hagberg & Tengan 2000; Savonnet-Guyot 1986).

At a very general level decentralisation is a distribution of power that is horizontal rather than hierarchical (Kasfir 1990, cited by Seely 2001), and depicts the transfer of power away from a central authority to lower levels in a territorial hierarchy. Yet, the transfer of power from a centre to a periphery involves the construction of such a periphery in the first place! In order to make the transfer of competences to local governments (*collectivités locales*) the latter must already exist as an administrative entity (Mback 2001). So, while decentralisation is the transfer of power a critical question is which are the institutions, structures and actors that should be granted this power. When local decision-making is advocated, the local is as much a social construction as other political categories and units.

In the mainstream debate on decentralisation a distinction is often made between deconcentration and devolution. The concept of deconcentration refers to the delegation of responsibility and authority to field units of the same department or level of government. It extends the reach of the central government to strengthen its authority "by moving executive agencies controlled by the centre down to lower levels in the political system" (Crook & Manor 1998:6). Yet what is called devolution has the opposite effect, "since it cedes control of such agencies and resources to political actors and institutions at lower levels" (Crook & Manor 1998:7). The concept of devolution indicates the transfer of authority to locally constituted units of government or special purpose authorities.

The distinction between deconcentration and devolution is reasonable for understanding the general concept of decentralisation. According to a legal-administrative perspective it makes a difference whether the central government rules through local representatives or the local government is invested with autonomous decision-making powers. Yet while at the policy level the distinction between deconcentration and devolution makes sense, once we move to actual practice the distinction is less clear-cut. Decentralisation is, like any other centrally implemented policy, subject to a multitude of local interpretations. While some political actors see decentralisation as part of a patrimonial agenda aimed at preserving the monopoly of power and ensuring control over resources, others pursue reformist objectives aimed at creating more transparency, accountability and efficiency in the management of local affairs (De Jong et al. 1999:5). For donors, decentralisation is supposed to open many doors: "decentralisation is not only supposed to lead to the introduction of local democracy and political accountability, it is also supposed to activate the dynamics of development at local level" (Bierschenk & Olivier de Sardan 2003:145). An unofficial interpretation of decentralisation says that "you decide on your affairs yourself"

(Mback 2003:36).[5] In Mali an impressive work was invested in the 1990s in order to find appropriate local notions for the concept of decentralisation. Two main terms in Bambara express power. While the term *mara* refers to the exercise of authority at all levels of society, the term *fanga* implies force, strength. The concept of decentralisation was translated into *mara ka ségi so*, that is, 'the power returns home' (Béridogo 1997:30). But the precise location and meaning of 'the home' was sometimes questioned, and gave rise to intense debates on political legitimacy. Once again we see that the construction of 'the local' (or 'the home') is central to decentralisation practices.

Invention and Mobilization

In this section I discuss how the ambiguous concept of the local is invented and mobilised by social actors. Localism is a common term used to denote a wide range of ideas and practices that support 'local production and consumption of goods', 'local control of government', and 'local culture and identity'. However, the local is not an unproblematic category, but rather a social and political construction that is filled with different meanings by various actors.

In classical anthropology ideas of locality and belonging were for a long time regarded as juxtaposed kindred concepts. Yet, as pointed out by David Parkin, "anthropologists can no longer assume that the people they study see themselves as attached to a particular, bounded locality" (Parkin 1998:ix). Rather than being a territorial reference point, locality could be a starting point for understanding concepts of origin, home, village and, ultimately, belonging. In the introduction to a volume on locality and belonging, Nadia Lovell develops how belonging to a particular locality evokes the loyalty to a place. Belonging is multifarious and related not only to social relations and rights, but also to emotions. "The exploration of how notions of belonging, localities and identities are constructed seems particularly relevant in current political contexts of 'globalisation', where the inter-

[5] "Vous déciderez vous-mêmes de vos affaires".

face between localised understandings of belonging, locality and identity often seem to conflict with wider national and international political, economic and social interests" (Lovell 1998:1). Gupta and Ferguson argue for an anthropology that is less an evocation of the local and more an exploration of the location. Anthropological fieldwork should be less of "a time-honoured commitment to the *local* but with an attentiveness to social, cultural, and political *location*" (Gupta & Ferguson 1997:5). Shifting our own location means that one may also explore links to other political or epistemological locations. That is why we need to represent the local in decentralisation practices as an *emic* concept. So, while all people are located, notions of the local are socially, politically, economically, and culturally constructed.

In colonial time the definition of administrative units was a critical task for state administration, mostly for reasons of governance and efficiency. The impact of colonial administration on ethnicity and belonging can hardly be contested today, but the relative importance of ethnicity in colonial statecraft is debatable. To my understanding ethnic identities were not only the result of colonialism, but, in Philip Burnham's words, the colonial period was "a particularly productive moment for ethnic political 'projects'" (Burnham 1996:158). In situations of dramatic change – the prime example is the colonial situation – one could expect that ethnic discourses react to change and rupture as to assert distinctions between 'Us' and 'Them'. Today's decentralisation and political pluralism could, I would argue, well be understood as another 'particularly productive moment for ethnic political projects'. It is in this context of socio-political and economic change that we may understand the construction – or, as I would prefer, the invention – of the local, because in 'democratic decentralisation' the interconnection between group and locality is given new political, economic and cultural meaning. When prominent members of an ethnic group see that they should occupy their 'own' municipality, issues of belonging and autochthony are likely to be ventured in party politics, associational life and economic infrastructure investment (Geschiere & Nyamnjoh 2000; Hagberg 2004a, 2006b; Lentz 2000; Zougouri 2008). In this process references to the local that result from the specific historical context also resonate with localism, because it is hard to argue against attempts to decentralise West African countries that have historically experienced such a high degree of centralism (cf.

Young 2003). Yet as shown in many recent writings on local arenas in West Africa (e.g. Bierschenk & Olivier de Sardan 2003; Hagberg 2004b, 2006b; Laurent et al. 2004; Zougouri 2008), decentralisation practices have often led to sharpened identity politics and community conflict. Today many actors see local democracy as synonymous with dispute and conflict. For instance, a local politician in Burkina Faso told me recently: "Since the municipal elections in 2006 my village is divided". Hence divide and rivalry rather than unity and understanding are associated with democracy. Freedom of speech is of particular importance; democracy has popularly come to imply that nowadays people may say whatever they want without consideration for other people.[6]

The struggle over definitions and boundaries of the local urge us to be cautious with the concept itself. With respect to decentralisation, Olivier de Sardan (2006:408) conceptualises the local as both an arena where heterogeneous actors intervene with local and external resources, and an emergent (and state-centred) public space where state representatives and representatives of the population (or citizens) interact around multiple norms with respect to access to public goods and services. To my mind, Olivier de Sardan's approach of the local as 'an arena' and 'a public space' has the methodological advantage that the local becomes tangible and possible to study. However, the local is more than that. It also pertains to political imagination, cultural representation and symbolic meaning. Therefore, I would to argue that the actors' perceptions of the local – the *emic* point of view – need to be integrated into our analysis.

The theme of this issue of the APAD-Bulletin is *Inventing and mobilising the local*. By inventing I would like to draw attention to the fact that the local does not exist 'out there' as a category itself, but must be constructed or created in order to make sense. Entities referred to as traditional or ancestral by social actors may be recent creations. The colonial entity of canton was most often a new creation albeit drawing bits and pieces of historical entities. A very telling example is that of Koné Gnagwan, a former interpreter

[6] A study on market women and taxi-drivers in urban Ghana describes that democracy is popularly defined as "I speak my mind, you speak your mind", that is, democracy is above all understood as a question of freedom of speech (Jennische 2009).

who, thanks to his political skilfulness, became the canton chief of Karaborola and Komono in the Banfora region of present-day Burkina Faso (Soma 2000; see also Hagberg 1998). From 1921, Koné Gnagwan, a Gouin from Bounouna, ruled over Karaboro 'country' and in 1938 his reign was extended to cover Komono and southern parts of Tiefo 'countries'.[7] Koné Gnagwan was feared and ruled over life and death because this was the time of forced labour. But, in 1946 he was removed due to power abuse (Hagberg 1998:93-94; Soma 2000). Still, Koné Gnagwan is today a legend of the Banfora region. Over the last decade a main political actor in Banfora was Koné's grandson, the late Mamadou Koné. Seen as a young dynamic private entrepreneur in the construction business, he also based his legitimacy on the ancestry. Mamadou Koné was an MP for the ruling party CDP[8] and then turned opposition politician for RDB[9]. In April 2006 he was elected mayor of Banfora against all odds as he contested the ruling CDP. With strong popular support and mobilisation Koné won the elections. However, unfortunately, he passed away later the same year suffering from an incurable disease. Some said Mamadou Koné died from cancer, whereas others held that political adversaries killed him by poison and/or witchcraft. In any case, the late Koné Mamadou based his power on his political dynamism and capacity to mobilise in conjunction with the historical legacy of his grand-father. In this example we see how invention is a process where political actors use the bits and pieces of political imagination, collective memory, and the pragmatics of power. While it is not 'pure invention', it results from the conscious attempts to create meaningful and workable political entities. Yet it is not enough to invent a historical legitimacy, one equally needs to have the capacity to mobilise. The example of the late Mamadou Koné therefore points towards the necessary combination of legality, legitimacy and dynamism of political actors in the process of inventing and mobilising the local.

The capacity to mobilise the local is a central challenge for any political actor. For instance, the visibility of political action is an important element for

[7] In Francophone Africa the notion of *pays* ('country') as to indicate the territory associated with a specific ethnic group finds an interesting parallel to decentralisation in France (Palard 2006).

[8] *Congrès pour la Démocratie et le Progrès*

[9] *Rassemblement pour le Développement du Burkina*

mobilising voters, state support and international donors. I have often heard how people refer to political actors in Burkina Faso along the following lines: "X est devenu une pièce incontournable pour toute intervention dans le village". The politician has great interest to become a gatekeeper or broker. A political actor who succeeds in becoming the broker able to mobilise actors and resources in 'the local', as well as actors and resources from 'the global' (most often in the form of state intervention and development aid) is likely to become the gatekeeper for any political action, development intervention and other collective action to be undertaken (Bierschenk et al. 2000; Lewis & Mosse 2006). The invention of the local therefore goes hand in hand with its mobilisation.

Dimensions of Decentralisation

Decentralisation processes carried out so far in Africa remain utterly contradictory. Despite the important steps taken, the strong policy focus obscures much of actual decentralisation practices. Firstly, the 'irreversibility' of decentralisation so often invoked is more of wishful thinking than grounded in empirical observation. The first decade of full-scale territorial communalisation in Burkina Faso, Mali and Niger currently shows sign of fatigue and increased questioning of decentralisation. One sign of this fatigue could be detected in the idealisation of the time of military presidents like Séyni Kountché 1974-87 (Niger) and Thomas Sankara 1983-87 (Burkina Faso) as it articulates local actors' longing for a central and powerful state. Secondly, while it is easy to be impressed by the social engineering in, for instance, Mali's decentralisation, a political analysis more than a policy analysis of decentralisation is needed to understand why ex-President Konaré pushed for its implementation (Seely 2001), whereas his successor Amadou Toumani Touré – popularly called ATT – has shown much less interest in decentralisation. Thirdly, attention must also be paid to less positive developments that prevail in the context of decentralisation. Despite Senegal's early decentralisation attempts, corruption is, in the words of Giorgio Blundo, a fact of decentralisation, not as a lack of mechanisms in its implementation, but as a mode of local governance (Blundo 2001). Fourthly, while decentralisation cannot be attributed all forms of transformations and diversions at work in municipalities across West Africa, the neo-liberal strive to 'de-scale' (Andrae), to 'disengage' (Körling), or to 'decentralise' (Mohamadou, Rudebeck) all involve the conscious politico-administrative transfer of power away from a centre to a periphery. In this section I discuss decentralisation processes in relation to how social actors in the local aim to acquire power, livelihoods and cultural meaning.

The first dimension of decentralisation is political as it goes without saying that decentralisation affects the distribution and the exercise of power within society. Therefore, the materialisation of decentralisation depends not only on policy and legislative reform, but also on the political will of the central government to transfer real, discretionary decision-making powers to local government bodies. An elected mayor in Mali told me in 2003 that "we cannot wait until the power and the resources are given to us by the central government, we have 'to pull out' the power". Another political aspect is related to the legitimacy of the local government. Local governments may well be legal in that they have acquired decision-making powers without being legitimate vis-à-vis other local power holders (particularly traditional chiefs). One notes, for instance, that land tenure is likely to be a contested issue; local governments may have the legal right to exercise power whereas traditional chiefs uphold legitimacy (Benjaminsen & Lund 2003; Juul & Lund 2002; Kuba & Lentz 2006; Lund 2006). But power is also central for understanding the relations between local governments, traditional institutions and the so-called civil society in terms of citizen participation, representation and accountability (Hagberg 2004a, 2006b). To some extent decentralisation complicates local political arenas, because rather than legislating away former power structures decentralisation represents a new layer of political institutions. Bierschenk and Olivier de Sardan argue that decentralisation is not a radical rift opening the way to good governance, but that "the current processes of decentralisation in Africa merely represent another moment in a long series of regime changes imposed from above by the state and experienced in Africa since the end of the Second World War" (Bierschenk & Olivier de Sardan 2003:167).

The second dimension of decentralisation concerns economics, or perhaps better, livelihoods and local economic development. Even though decentralisation introduces new political relations between the electors and the elected, its *raison d'être* largely relies on newly elected government bodies' abilities to support the livelihoods of local people and to address everyday problems of poor health and education facilities, inadequate water supplies, and lack of employment, marketing and investment opportunities. This requires ensuring effective management of natural resources, the provision of appropriate, efficient and affordable services, the seizing of new economic opportunities, and the reconciling of competing interests of different social groups. In economic terms decentralisation has, positively or negatively, an impact on people's livelihoods. The paying of taxes and the increased control over people's livelihoods through land tenure and cattle markets are likely to have implications for rural producers' capacities to subsist. However, the logics of micro-projects seem to be more oriented towards 'the management of poverty' (Mback 2001:110-111). Donors that have been supporting decentralisation processes often undermine local governments by channelling public aid through NGOs, leaving district assemblies with scarce resources. Another economic aspect is the decentralisation of patrimonial networks. Giorgio Blundo identifies the decentralisation of corrupt practices, what he terms *décentralisation détournée*, as emanating from the logics of bureaucratic predation coupled with the logics of factional sharing of the resources that are administered by members of local governments (Blundo 2001:124). And in local discourses on corruption, the corrupted is not the one who has eaten *per se*, but the one who has eaten in an egoistic manner (see also Blundo & Olivier de Sardan 2006).

The third dimension of decentralisation is cultural in the sense that it involves people's perceptions of, and meanings attributed to, decentralisation. Beyond political and economic practices of decentralisation, there is a need to better understand the cultural meaning of decentralisation (Hagberg 2004b; Laurent at al. 2004). Even though it is generally admitted that cultural practices of decentralisation are important, these practices are rarely addressed in any systematic manner. Decentralisation may enable a re-appropriation not only of local resources but also of local cultural identities and values. It could allow for local arrangements building on local rules and institutions (Djiré & Dicko 2007). By devolving more power to local communities decentralisation may help make sense of the postcolonial state administration and, at best, favour the emergence of local democratic culture. In Mali the elected mayor rather than the former *sous-préfet*, who is appointed by the state, is nowadays the strong political actor. This represents a radical shift in terms of power, but it has cultural bearings as well. The tricky issue of how to draw politico-administrative boundaries prevails in most countries and articulates with belonging and exclusion. Niger has opted for preserving the former canton boundaries whereas Mali has had serious problems in getting economically viable communes and has instead seen the creation of micro-communes (Koné 1997a; Koné 1997b). The re-shuffling of provincial boundaries has often been interpreted culturally in the sense that those on the other side of the border are different. A hunter leader explained to me when a hunters' association had been divided into two as a consequence of decentralisation's new provincial boundaries: "It is good because of languages. We do not understand them. We the Karaboro, Gouin and other peoples here [in the Comoé Province] we understand each other but not them [that is those in the new Léraba Province][…] But the government has regrouped us. Now we are divided and it is not bad" (Hagberg 2004b). In other words, the politico-administrative reshuffling was justified culturally by this hunter leader.

In addition, 'culture' may be manipulated by local elites to back their claims over local power and resources in the process of the invention of tradition (Hobsbawm & Ranger 1983; Ranger 1983; Buur & Kyed 2007; Perrot & Fauvelle-Aymar 2003; Hagberg 2004a, 2006a, 2006b, 2007). This has been articulated as 'the return of the kings' (Perrot & Fauvelle-Aymar 2003) or as 'power returns home' (Béridogo 2006; Kassibo 2006; Koné 1997b). The Nigerien case is most obvious where the canton chiefs are still on the payroll of the state. But it is a common feature that descendants of the former canton chiefs are among today's power-holders in the capacity of mayors and municipal advisors. In Burkina Faso, the Emir of Liptaako was mayor of Dori 1995-2000 and the traditional chief Pô Pê was the mayor of Pô in the early 2000s. And when the chief himself remains outside the local government, a younger brother, a son or another close relative is likely to be among the local power-holders. But in this process traditional chiefs are not exempt from the public gaze. In 2000-2001, Burkina Faso experienced three cases of political violence in which chiefs were deeply involved (Hagberg 2007). In these cases the fuzzy boundary between traditional power and modern politics was one key element. Another was that these chiefs became publicly criticised for acting far beyond the limits of the rule of law.

The cultural dimension of decentralisation practices is thus ambiguous. Decentralisation provides the opportunity for chiefs, legitimised by tradition and culture, to access new political and economic resources, but decentralisation also exposes tradition and culture to public scrutiny, debate and contest. Cultural practices of decentralisation fundamentally concern exclusion. Some political actors are defined as legitimate and apt for political offices, while others are excluded. Social categories, such as women, nomads, latecomers and various groups of casted peoples are particularly vulnerable when 'culture' is instrumentally fed into local governments.

Women in the local

In current decentralisation practices women are ambiguously portrayed and represented in local mobilisation. Initially women tend to loose out when power is transferred to the local, but given the strong advocacy for gender and development they simultaneously seem to gain weight with decentralisation. In this section I elaborate on two examples of women in the local so as to reflect upon the constraints and opportunities of moving beyond what I would like to label 'the female space'.

The first example illustrates that decentralisation not only implies the devolution of power but also a re-centralisation at local level. When local administration is strengthened, citizens get closer to public authorities. But the public and administrative sphere of people's life is simultaneously enlarged, formalised and recentred by decentralisation. In committees and councils one or two seats are generally reserved for women, but as a matter of fact they do not compete for political power with the male actors. Similarly, in municipal elections women tend to be less represented locally than in national assembly. And, still, political competition between women tends to be seen as 'a women's affair'.

In recent years there has been a fierce struggle among women's political leadership in Burkina Faso's second city Bobo-Dioulasso. With legislative elections in 2007 there was competition about which one among leading women politicians of the city who was to be on an eligible position of the majority party CDP's list. In 2008 the competition was once again launched when the coordinating structure for women's associations under the Ministry of Women's Promotion was to be elected. One faction was led by a female MP, who has for long time been a leading personality of the city and who is the president of a collective of HIV/AIDS associations. The other faction was led by the deputy mayor of Bobo-Dioulasso and who is also the president of a collective of environmental associations. Both women leaders represented the ruling party CDP, because at least officially the struggle concerned a civil society organisation (*la coordination provinciale des associations féminines*) under the umbrella of the ministry. In fact this structure is positioned at the interface of party politics, state administration and civil society.

While the battle included many intricate details that I will describe elsewhere, suffice to note that the battle was about *who* should be the women's leader in the city rather than *how* to increase the number of women in politics. The two factions were competing for the space available for women in the local, while leaving the remaining male-dominated largely space untouched. This observation would perhaps lead to a pessimistic conclusion of the possibilities to enhance women's political participation. But the case of women's factional battle could also represent a shift in which women leave the public political category of caring mothers and sisters, and bring the fierce battle and factional fight to the fore.

The second example demonstrates that when women in the local are able to influence politics and development, they are often legitimised in terms of their husband, father or other male relatives. A dispute around a cereal mill offered to women in Gongasso in Southern Mali is particularly revelatory. Different women's associations and groups entered into conflict about the management of the mill. The mill was a donation to 'the women of the village'. While according to one version the mill came from a local organisation called *Centre de Santé Communautaire* (CSCOM), another version held that the mill was a gift from the ruling political party *Alliance pour la démocratie au Mali* (ADEMA, party in power since the early 1990s). The prominent women leaders in Gongasso were 'the wife of the village chief', 'the wife of the mayor', 'the wife of the Imam' and 'the wife of the schoolteacher'. Although such labelling does not necessarily exclude these women's agency outside their husbands' influence, women do gain legitimacy through their matrimonial position (Hagberg et al. 2009). In addition, many actors take on the task to speak 'in the name of women', especially given the fact that international development agencies give priority to fund women's activities. However, the mill that was donated to the village women was later captured by political actors and outside women's control. It ultimately ended at the village chief's courtyard. This example shows that while many actors speak in the name of women, local women are often unable to influence key management decisions when it comes to decentralisation and development.

These two cases clearly exemplify the problems related to women in the local and the importance of looking at processes of exclusion in decentralisation practices. Yet it should also be stated that the politics of exclusion has also meant that public debate and discussion increasingly highlight those who are loosing out. In Burkina Faso women's representation on electoral lists has become an issue and in the 2006 elections the ruling party CDP decided a quota on electoral lists. In 2009 a law on quotas was enacted by parliament meaning that at least 30% of eligible seats on the electoral list should be reserved for women. These steps are important in the sense that they prepare the ground for increased political participation of women, but resistance is continuously strong in local arenas.

Everyday Decentralisation and Development

The articles of this APAD-Bulletin represent various scholarly, geographical and thematic locations, but they are all held together by a concern for how the local is mobilised in daily political and development actions. Human geographer Gunilla Andrae draws upon fieldwork from Kano in Nigeria to raise the issue of water provision and decentralisation by default. She points to how the liberalisation of water supplies has dramatically changed the provisioning patterns in African cities. The dominating form for liberalisation of urban water supplies has been the take-over by transnational companies of previously publicly owned water utilities. With support of the World Bank, State authorities have let go supply functions as well as regulating functions concerning water supplies, especially targeting poor populations in urban peripheries. As a consequence, the field has opened up for a wide range of other actors outside state control, meaning that water provision is "de-scaled without democratic substance". Andrae investigates different modes of regulations of water supplies in present-day Kano. In addition to state actors we observe several commercial and neo-traditional actors involved in water provision. Three main forms of regulation are identified: the secular state, the leaders of community organisations, and the neo-traditional rulers. Andrae concludes that the degree of popular influence around water supplies is not particularly democratic, neither by standards of electoral parliamentary democracy nor of direct 'substantial' democracy. This is not the intention of decentralisation policies, but these practices are the consequence of liberalisation by default. In this process the local is mobilised so as to counteract the withdrawal of the State.

The democratic substance is also the concern of political scientist Lars Rudebeck who looks into electoral processes and politics in the village of Kandjadja in Guinea-Bissau. The article deals with 'substantial democracy' as to integrate constitutional, minimalistically defined democracy and political equality in practice. Substantial democracy is about political power being more equally distributed between citizens in a process where constitutional rules and actual practice are mutually supportive. Rudebeck, who has followed the village of Kandjadja in Guinea-Bissau since 1976, provides a diachronic account of local politics. The central paradox explored is that while the whole area is practically untouched by development interventions and literally no benefits of national policy have reached the village since the last school teacher left in 1989, the ruling party PAIGC[10] and state power under PAIGC have always received political support in the Kandjadja area. The most common explanation is that "this is an old liberated area", possibly indicating that the only political contacts between the village and the capital go through PAIGC. So, although people hold that they have been left "in a hole" and instead demand for change, in elections more votes were cast for PAIGC than any of the other parties. Rudebeck suggests that the support also originates in the 1960s during the liberation war, when the PAIGC political structure was grafted onto local 'traditional' socio-political

[10] Former liberation movement and present-day ruling party is *Partido Africano da Independência de Guiné e Cabo Verde* (PAIGC).

structure. Politics in Kandjadja is furthermore linked to ethnicities, because Rudebeck observes how in the elections in 1999 'Mandinga' of Kandjadja lined up against a presidential candidate of 'Balanta' origin. Thus, the case of Kandjadja is instructive both by demonstrating how little local people get in return for their political support, and by suggesting the limits of their patience. It also exemplifies how a specific form of the local was invented in the 1960s when PAIGC used local political structures to mobilise the area for the liberation war, and the power of that invention despite the fact that socio-economic betterment has yet to come.

Marginalisation and exclusion are central aspects described in the article by anthropologist Abdoulaye Mohamadou. He analyses how pastoral peoples are marginalised in decentralisation and, in consequence, how they seek to territorialise their claims. Decentralisation has meant that various forms of chieftaincy have provided primacy to sedentary groups in contrast to mobile ones. In Dakoro, Niger, pastoralists have engaged in settlement logics as to obtain chieftaincies and territories on the municipal level. These logics include the creation of socio-economic infrastructures (wells, schools, cereal and fodder banks etc.) and changing transhumance patterns according to which family members settle permanently in the home area to avoid that farmers settle there. Traditional chieftaincy is administratively recognised in Niger, and chiefs are major actors in local arenas. But Mohamadou demonstrates that today chiefs do not "speak with one voice" any longer, due to the growing impact of development projects and programmes. Managers of projects have become a local noblesse, building legitimacy through NGOs and development agencies. The case of Dakoro is illuminating when it comes to what I call the invention of the local. The district was delimited in 1947 to form part of the Maradi Cercle. Dakoro was then divided into an agricultural zone on which *chefs de canton* exercised power and authority, and a pastoral zone inhabited by nomads. While farmers and nomads had different chieftaincies, the nomads did not have legally recognised territories. The difference with regard to territorial claims prevailed through colonial and postcolonial eras. With decentralisation the issue of territorial claims and land rights has become a central concern that articulates political stakes around the local. The overlapping of administrative and customary territories awakened old rivalries between local notabilities as well as between agriculturalists and pastoralists, and pastoralists used decentralisation as a pretext to delimit the boundaries of their territories in a conflict-ridden agro-pastoral zone. Beyond the invention of the local decentralisation articulates the problem of State building: the disengagement of the State has given way to traditional chieftaincy with a patrimonial and extractive mode of governance.

In another article on Niger anthropologist Gabriella Körling looks into the education sector, and follows the rise and fall of a school in the periphery of Niamey. The article highlights how the Millennium Development Goals, notably to achieve universal primary education, interact with social, political and economic stakes around schools in local arenas. Schooling is a key strategy for donors, whereas the neo-liberal paradigm of a disengaged State seems to be in conflict with education for all. Körling details how various local stakeholders (e.g. parents' associations, management committees and chiefs) got involved in the creation of a new school in the village of Saga, and how the classrooms, due to the lack of basic infrastructure, were built of straw. The 'action plan' of the committee was to ensure that pupils would at least get such classrooms. The principal of the school, employed by the State, had to rely on the mobilisation of local resources and hope for 'development projects' (in this case Canadian and Chinese organisations) to finance this basic infrastructure. With a thick ethnographic description Körling shows how by the end of the school year the classrooms were taken down and stored until next school year. For people in Saga the disengagement of the State concretely meant increasing personal costs of education for school books, school material, uniforms etc. Or, as Körling's informants put it: "we have done everything and the State has done nothing." In the context of a disengaged State we see how the local is mobilised to raise funding among local socio-political actors. Körling's example of the Chinese development project that was to come, but never arrived, furthermore illustrates how local actors are squeezed in-between donors and rumours.

Conclusion

So far I have discussed different ways in which the local is invented and mobilised. I have argued that the local must not only be conceptualised as an arena and a public space but also as an *emic* category that is invented and mobilised by social and political actors. When mobilising the local certain social categories tend to be included and portrayed as 'local people', 'the population' or 'stakeholders', while excluding others that are defined as 'strangers' or 'outsiders'. In line with this I would like to emphasise that we see not only political and economic transformations in decentralisation practices but also cultural ones. It is therefore necessary to rethink cultural dimensions of decentralisation, not as a culturalist explanatory model (Olivier de Sardan 2005) but as how people live culturally and invest in what they see as culturally meaningful projects in situations where the economic and political benefits remain uncertain. A cultural analysis is needed to understand why successful individuals on a national and sometimes international arena opt to return to the local and compete to become mayor of a rural municipality. To do something concrete and meaningful for the home area and to search of recognition from people back home seem to be driving forces. But such a cultural analysis also depicts the manipulation of, and fight over, cultural categories. In this vein, I propose that the local is also an *emic* category and a locus of political imagination, cultural representation and symbolic meaning.

Although historically associated with the creation of urban communes and its consequence local government, current decentralisation practices seek to create rural communes far away from urban centres. There is a strong historical record of reproducing distinctions between urban citizens and rural populations, that is, the bifurcated State of citizens and subjects (Mamdani 1996). Mahmood Mamdani argues that such a divide of citizens and subjects was a central feature of the colonial state. Citizenship would be a privilege of the civilised, whereas the uncivilised would be subject to an all-round tutelage: "The rights of free association and free publicity, and eventually of political representation, were the rights of citizens under direct rule, not of subjects indirectly ruled by a customarily organized tribal authority" (Mamdani 1996:19). So, in a way it could be argued that decentralisation constitutes an attempt to overcome the historical divide between urbanites and rural dwellers, and between citizens and subjects. But, citizenship is far more than a legal category. It also includes rights and access to basic goods and services, and the case-studies clearly show that this is far from certain in contemporary West Africa.

Decentralisation practices concern the fundamental relations between citizens and the State. Key relations include the ways in which the local are invented and mobilised, presenting new ways in which the postcolonial state is re-appropriated. The return to 'the local' or 'the home' could therefore also be expressed as the celebration of rurality in an urban context, representing emerging West African urbanities. But decentralisation should first and foremost be approached as the most recent layers of political and administrative reform to which local actors need to adjust, or to resist. Far from irreversible, it is my contention that decentralisation practices may well give way to the return of the strong, central State with financial and political resources to implement policies. That is why historically grounded and ethnographically dense analyses, aptly illustrated by the four case-studies of this APAD-Bulletin, are needed for understanding how policy is translated into the daily practices of citizens of West African municipalities.

References

Amanor, K. & J. Annan. 1999. *Linkages between Decentralisation and Decentralised Cooperation in Ghana.* Maastricht: The European Centre for Development Policy Management. ECDPM Discussion Paper 9.

mselle, J.-L. & E. M'Bokolo (eds) 1985. *Au coeur de l'ethnie: Ethnies, tribalisme et État en Afrique.* Paris: Editions La Découverte.

Ayee, J.R.A. 1996. The measurement of decentralization: The Ghanaian Experience, 1988-92. *African Affairs* 95, 31-50.

Benjaminsen, T.A. & C. Lund (eds) 2003. *Securing Land Rights in Africa.* London & Portland, Or.: Frank Cass.

Béridogo, B. 1997. Processus de décentralisation au Mali et couches sociales marginalisées. *APAD-Bulletin* 14, 21-33: "La décentralisation au Mali: état des lieux" (ed.) B. Kassibo.

Béridogo, B. 2006. Processus de décentralisation et pluralité de logiques des acteurs au Mali. In *Décentralisation et pouvoirs en Afrique: En contrepoint, modèles territoriaux français* (eds) C. Fay, Y.F. Koné & C. Quiminal. Paris: Institut de Recherche pour le Développement (IRD).

Bierschenk, T., J.-P. Chauveau & J.-P. Olivier de Sardan (eds) 2000. *Courtiers en développement: les villages africains en quête de projets.* Paris: Karthala.

Bierschenk, T. & J.-P. Olivier de Sardan. 2003. Powers in the village: Rural Benin between democratisation and decentralisation. *Africa* 73, 145-173.

Blundo, G. 2001. La corruption comme mode de gouvernance locale: trois décennies de décentralisation au Sénégal. *Afrique contemporaine* 199, 115-127.

Blundo, G. & J.-P. Olivier de Sardan 2006. *Everyday Corruption and the State: Citizens and Public Officials in Africa.* New York & London: ZED Books.

Buur, L. & M.H. Kyed (eds) 2007. *State Recognition and Democratization in Sub-Saharan Africa: A new dawn for traditional authorities?* New York: Palgrave Macmillan.

Camara, S. 2006. Terre, pouvoir et décentralisation au Manden. In *Décentralisation et pouvoirs en Afrique: En contrepoint, modèles territoriaux français* (eds) C. Fay, Y.F. Koné & C. Quiminal. Paris: Institut de Recherche pour le Développement (IRD).

Crook, R.C. & J. Manor 1998. *Democracy and Decentralisation in South Asia and West Africa: Participation, Accountability and Performance*. Cambridge: Cambridge University Press.

Dahou, K. 2003. La bonne gouvernance selon la Banque mondiale: au-delà de l'habillage juridique. In *La décentralisation en Afrique de l'Ouest: entre politique et développement* (eds) M. Totté, T. Dahou & R. Billaz. Paris: Karthala.

De Jong, K., C. Loquai & I. Soiri. 1999. *Decentralisation and Poverty Reduction: Exploring Linkages*. Helsinki: Institute of Development Studies, University of Helsinki.

Djiré, M. & A.K. Dicko. 2007. *Les conventions locales face aux enjeux de la décentralisation au Mali*. Paris: Karthala.

Fay, C., Y.F. Koné & C. Quiminal (eds) 2006. *Décentralisation et pouvoirs en Afrique: En contrepoint, modèles territoriaux français*. Paris: Institut de Recherche pour le Développement (IRD).

Ferguson, J. 1994. *The Anti-Politics Machine: 'Development', Depoliticization, and Bureaucratic Power in Lesotho*. Minneapolis & London: University of Minnesota Press.

Fourchard, L. 2001. *De la ville coloniale à la cour africaine: espaces, pouvoirs et sociétés à Ouagadougou et à Bobo-Dioulasso (Haute-Volta) fin XIXe siècle-1960*. Paris: L'Harmattan.

Geschiere, P. & J. Gugler (eds) 1998. The Politics of Primary Patriotism. *Africa* 68, Special Issue.

Geschiere, P. & F.B. Nyamnjoh 2000. Capitalism and Autochthony: The Seesaw of Mobility and Belonging. *Public Culture* 12 (2), 423-452.

Gupta, A. & J. Ferguson (eds) 1997. *Anthropological Locations: Boundaries and Grounds of a Field Science*. Berkeley & London: University of California Press.

Hagberg, S. 1998. *Between Peace and Justice: Dispute Settlement between Karaboro agriculturalists and Fulbe agro-pastoralists in Burkina Faso*. Uppsala Studies in Cultural Anthropology 25. Uppsala: Acta Universitatis Upsaliensis.

—. 2001. *Poverty in Burkina Faso: Representations and Realities*. ULRICA 1. Uppsala: Department of Cultural Anthropology & Ethnology, Uppsala University.

—. 2002. Learning to Live or to Leave? Education and Identity in Burkina Faso. *African Sociological Review* 6 (2), 28-46.

—. 2004a. Ethnic Identification in Voluntary Associations: The Politics of Development and Culture in Burkina Faso. In *Rights and the Politics of Recognition in Africa* (eds) H. Englund & F.B. Nyamnjoh. London & New York: ZED Books.

—. 2004b. Political Decentralization and Traditional Leadership in the Benkadi Hunters' Association of Western Burkina Faso. *Africa Today*, 50 (4), 51-70.

—. 2005. Dealing with Dilemmas: Violent Farmer-Pastoralist Conflicts in Burkina Faso. In *No Peace, No War: An Anthropology of Contemporary Armed Conflicts* (ed) P. Richards. London & New York: James Currey.

—. 2006a. 'Bobo buveurs, Yarse colporteurs': Parenté à plaisanterie dans le débat public burkinabè. *Cahiers d'Etudes africaines* 184, XLVI (4), 861-881.

—. 2006b. The Politics of Joking Relationships in Burkina Faso. *Zeitschrift für Ethnologie* 131 (2), 197-214.

—. 2007. Traditional Chieftaincy, Party Politics, and Political Violence in Burkina Faso. In *State Recognition and Democratization in Sub-Saharan Africa: A new dawn for traditional authorities?* (eds) L. Buur & M.H. Kyed. New York: Palgrave Macmillan.

Hagberg, S. & A.B. Tengan (eds) 2000. *Bonds and Boundaries in Northern Ghana and Southern Burkina Faso*. Uppsala: Acta Universitatis Upsaliensis.

Hagberg, S., Y. F. Koné & K. Elfving en collaboration avec B. Koné, N. Traoré & M. Diallo 2009. *Analyse sociale au Mali : inclusion et exclusion à travers les opportunités du travail et de l'emploi*. Swedish International Development Cooperation Agency.

Hahonou, E.K. 2006. Une communauté 'nomade' face à la décentralisation. In *Décentralisation et pouvoirs en Afrique: En contrepoint, modèles territoriaux français* (eds) C. Fay, Y.F. Koné & C. Quiminal. Paris: Institut de Recherche pour le Développement (IRD).

Hilgers, M. & J. Mazzocchetti (eds) 2006. Le Burkina Faso : l'alternance impossible. *Politique africaine* 101.

Hobart, M. 1993. Introduction: The Growth of Ignorance? In *An Anthropological Critique of Development: The Growth of Ignorance* (ed.) M. Hobart. London & New York: Routledge.

Hobsbawm, E. & T. Ranger (eds) 1983. *The Invention of Tradition*. Cambridge: Cambridge University Press.

Jennische, U. 2009. Civil Society and Political Debate among Drivers and Traders in Urban Ghana: The Koforidua Central Market and Taxi Station. Master Theses in Cultural Anthropology 21. Uppsala: Uppsala University.

Juul, K. & C. Lund (eds) 2002. *Negotiating Property in Africa*. Portsmouth, NH: Heinemann.

Kambou-Ferrand, J. 1993. *Peuples voltaïques et conquête coloniale 1885-1914: Burkina Faso*. Paris: L'Harmattan.

Kasfir, N. 1990. Introduction. In *The Failure of the Centralized State: Institutions and Self-government in Africa* (eds) D. Oluwo & J Wunsch. Boulder, CO: Westview.

Kassibo, B. 1997. La décentralisation au Mali: état des lieux. *APAD-Bulletin* 14, 1-20: "La décentralisation au Mali: état des lieux" (ed.) B. Kassibo.

Koné, S. 1997a. La décentralisation face à l'ordre ancien. *APAD-Bulletin* 14, 67-75: "La décentralisation au Mali: état des lieux" (ed.) B. Kassibo.

Koné, Y.F. 1997b. Les micro-communes: expression des logiques locales. *APAD-Bulletin* 14, 59-66: "La décentralisation au Mali: état des lieux" (ed.) B. Kassibo.

Kuba, R. & C. Lentz (eds) 2006. *Land and the Politics of Belonging in West Africa*. Leiden & Boston: Brill.

Laurent, P.-J. 1995. *Les pouvoirs politiques locaux et la décentralisation au Burkina Faso*. Louvain-la-Neuve & Paris: Cahiers du CIDEP 26, Académia-L'Harmattan.

Laurent, P.-J., A. Nyamba, F. Dassetto, B. Ouédraogo & P. Sebahara (eds) 2004. *Décentralisation et citoyenneté au Burkina Faso: Le cas de Ziniaré*. Paris: L'Harmattan.

Lentz, C. 2000. Chieftaincy has come to stay: La chefferie dans les sociétés acéphales du Nord-Ouest Ghana. *Cahiers d'Études africaines* 159, 593-613.

Lentz. C. 2006. La décentralisation dans le nord-ouest du Ghana: Des frontières contestées. In *Décentralisation et pouvoirs en Afrique: En contrepoint, modèles territoriaux français* (eds) C. Fay, Y.F. Koné & C. Quiminal. Paris: Institut de Recherche pour le Développement (IRD).

Lewis, D. & D. Mosse (eds) 2006. *Development Brokers and Translators: The Ethnography of Aid and Agencies*. Bloomfield: Kumarian Press.

Lovell, N. 1998. Introduction: Belonging in need of emplacement. In *Locality and Belonging* (ed.) N. Lovell. London & New York: Routledge.

Lund, C. (ed.) 2006. *Twilight Institutions: Public authority and local politics in Africa*. Malden, MA: Blackwells.

Mamdani, M. 1996. Citizen and Subject: Contemporary Africa and the Legacy of late Colonialism. Kampala, Cape Town & London: Fountain Publishers, David Philip & James Currey.

Mback, C.N. 2001. La décentralisation en Afrique: Enjeux et perspectives. *Afrique contemporaine* 199, 95-114.

Mback, C.N. 2003. *Démocratisation et décentralisation: Genèse et dynamiques comparés des processus de décentralisation en Afrique subsaharienne*. Paris: Karthala.

Olivier de Sardan, J.-P. 2005. Classic Ethnology and the socio-anthropology of public spaces: New themes and old methods in European African Studies. *Africa Spectrum* 40 (3), 485-497.

Olivier de Sardan, J.-P. 2006. Des pouvoirs locaux dans l'attente de la décentralisation. In *Décentralisation et pouvoirs en Afrique: En contrepoint, modèles territoriaux français* (eds) C. Fay, Y.F. Koné & C. Quiminal. Paris: Institut de Recherche pour le Développement (IRD).

Olowu, B. 2001. *African Decentralisation Policies and Practices from 1980s and Beyond.* Working Paper Series 334. The Hague: Institute of Social Studies.

Palard, J. 2006. Le 'pays' dans le processus français de décentralisation. In *Décentralisation et pouvoirs en Afrique: En contrepoint, modèles territoriaux français* (eds) C. Fay, Y.F. Koné & C. Quiminal. Paris: Institut de Recherche pour le Développement (IRD).

Parkin, D. 1998. Foreword. In *Locality and Belonging* (ed.) N. Lovell. London & New York: Routledge.

Perrot, C.-H. & F.-X. Fauvelle-Aymar (eds) 2003. *Le retour des rois: Les autorités traditionnelles et l'Etat en Afrique contemporaine.* Paris: Karthala.

Ranger, T. 1983. The Invention of tradition in colonial Africa. In *The Invention of Tradition* (eds) E. Hobsbawm & T. Ranger. Cambridge: Cambridge University Press.

Sawadogo, A.R. 2001. L'État africain face à la décentralisation. Paris: Karthala.

Savonnet-Guyot, C. 1986. *Etat et sociétés au Burkina: Essai sur le politique africain.* Paris: Editions Karthala.

Seely, J.C. 2001. A political analysis of decentralisation: coopting the Tuareg threat in Mali. *Journal of Modern African Studies* 39, 499-524.

Soma, L. 2000. Nyangu'wan Koné: chef de canton du karaborola et du komono (1921-1946) dans le cercle de Bobo-Dioulasso. Mémoire de maîtrise, Département d'Histoire et Archéologie 1999-2000. Université de Ouagadougou.

Totté, M., T. Dahou & R. Billaz (eds) 2003. *La décentralisation en Afrique de l'Ouest: Entre politique et développement.* Paris: Karthala.

Van Rouveroy van Nieuwaal, E.A. 2000. *L'Etat en Afrique face á la chefferie.* Paris: Karthala.

Van Rouveroy van Nieuwaal, E.A.B. & R. van Dijk (eds) 1999. *African Chieftaincy in a New Socio-Political Landscape.* Hamburg: LIT.

Young, T. (ed.) 2003. *Readings in African Politics*. Bloomington & Indianapolis: Indiana University Press; Oxford: James Currey.

Zougouri, S. 2008. *Derrière la vitrine du développement : Aménagement forestier et pouvoir local au Burkina Faso*. Uppsala Studies in Cultural Anthropology 44. Uppsala: Acta Universitatis Upsaliensis.

De-scaling without Democratic Substance

Water Provisioning in Peripheral Kano, Nigeria

Gunilla Andrae[1]

The case of water provisioning in Tudun Murtala, a peripheral low income area in Kano, Nigeria, is used to highlight an expanding form of decentralisation in infrastructure provision in African cities and the democratic problems associated with it. I look at the decentralisation 'by default' that is connected with the type of liberalisation that takes the form of informalisation of supplies. The concurrent separation of supply from state regulation means that the regulation of relations between suppliers and users escapes from public control at the municipal and local government level into traditional hands at the community level. For users, this entails a revived dependence on neo-traditional politics, rather than the development of the parliamentary system, as a mode of influencing the conditions of access to water provisioning.

Le cas de l'approvisionnement en eau de Tudun Murtala, une zone périphérique modeste de Kano, Nigeria, est utilisé pour analyser une forme émergente de décentralisation de l'approvisionnement en eau des villes africaines et les problèmes démocratiques associés à celle-ci. J'étudie la décentralisation « par défaut » qui est liée au type de libéralisation favorisant une informalisation de l'offre. La séparation de l'offre et du règlement de l'État, implique que la régulation des rapports entre fournisseurs et utilisateurs échappe au contrôle public communal et local pour aboutir au contrôle des institutions traditionnelles. Pour les utilisateurs, cet état des choses implique une dépendance ravivée de la politique néo-traditionnelle plutôt que le développement d'un système parlémentaire, comme mode d'influence des conditions d'accès à l'eau.

Introduction

Research Questions

Liberalisation of water supplies in a situation of rapid urban expansion has made for great changes in water provisioning patterns in many African cities. While publicly controlled utilities with piped systems for distribution

[1] Reader in Human Geography, Stockholm University: gunilla.andrae@humangeo.su.se

continue to serve the formal economy and the well-to-do citizens, they have increasingly been supplemented with various other modes of provision for and by the poor. Highly fragmented and largely informalised structures are playing an increasing role, not only in practice but also as a recognized and expanding form for satisfying basic needs of the urban masses. Such fragmented supply structures have made for highly dispersed forms of provisioning. Located at scale levels below the municipal and even beyond the reach of local governments, these dispersed small-scale providers commonly show new forms of regulation and new relations between providers, users and concerned citizens. In this situation, agents concerned with the process of democratisation and the introduction of a human rights perspective to the provision of basic services have put popular access and influence over matters of access high on the agenda. As a result, the issue of the nature of community level governance has come to the fore, in particular as it relates to the scope for democratic modes of popular influence in locations where state authority is weak.

These matters are discussed in this article using a case study of the peripheral low-income community of Tudun Murtala in the large old city of Kano on the savannah of northern Nigeria in West Africa as the point of departure. My assumption is that for state backed democratic regulation of water provision for the poor to be realized, the regulatory powers of the state will need to reach beyond the local government level, which is where decentralisation policies are currently targeted. To effectively regulate the actual conditions of supply, these powers need to reach even further down, to the level of the community, where their current weakness leaves uncontested scope for alternative forces which do not necessarily cater for the interests of the low-income population. In the community studied here, legacies of colonial indirect rule remain in the form of neo-traditional modes of regulation of popular access to livelihood resources, and in a weak tradition of collective action, even on issues of provision of basic services. We may consider parliamentary democracy as the main guarantor of democratic representation in the realization of popular rights of access to water, or leave the door open for alternative 'substantial' modes of popular influence on access. Probing the place specific forms of governance at the community level, and in particular the forms of articulation between state based institutions and other forms for deliberation, will contribute necessary understanding of use in realizing democratic access to water in an era when provision of this service is increasingly fragmented and dispersed.

Research Context and Data: 'People, Provisioning and Place in African Cities'

The Nigerian case study reported here was carried out in the context of a series of studies of contemporary changes in urban service and livelihood in Africa at the Department of Human Geography at Stockholm University during 1998-2007. The focus of this programme, *People, Provisioning and Place in African Cities*[2], was the implications of liberalisation and globalisation for agency of provision and regulation of basic means of livelihood in the cities. In some of the studies the changes in modes of popular influence on distribution and access to resources, under variable local conditions, have been explored. The programme contained studies of different African cities and on different sectors of livelihood and service provision, with similar analytical departures, among these are Adama (2007), Appelblad, (2008), Cadstedt (2006), Kjellén (2006). My own case study concerns patterns of water provisioning[3] in one expanding peripheral low-income area in Kano. A fuller empirical account of the agents and relations of water provisioning there has been published as Andrae (2005) where fuller references to its source materials are also given. The sources include qualitative interviews with key informants in Tudun Murtala; at Kano State Water Board; Kano State Environment Planning and Protection Agency, KASEPPA; and Community Action for Popular Participation, CAPP, in 2000 and 2002. They also include two consultancy reports made for Kano Water Board that were the basis for external donors to fund reforms at the dysfunctional central public utility.[4] I further rely on my networks from earlier studies on Kano over the past decades (Andrae & Beckman 1985,

---

[2] This programme has received generous funding from the Swedish International Development Cooperation Agency (Sida) which is hereby acknowledged.

[3] The form 'provision' is used in the general sense of the word while 'provisioning' is meant to emphasize a connotation of agency.

[4] Regarding the earlier institutional context of water supplies for Kano see also WUP (n.d./late 1990s).

1998). Preliminaries to the present article were presented at conferences on *Decentralisation in Practice* in Uppsala 2004[5] and on *Human Rights Movements in Nigeria* held in Kano in 2007 (Andrae 2007). The present article is a more analytical development of these empirical presentations, where the main contribution is to problematise the implications for democratic popular influence of the de-scaling of water provision in a situation where secular organisation at the community level is weak and largely pre-empted by the strength of neo-traditional powers. Renewed contacts with informants in Tudun Murtala in 2007 confirmed that, apart from a colossal expansion of local private boreholes, the same basic provisioning model remained in place.

Analytical Framework and Relation to Current Discourses

Historically in African urban water provision, public utilities managed at the municipal level have a central role (Nilsson 2006). With the break-up of state monopolies into several components with different ownership, we can clearly see that there is a spatial dimension to change. Degree of dispersal and patterns of location relate to the altered structures of supply and regulation. The changes in supply structures, in forms for regulation, and in location patterns, are also reflected in changes in provisioning relations to users and citizens. These in turn will entail different conditions for democratic popular influence. The role of, and scope for, parliamentary forms for democratic regulation versus 'substantial' democracy modes depend on historic place specific factors that may fruitfully be sought through comparative case oriented research. While there may be general logics of location and of governance associated with the scale of administration and management, we can also expect to find particular scale and place specific logics, where socio-cultural and political factors operating at different levels in the spatial systems influence the outcome. Some elaboration is in order.

---

[5] Documented on CD in *Decentralisation in Practice: Power, Livelihoods and Cultural Meaning in West Africa*, International Workshop Highlights, Uppsala, Sweden, May 4-6, 2004, International Institute for Environment and Development (IIED), London & Dept. of Cultural Anthropology and Ethnology, Uppsala University, Uppsala (brochure + CD-ROM).

The dominating form for liberalisation of urban water supplies in Africa, that has been commonly adopted in national government policies and eagerly championed by the World Bank, has been the take-over by transnational companies of ownership or management in previously publicly owned water utilities. While this was a rather aggressive development running through the 1990s (Hall, Bayliss & Lobina 2002; UNDP 2006), it seems that we may already be entering a post-privatisation era at this level of large-scale supplies. With increasing popular resistance (Hall et al. 2005), and as the costs of operating the run-down public pipe-born systems are rapidly becoming evident to the transnational companies, the thrust for privatisation on this model is increasingly giving way to re-nationalisation. One example of this is Tanzania (Kjellén 2006). We are also beginning to see various other forms for commercialisation, still under public control, as in the case of Uganda (Appelblad 2008). All along we have, however, seen another parallel and still ongoing process of establishment of small and fragmented non-public suppliers. It occurs in replacement of the breaking-down public systems of water supply (which often date back to early colonial times), and has come to constitute a major mode of provision for the needs of the masses of the urban poor in many African cities. It is a development that connects with what was for a long-time the only available form for developing supplies in the rapidly expanding peripheral and often unplanned areas of cities. Covered by Kjellén and McGranahan (2006) this small-scale and mainly informally organised privatisation of provision for the urban poor, already described by Solo (1999), has attracted continued attention in conjunction with recent movements at the international level to enforce the access to water as a human right (UN Economic and Social Council, 2003). It includes renewed concerns, mainly on the part of international agencies and donors and more rarely of national government authorities, for the need to extend public responsibilities for service provision beyond the wealthy elites to these majorities, if not by supply then at least by regulation of the relations of provision. The 2006 UNDP World Development Report dealing with water thus puts strong emphasis on the problem of governance (UNDP 2006).

The modes of poor people's provisioning and the politics involved in these are attracting increased attention within the research community. Remembering that even rights-based regimes do not preclude the need for the urban poor to actively contest their rights of access, there are strong pressures on researchers to contribute better understandings of the modes of insertion of the poor in existing and developing provisioning regimes, and to provide knowledge that is of use for their struggles for better access. Seen as a matter of empowerment, the political dimension must not be allowed to be concealed in top-down modes of provision under the concept of participatory management.

The large-scale utility systems typical of the pipe-born supplies inherited from colonial times are commonly run from the metropolitan level, obeying the logics of 'natural monopolies' with potentials for large economies of scale to be gained by concentration of processing, distribution and administration (Belli 1997; Kjellén 2006; Nilsson 2006: Article 3). In the peripheral areas where the metropolitan grid no longer reaches, or where it is no longer functional due to lack of maintenance, the smaller-scale providers take over as suppliers in highly fragmented structures of establishments located at the level of the neighbourhood community. With current rapid expansion in the peripheries of the cities, this type of supplier already dominates in supplying the poor populations

Our concern here is that in much of Africa, the state authorities have not only let go of their supply functions, legitimized by reigning neo-liberal ideologies as promoted notably by the World Bank. They have also lost their regulating functions concerning service supplies that are targeting the urban poor, as they have been allowed to develop in distant peripheries by a largely unregistered mass of providers. We can then expect to find that regulation of relations around these peripheral supply points will be in the hands of forces other than the local government, as these will take place in communities where the powers of the 'secular' state hardly reach. The result will be a kind of decentralisation of regulation 'by default', driven by the de-scaling of supplies through expansion of small-scale and informal forms of provision.

Strategies of decentralisation of service provision as a policy option have become a common component of liberalisation policies and rhetoric, and have usually been based on ideas of the democratic potentials that can be realised by moving control over basic livelihood services closer to the people. Such ideas have been championed by the global donor community in furtherance of impacts on efficiency, resource mobilisation, local relevance and popular participation (see Cheema 2005; Chikulo 1998; and for Nigeria, Crook & Manor 1993; Gboyega 1998). The need for renewed awareness of the significance of the spatial level below that of the local government, the community level, in the decentralisation problematic concerning regulation of service provision is underlined by the community case I have chosen to study (Andrae 2005). Clearly the currently popular notions of 'Spaces for Democracy' (Barnett & Low 2006) and 'Spaces for Change' (Cornwall and Coelho 2007) need to be applied in the literal sense of *where* the power game around access to services by the poor is actually played out, since this has implications for who regulates access, influence and empowerment to whose benefit. In this context it is pertinent to maintain that concern with community level governance will need to move to a more central place in this analysis.

The character of alternative community level regulation structures is of course variable, and the conditions of variation are matters that we need to further explore empirically. The definition of place specificities and variations of local patterns in the different institutional, socio-political and physical contexts are pressing challenges for geographical research, not least if the arguments are to be effective against the generalised policies and loan conditionality pushed by the powerful global finance institutions. Contributions of case studies may produce a basis for defining relevant parameters for comparative studies. This is thus one purpose of the analysis of the case presented here.

We apply a concept of governance that, in this context, looks as follows.[6] With the rapid fragmentation of water supplies, we observe a growing number of forms of water provision with different conditions of access. Whether mediated by the market, or by public or communal supply, access will be influenced by the regulation by powers that may rest with the state, private owners collective organisations of users, or of other citizens who support their cause. These rule-setting agents are, however, only one side of the governing relation. Successful regulation rests on relations to the users, or other citizens, with political interest in the supply, and depends on their

---

[6] For the concept of governance applied in a service provisioning context in the global South see Devas (2004)

legitimisation of the arrangement of supply. The resulting structure of provisioning relations is what we term a *mode of governance.* Operationally we may delimit these relationships by looking for the users of the various supplies, and particularly their agency of demand-making, on the one hand, and then, on the other hand, define the authorities that enter into regulating relations, for groups of suppliers, with the demand making users (and their political allies)[7]. This is the approach applied in the case treated here.

There is a spatial dimension to the mode of governance. The holders of rule-setting power may relate to the concerned population from and over different scale levels. Since administrative state structures are important in regulation of services, the notions of space and scale may in this case follow these state administrative structures. From the point of view of one particular spatial level we may talk of 'multi-level governance' (Elander 2002). We may finally expect a variation in governance according to specific conditions in particular places.

The regulating structures that we expect in the African context are, first of all, the public authorities, which come in very different shapes. Mamdani (1996) has drawn attention to the existence of the bi-furcated state, where the colonial powers have left legacies of their neo-traditional systems of indirect rule, which in some places still remain. Lund (2006) has developed the notion of the 'twilight state' indicating the range of forms of public authority structures that may perform state-like functions. And Buur and Kyed (2006) in the above publication by Lund, have given us interesting examples of alternative agents performing such functions in the context of weak or destroyed state authority (e.g. in post-war Mocambique). The blurred nature of state authority will be particularly pertinent at the local level, where the presence of the modern states has usually been particularly weak. Policies of decentralisation of state functions have usually been aimed at addressing this structural phenomenon, while usually considering the local government level low enough for reaching the whole population.

A specific condition in the case of Northern Nigeria in general, and Kano in particular, is then the strength of its heritage of neo-traditional rule, once

[7] We may refer to all of them as 'users' for short.

the very model for British colonial *indirect rule*, and the viability of its remnants. The implications of this for the mode of governance and the potentials for popular influence over water provisioning gives the chosen case its very specific character, well suited for demonstrating the significance of local conditions for the relations of service provision.

When it comes to popular influence over access and conditions of access, it is clear that the clientilistic relations between neo-traditional authorities and community residents are not favourable for collective organising. In other situations where the conditions for civic organising have been strong, as in South Africa, they have been shown to hold potentials for channelling real influence, as demonstrated by Stokke and Oldfield (2002). The experience is that where these are restricted or historically weak, the 'space' for alternative modes of 'substantial' democratic influences is considerably narrowed (see Gaventa 2004 and also Harriss et al. 2004, where the contribution by Törnquist is of particular relevance). This puts great weight on the functioning of parliamentary modes of representation of popular interests, and on the structure of the state institutions for fair regulation of the provision of a basic needs service, such as water. Alternatively the recent search for functioning modes of 'deliberative democracy' à la Habermas and 'new forms of citizenship' must continue (as discussed by Gaventa 2007, who rather uses the term 'substantive democracy').

Departing from the observation of the recently de-scaled location of water supply to the low-income community of Tudun Murtala, we have thus set out to probe the spatial structure of the relations of regulation over water as seen from the perspective of this community. We note that these relations result in a spatially skewed governance structure, where the regulation of supplies has to a very high degree come to be played out at the community level. The question in focus, then, concerns the implications that this structure of relations will have for the democratic influence that users and citizens may exert on their access to household water.

The Case of Tudun Murtala, Kano

Research Area

The area of our case study, Tudun Murtala, was a rapidly expanding low-income community of some 20,000 inhabitants at the time of this study, in 2000 and 2002. It is situated on the north-eastern outskirts of the city of Kano. With over two million inhabitants, this is the second city of Nigeria, located in the far north of the country. It is an industrial and administrative centre with long historical standing as a Muslim cultural and religious node in the Nigerian North and the surrounding Sudan region. It is a city within Kano State, which is one of 36 states (or provinces) in the Nigerian Federation. These are divided into local government areas, each with its own local government council. Tudun Murtala is part of Nassarawa local government area. The parallel neo-traditional authority structure contains the Emir of Kano to which a number of district-heads, appointed by him, report. The districts are divided into wards with ward heads who are popularly elected for life. At the time of my study Tudun Murtala had recently been expanded from one ward with one head to four wards, each with their own ward head. Of these, one was particularly vocal and enterprising and was one of my respondents. His information on the role of ward heads as agents in the provisioning game at this level is amply used in this case.[8]

The origin of the community is as a resettlement area of people who were earlier living in the adjacent Bompai area, which was designated an industrial area half a century ago. The core of the population today is of Muslim Hausa origin, from Kano and its surrounding rural regions, with smaller numbers of southern immigrants that belong to a Christian religion.

De-scaled Supply and Decentralised Regulation

In Kano the colonial piped water utility, built in the 1930s, has been allowed by the city level public authorities to deteriorate, particularly in low-income residential areas outside the walled historic inner City and the cen-

[8] Interviews Sabo Munkaila (2000 and 2002)

tral high-income Government Residential Areas (GRAs). In the old outer areas most of the piped public supply has, as it has gradually broken down, been replaced by a host of non-public sources of supply. Similar sources of supply are also emerging in the rapidly growing new expansion areas of these same communities. It is this process of privatisation by fragmentation and informalisation from the previously centralised city level public supply that can be shown to have resulted in a de-scaling in agency of supply down to the community level. The result is summarised in Table 1, which thus shows the situation in the community of Tudun Murtala in the first years of this century.

Table 1: Agents involved in supply by scale level and mode of regulation

Mode of Regulation	**Scale level of supply**		
	Community	*Local Govt.*	*City*
State	Water tap	Self-help Funding	Pipe grid
State through formal market	Tap operator Bore hole	Competing industry	
Informal market	Vendors		
Neo-traditional	Mosque Communal Well		Philanthropy
Household/Self	House wells Self-help labour		

Reading down the columns we see the various agents involved in supplying water that are found at different spatial levels from community through local government to city level. In the rows in the table these sources are categorized according to principles of regulation which have replaced the increasingly deficient state regulated supplies. I have termed these principles *modes of regulation* and they are shown to range from state to formal (state regulated) and informal market, neo-traditional and finally household/self regulation. We will look at the supply structures and regulation structures in turn.[9]

The public piped water source, which previously supplied the central sections of the community of Tudun Murtala from a handful of community stand-pipes, had by the year 2002 been reduced to a single commercially operated water tap at the entrance to the area. Operators of commercial deep bore-holes, and independently working water vendors distributing the water from these outlets and from the only functioning local tap on the metropolitan grid, are now major providers, who have stepped in to supplement the common shallow hand-dug house wells and a few wells provided by the mosque and by the community. Together they form the core of a supply system that has thus moved from a highly centralised publicly controlled one to a highly decentralised one involving a multitude of non-state providers.

The community-based supplies are supplemented by those initiated at the city and local government levels. These involve the services of self-help groups and the 'philanthropists' of religious and political motivation. Self-help groups are a form for co-operation between community groups and the local government in the field of physical water regulation with focus on prevention of further erosion along the drainage channels. It is in this case manifested in public sponsorship and financial support for a community based group with a chairman who is locally elected through the mediation of and dependence on patronage from the neo-traditional ward heads. The motive behind this public support for water management lies primarily in the prevention of pollution of household wells. It is one of the few contact points between local government and the community regarding water supplies.

[9] For a fuller account, see Andrae 2005

Supply by philanthropists along neo-traditional lines, e.g. by donation of water by tanks, has been a possibility that has kept local agents of negotiation alert, as it has had considerable impact in the neighbouring area of Tudun Wada. The main source of such supply is wealthy men at the city level. Similarly, gifts for political patronage have been received all the way from the national level. As an example, in the 1999 election campaign, gifts of electrical equipment of use for mechanical bore holes were received from a national politician. The possibility of supplies of such services caused local power brokers to pay attention to the relevant networks outside their community.

But the supply picture also includes external limitations on supply of water. Shortages due to intermittent periods of drought have lead to swings in ground water supplies. These have also affected the neighbouring industry, which has tended to make demands on the water of the residential community which is located further down the same main municipal pipe, thus aggravating the shortage there. It has led to the need for negotiation on behalf of the whole community, again with active mediation of the ward heads, but also of other representatives of the civil society that relate to these. Industrial pollution of the water from the natural stream running through the community, has further affected some of the neighbouring household wells. This is another concern where the community needs to negotiate as a unit with the industry.

We understand this supply structure as being the result of what we may speak of as a process of de-scaling of supply 'by default', and as a by-product of the process of privatisation which can in this case also be characterised as having occurred by default (following the breakdown of the infrastructure). Supply is de-scaled largely through the logics of location tied to the informalisation of services, and by dependence on small-scale suppliers. This mode of privatisation supplements the more programmatic policy proclaimed from the national level as a condition for World Bank loans that were offered at this time for the overhaul of the public utility and the piped supply of the more central areas of the city. Though proclaimed, they were implemented only in the form of one small pilot purification plant to serve the industry. What remains of the central municipal utility continues to supply central high-income residential, commercial and public administration areas.

Let us then move to looking at the regulation structures. In the social life of Tudun Murtala issues of water supply constantly require mediation and regulation between different interests. When most of the water consumed at the household level could be drawn from the supplies administrated by the Kano Water Board through the piped system, this administering authority was the target of negotiation regarding claims for better supplies. Claims could (in theory) be channelled through the parliamentary system through the locally elected local government councillors representing the wards. They were probably just as often carried forth by direct approaches to the supplier from lobbying coalitions of local representatives, as we shall see below.

The changing agency structure of supply has led to adjusted patterns of negotiation and brokerage where the pattern of location plays a part. The rows in Table 1, above, indicating the dimension of modes of regulation, enable us to summarize the complexity of the spatial dimension of the combined supply and regulation structure. It helps us to see how large sections of community level supplies have come to be controlled by the informal market regulators, traditional authorities and by households, who to a large extent lead their lives outside the formal economy.

Apart from privatisation of small-scale supplies, by design and by default, the other main process in the provisioning game in the recent times of liberalisation is the separation of regulation from supplies. Even when the supply function gets devolved to levels nearer to the users, this leaves a measure of regulating functions still in the hands of the state, but largely devolved to lower scale levels. Public regulation and management have in this process been largely devolved to the local government level in the form of certain control functions. Licensing of the new and rapidly expanding commercial and privately owned deep 'mechanical' wells is thus done by the local government, and is followed by intermittent inspections of water quality by the same agent. In addition there are said to be occasional checks of the common household wells, particularly when there are outbreaks of cholera, as in 2001. Public regulation by the local government ends there, however.

The essence of this development is that with the de-scaling of supplies, other regulating functions have taken hold of the community level supplies, which implies that these have, to the same extent, escaped from the reach of the local government. Here the situation in Kano has its own characteristics. The colonial heritage of indirect rule that existed there up to Independence in 1960 has resulted in a division of labour with neo-traditional authorities still in control of basic livelihood conditions at the community level, particularly in low income areas. As reported by Gboyega (1998), a series of reforms for the dismantling of indirect rule have since sought to limit the formal powers of the neo-traditional office bearers to the mediation of 'peace and harmony' in the spheres of community – household relations. Some very basic functions have, however, remained in the hands of the neo-traditional ward heads. In Tudun Murtala, for instance, they still took care of the registration of land transfers according to officials at the Kano state planning authority, KASEPPA (interview 2002). The recent process of small-scale development and informalisation of service provision in the case of water has the result of pushing this balance of regulation even further in favour of neo-traditional authorities at the community level. This becomes visible when we look at the ways local users and citizens articulate their demands for access and influence over access to water, and to whom their demands are directed.

My study of the patterns of demand-making over issues of access to water in Tudun Murtala shows that it is when it comes to conflicts between community based commercial providers, such as formal deep-well managers and informal vendors, on the one hand, and the water-using residents of the community, on the other, that the capacity and the legitimacy of neo-traditional authorities to handle the regulation of these conflicts become visible.[10] The ward heads play a part in mediating between agents of supply, internal and external to the community, and their authority is difficult to circumvent for community residents.[11]

Their methods of regulation and the modes of demand making that they engender lead me to link the process of decentralisation of supplies to the area of local politics, and at least tentatively suggest that it works against the

[10] Again, see Andrae 2005 for greater detail.

[11] In analysing this I refer to the time immediately after the replacement of a single ward with four different ones for this community. I perceived the old single office bearers to continue to be rather hegemonic in acting as representatives of the whole community.

process of democratisation. We therefore proceed to look at the various actors involved in concrete situations of negotiation, starting with the modes of demand making applied by users and others who seek to influence supplies as citizens residing in the community.

When individuals want to change their access to water within the new supply system, they use a range of strategies. They may step up individual supplies by digging deeper household wells or walking further to fetch water from the few remaining natural streams. Most strategies are, however, directed at influencing other agents of supply or regulation. I found cases where violence had been used, as when in the late 1990s one bore-hole owner was killed in an armed robbery commonly attributed to his profiting from water shortages at a time of drought. Another event that I documented was a conflict when consumers threatened to smash the equipment of the water vendors, when these had raised the price of water following the closing of a crucial tap connected to the public pipes running through the community. When the vendors organised a strike lasting several days, it was the leading ward head of the community that could muster the authority and legitimacy to step in as the mediator. In that instance, he arbitrated in favour of the vendors, with the acquiescence of the community, as further violence was prevented.

Users of water also form groups for collective action. The formation and activities of the self-help groups referred to above is one example that involves participatory management at the initiative of, and with support from, the local government. More pertinent as a regulating agent was Tudun Murtala Development Association (TUDA) which was at this time the most established town organisation. Originally formed by some young educated residents for the purpose of external lobbying, TUDA also works in support of community development and 'peace and harmony' internally.

Intervention in support of formal democratic procedures was also made by the local chapter of the Community Action for Popular Participation (CAPP). This was a branch of a national NGO with an agenda to mobilise members in the local community to challenge the agency of local government in the field of water. The main activity was to educate citizens to use the parliamentary process to its full potential. During 2000, the general focus of their city-wide campaign was on water, and in particular industrial pollution of water. Their mode of operation was public mobilisation and voters' education in the local elections, inducing people to take up water pollution as an election issue. Later, they organised meetings of groups of citizens, including those from Tudun Murtala, with local government officials, who were repeatedly interrogated concerning implementation of election promises between elections.[12]

But, more spontaneous interest group organising was rare, of limited success, unless played out in coalition with the neo-traditional rulers or with TUDA, which operated very close to the rulers. This was illustrated by the case of one experienced trade union organiser, a long-time resident in the community, and his frustrated attempts at gathering his neighbouring households in an independent protest. The issue of concern was the negative impact that newly drilled deep mechanical bore-holes in central parts of Tudun Murtala had on the water level in the local house wells. In his own interpretation of events, it was the fact that he did not ally with the neo-traditional community authorities that inhibited his neighbours from joining his campaign.[13] Nevertheless, we did find the same man, also as the local organiser and trainer for this community, behind the explicit efforts of the above-mentioned CAPP to widen the arena for secular organisation. Together, his efforts show us the seed for a more secular form for organisation as part of a local politics of provision independent of neo-traditional authorities.[14]

Notable for its absence is the influence of women as a group, and as individuals. For the majority of housewives in seclusion, the main managers of household-water, the development of the new water 'regime' that we have described here has meant a reversal to a neo-traditional dependence on their husbands for their access. Their previous control over supplies from public taps, that they exercised by sending younger girls to queue up to collect water, has been replaced by complete dependence on their husbands' duty to supply them from whatever source they choose. Usually this was done

---

[12] Interview Yunuza Yau 2002, one time National President of CAPP. More detailed information on CAPP and its role in water provisioning is given in Andrae (2007).

[13] But in 2007 we did hear of another, more successful neighbourhood protest on similar issues, where we do not, however, have information of the conditions of struggle.

[14] Interview in 2002 with Ibrahim Yusuf, the one-time chairman of the local chapter of CAPP.

through sending water vendors to their door with their vans. The regulation of the conflicts in household relations that may then ensue is another area where neo-traditional authorities have considerable influence. But, the housewives also enter the supplier trade in the capacity of vending cart owners. Non-Muslim female southerners may and do participate as entrepreneurs of distribution. And, even among those in seclusion, I met women who raised income from renting out water vending carts. The money earned was said to be used for instalments in the mutual saving societies, to which many women belong.

The parliamentary system offers vehicles for channelling grievances, by voting for and by approaching the Councillors for the wards, who were elected through a multi-party process. As representatives of the community, their field of influence also includes the regulation of appropriation and pollution of the available water by the competing industry, as well as matters of licensing and quality inspection handled by the local government, through the Council.

Also at the extra-community level the use of lobbying was at least as important as a mode of influencing provision and has typically involved delegations to the Water Board, to competing industries and to philanthropists. These delegations were found to include coalitions of representatives of the town association (TUDA), the self-help groups, and importantly and unavoidably a representative of the neo-traditional ward heads. A local government councillor, would sometimes also be included, particularly as, at this time, his origin was in the other groups (self-help and TUDA), which had recently formed the recruitment base for this function. This form for channelling grievances made the non-parliamentary forms for influence, including those of the neo-traditional rulers, important also in relations outside the community.

We thus find that in the case of water provision in Tudun Murtala at the time of this field study, the neo-traditional ward head had a hand in very many of the modes of interest promotion and demand making taking place. Internally, in Tudun Murtala, we find him not only as a social advisor to individuals, but also as a mediator in conflicts between groups of citizens, e.g. in the case of the conflict of users vs. water vendors. Although elected (for life) by the residents, his inherited neo-traditional role as a keeper of 'peace and harmony' gave him particular authority in such situations. In external relations we rather find him as a co-ordinating lobbyist in coalitions of TUDA, self-help groups and even the local government council. He played this role in parties negotiating better terms with the industries as they competed for access to their water, and with the Water Board on the closure and mismanagement of communal water taps on the piped grid. We were also told of his role in alliance with neo-traditional district authorities in approaching philanthropists at the city level and negotiating shares in their ritual gifts of water. We can thus single him out as a very important regulator of relations with suppliers at spatial levels internal and external to the community.

However, he was not the only regulator. In the case of the self-help groups we have seen that their interventions are rather on the initiative of the local government. Negotiating with the community, their representatives, however, have to relate to the ward heads as brokers. The local government councillors have, of course, their own power base in the secular parliamentary system. But, there is considerable scope for neo-traditional authority meddling into the operation of this system through election rigging and lobbying for candidates, as was openly acknowledged by my ward head respondent. With decreasing municipal water supplies and with interventions from the local government being limited to the licensing of boreholes (said in 2007 to be increasingly evaded by drillers), and to highly intermittent health inspections, the regulating powers of the parliamentary representative were also becoming more and more marginal. Thus we do find co-operating and competing agents of regulation representing different social forces, and have to conclude that the local neo-traditional rulers are without doubt important holders of power. Indeed, the few attempts that have been made to organise outside of them, have been largely abortive, as in the case of the mobilisation of resistance to a deep bore hole by the resident unionist.

It is of interest to note (see Table 1) that the different scale-levels that are targeted have their distinct profiles with regard to agents and methods of demand-making and regulation. It seems that it is the role as conflict mediator between users and suppliers inside the community, which gives the neo-traditional ruler the particular powers that merit his inclusion as the formal head of the lobbying coalitions for external negotiations. We may add that these powers may have been enhanced by his role in mediating between interests of people in different parts of his ward. In an earlier phase, those residents in different locations in relation to the decreasing number of functioning taps on the grid represented such interest groups between which he was said to mediate. We can thus find matters of spatial contradiction also internal to the community.

The position of the neo-traditional authorities is further enhanced by their straddling different political realms. Above the ward-head in the traditional hierarchy is the district head, who has an office in the local government headquarters and who is appointed by the Emir of Kano. Access of the ward-head to these power holders will also facilitate his access to the Muslim philanthropists.

A Hybrid Governance Pattern and its Democratic Content

It thus appears that in the context of Tudun Murtala, we can count three main forms of regulation combined in a hybrid mode of governance. The secular state (at various levels), the leaders of community organisations and the neo-traditional rulers are the regulators that combine to form one side of the community governance system. The legitimacy of each is based on the resident citizens who relate to them by more or less democratic means. Each regulator has their particular legitimacy base in the users and other citizens who are prepared to ally with them. These persons make up the other side of the mode of governance around water in this community.

The particular mode by which they each relate to users and other local residents can be scrutinized with regard to the democratic content of the relationship. Representation through the state and the electoral system is shown to be weak. Water issues are given very low attention in the election of ward councillors. Their influence on water provisioning issues in local government is also weak, and these issues are not given strong attention by them. Their representation of popular interests is also marred by the fact that elections of ward councillors are highly manipulated by neo-traditional rulers.

The channelling of demands and opinions via civil society organisations is a mode for popular influence that is not well anchored in local traditions. Secular, non-traditional, forms for community action, as when initiated by a man with union experience and affiliation to a 'secular' NGO, was not met with great response. It was suggested that popular support was given only to organisations that were sanctioned by neo-traditional rulers and which involved commitment to supporting their modes of regulation. This does not open for the practice of 'substantial' forms of democracy to any extent. The role of such forms in deepening the democratic deficit thus does not appear to be of immediate importance in this place context, with its particular historical and institutional set-up.

Neo-traditional rulers are elected for life and have strong allegiance to the parallel authority system of the Emir. They are allowed to exercise power by paternalistic means and are approached through clientilistic relations by individuals or collectives that submit to their authority. There is complete lack of transparency and accountability in their regulation of internal conflict. They are known to manipulate the electoral system of representation through illicit influence on nomination and voting. They have powers to lobby external regulators through direct contacts, individually as in contacts with the industry, and in combination with the other regulators. They do not encourage independent popular organisation around internal community interests, particularly not outside their own spheres of regulation. They certainly do not support the independent agency of women in provisioning relations outside the home.

We may thus conclude that the degree of popular influence around water provisioning in Tudun Murtala cannot, on the basis of this material, be characterized as particularly democratic, neither by standards of electoral parliamentary democracy nor of direct 'substantial' democracy. One may even perceive of this mode of governance as a virtual reversal of the vision of democratisation of local governance of service provision that is commonly the aim of the policy discourse on the benefits of decentralised provision. But then this decentralisation is not really an intended one, but rather the location consequence of the process of liberalisation by default.

Conclusions

The Kano case shows us a process of de-scaling of water provision to the community level without corresponding adjustments in modes of state regulation. In this case this leaves citizens with very weak 'secular' democratic means of influence over access and conditions of access. In a situation where civil organizing is not developed, it is difficult to identify much immediate scope for 'substantial' democratic alternatives. Meanwhile, it is clear that the actual powers of influence of poor residents within the parliamentary regulation system are not very large either.

As a place, Kano is special in the continued strength of the neo-traditional regulation sphere, based on a still viable Emir-centred authority structure, and its heritage as a centre for Islamic culture in a range of respects. It is also true that it is located in one of the Nigerian states (provinces) that have in the past decade (in 1999) introduced the *shari'a* criminal laws. The generally interesting circumstance is, however, the way in which these conditions have historically interacted in very particular ways with the locally and regionally specific forms of capitalist development that we see in this city (see e.g., Lubeck 1995 and Watts 1996). Probing the specific features of community level governance that this has yielded has served our main purpose, to demonstrate the relevance of considering the scale specific nature of the conditions of political organisation that influences popular access to livelihood resources when liberalisation has taken the form it has in this case. If we compare with conditions in cities in other parts of Africa or, even only in Southern Nigeria, where the neo-traditional powers have a different history of articulation with modern economic development, we are certain to find very distinct specificities in the ways they manifest themselves in provisioning politics at the community level. These are specificities that add to the characteristics of climate, hydrology, demography, economy and political culture in their historical and geographical contexts which explain the patterns that we find. The scope for comparative studies aiming for further generalisations is great in this field.

Of course, the empirical study reported here could be expanded to confirm and deepen what we have seen so far. Some immediate questions concern first the actual relations between traditional rulers and residents which might also be differentiated in several categories. By what means do residents negotiate with the authority of regulation and influence? Who gains and who loses in the paternalistic system of contestation between them and informally and traditionally regulating agents? In the short run, the close knowledge of conditions of poor residents held by the local neo-traditional power holders, together with their greater legitimacy as mediators between many locally based agents, may make them well equipped to represent their interests outside the community and to intervene internally in this conflict-prone and commonly riot-exposed context. We must concede that our tools might need to be refined in order to catch this 'substantial' dimension of representation as well. Experiences from the neighbouring country of Niger, in the related Hausa society, where traditional authority is still formally recognized (and from where notably many water vendors in Tudun Murtala are said to be recruited), would be of interest to bring in for comparison. Further documentation might tie on to recent interesting research on the agents of regulation that develop in the 'twilight' zone between weak state institutions and other local authorities in places with differing conditions, as documented in the studies referred to above and reported in Lund (2006).

Conditions for forming collective organisations of shorter and longer duration, and the nature of their relations to neo-traditional authorities, are further themes for research. Points of departure originating from this study would include the close allegiance we noted of the town association (TUDA) to the neo-traditional authority, while modern secular organisations, such as CAPP and its related activists, have legitimacy problems. The historically low propensity for collective organisation may well be on its way to change. This may well happen under the influence of external NGOs, which sometimes have international funding connections as a basis for influence, as was the case with CAPP. It might be fruitful to look deeper into the occurrence of organisations in associated fields of service provision and material livelihood concerns. I saw in Tudun Murtala a number of community based organisations concerned with prevention of erosion along the central drainage canal running through the community. It is likely that their collective experience of organisation might have a spread effect. Connection with Islamic networks and their development is another phenomenon one might like to probe further.

While stressing the goals of satisfying human rights principles with respect to access to water, and recognizing the continued need for contestation among popular users and agents of influence over access, there is need to ask how the system can be made more respectful of popular interests in access and influence through a more democratic mode of provision. Responsibilities for furthering such goals will in some sense be spread over the social forces that participate in the game of water provisioning, both those on the regulating and on the demand-making sides. It would seem that public institutions at the city level, while of course circumscribed by national and provincial agents, are however in particular positions to act based on the comparative strength of their regulation powers.

Focusing on the public agents of regulation, our analysis in this case leads us to formulate a number of alternative policy options. They could strengthen the reach and presence of 'secular' democratic institutions of regulation at the community level, if this is where supply and regulation actually take place. They could further support forces of civil society organisation, to realize not only participatory management, but also political influence as part of the modes of provision. Finally, they could pay attention to the democratic problems associated with the remaining and possibly expanding powers of neo-traditional forces of regulation.

A challenging question to pursue is what difference a more decentralised state regulation structure, built on closer public presence at the community level, could make in this particular case. We certainly have no reason to romanticise the democratic qualities of the secular parliamentary system and its modes of regulating service and infrastructure provision in Nigerian cities. Still, after decades of oppressive military rule in Nigeria, elections to the local governments have been somehow revitalised, returning representatives from communities at the urban ward level to the secular parliamentary system of representation. Although these elections usually do not concern the concrete livelihood issues, that e.g., CAPP has tried to mobilise around and train citizens for, at least they do, with all their flaws and shortcomings, provide channels for popular demand-making on matters of urgent popular interest.

In a different approach, one option is of course to return to the basic matter of the modes of liberalisation or commercialisation practised at the city level. The possibility might still be there to reverse the fragmented and informalised modes of provision and seriously consider the scope for overhauling the central, city level utilities of water processing and distribution. In case these utilities were state controlled, if not by ownership at least by effective regulation, and the task of supplying the whole city area with processed water were taken seriously, the potential to facilitate equalisation of access including the peripheral low income areas might still be there. Just as much in favour of this alternative may be the argument of the powerful economies of scale that are usually associated with provision through central purification plants and city wide pipe-systems of distribution. In a city like Kano, where comparatively abundant sources of water are available in the Kano River combined with conditions of a sensitive ground-water table, the option of expansion of supplies by deep bore-holes may compare very negatively with expansion by dependence on central intakes from Kano River. But, of course, in the final analysis it all boils down to the conditions set by the political economy of the particular place, as inserted in the national and global context.

References

Adama, O. 2007. *Governing from Above. Solid Waste Management in Nigeria's New Capital City of Abuja*. Stockholm: Stockholm Studies in Human Geography 17.

Andrae, G. 2007. Local Level Democratisation: CAPP and the traditionalisation of Water Provision in Tudun Murtala, Kano. Draft paper to CDR and CDRT conference on *The Human Rights Movement in Nigeria*. Kano 20-21 February 2007.

Andrae, G. 2005. Wanting Water: Popular Politics in Response to Changing Agency in a Peripheral Low-Income Area in Kano, Nigeria. In *Space and Place in Development Geography* (eds) A. Broekhuis, G. Nijenhuis & G. Van Westen. Amsterdam: Rozenberg Publishers, Thela Thesis.

Andrae, G. & B. Beckman 1985. *The Wheat Trap: Bread and Underdevelopment in Nigeria*. London. Zed Books.

Andrae, G. & B. Beckman 1998. *Union Power: Labour Regime and Adjustment in the Nigerian Textile Industry*. Uppsala: The Nordic Africa Institute; Somerset, NJ: Transaction Publishers; Kano: Centre for Research and Documentation.

Appelblad, J. 2008. Parting from the Privatisation Path? Public Reform Strategies in the Ugandan Urban Water Sector. In *The Provision and Politics of Public Services – Urban Governance in Uganda*. Licentiate Thesis, Department of Human Geography, Stockholm University. Stockholm.

Belli, P. 1997. *The Comparative Advantage of Government*. Washington DC: World Bank.

Buur, L. & H.M. Kyed 2006. Contested Sources of Authority: Reclaiming State sovereignty by Formalizing Traditional authority in Mozambique. *Development and Change* 37 (4): 847-869.

Cadstedt, J. 2006. *Influence and Invisibility: Tenants in Housing Provision in Mwanza City, Tanzania*. Stockholm: Stockholm Studies in Human Geography 14.

Cheema, G. S. 2005. *Building Democratic Institutions: Governance Reform in Developing countries*. Bloomfield, CT, USA: Kumarian Press, Inc.

Chikulo, B.C. 1998. Decentralisation and the Role of the State in the Future. In *Governance and Human Development in Southern Africa* (ed.) I. Mandaza. Harare: SAPES Books.

Cornwall, A. & V. Schattan Coelho 2007. *Spaces for Change: The politics of Citizen Participation in New Democratic Arenas*. London: Zed Books.

Crook, R.C. & J. Manor (eds) 1998. *Democracy and Decentralisation in South Asia and West Africa: Participation, Accountability and Performance*. Cambridge: Cambridge University Press.

Devas, N. (ed.) 2004. *Urban Governance, Voice and Poverty in the Developing World*. London: Earthscan.

Elander, I. 2002. Partnerships and Urban Governance. *International Social Science Journal* 172 (June): 191-204.

Gaventa, J. 2006. Triumph, Deficit or Contestation? Deepening the 'Deepening Democracy' Debate. IDS Working Paper 264. Brighton: Institute of Development Studies.

Gaventa, J. 2007. Foreword. In *Spaces for Change: The politics of Citizen Participation in New Democratic Arenas* A. Cornwall & V. Schattan Coelho London: Zed Books.

Gboyega, A. 1998. *Decentralisation and Local Autonomy in Nigeria's Federal System*. Dept. of Political Science: Occasional Paper 49. Ibadan: University of Ibadan.

Hall, D., K. Bayliss & E. Lobina 2002. Water privatisation in Africa. Paper presented at' Municipal Services Project Conference', Witwatersrand University: Johannesburg (May 2002). London: Public Services International Research Unit (PSIRU).

Hall, D., E. Lobina & R. de la Motte 2005. Public Resistance to privatisation in water and energy. *Development in Practice* 15 (3-4), June 2005, 286-301.

Harriss, J., K. Stokke & O. Törnqvist 2004. *Politicising Democracy: The New Local Politics of Democratisation*. Basingstoke: Palgrave Macmillan.

Kjellén, M. 2006. *From Public Pipes to Private Hands: Water Provision in Dar es Salaam*. Stockholm: Stockholm Studies in Human Geography 15.

Kjellén, M. & G. McGranahan 2006. *Informal Water Vendors and the Urban Poor.* Human Settlements Discussion Paper Series Theme: Water-3. London, International Institute for Environment and Development (IIED) (http://www.iied.org/pubs/pdf/full/10529IIED.pdf)

Lund, C. 2006. Twilight Institutions: Public Authority and Local Politics in Africa. *Development and Change* 37 (4): 685-705.

Lourenco-Lindell, I. 2002. *Walking the Tight-Rope: Informal Livelihoods in a West African City*. Stockholm: Stockholm Studies in Human Geography 9.

Mahwood, P. (ed.) 1993. *Local Government in the Third World: The Experience of Decentralisation in Tropical Africa.* Chicester, South: John Wiley and Sons.

Nilsson, D. 2006. *Water for a Few: A History of Urban Water and Sanitation in East Africa.* Licentiate dissertation, School of Architecture and the built environment, Royal Institute of Technology, KTH. Stockholm.

Oldfield, S. & K. Stokke 2004. New Social Movements and Substantial Democratisation in South Africa. In *Politicising Democracy: The New Local Politics of Democratisation* (eds) J. Harriss, K. Stokke & O. Törnquist. Basingstoke: Palgrave Macmillan.

Solo, T.M. 1999. Small-scale entrepreneurs in the urban water and sanitation market. *Environment and Urbanisation* 11 (1) April, 117-132.

Törnquist, O. 2004. The Political Deficit of Substantial Democratisation. In *Politicising Democracy: The New Local Politics of Democratisation* (eds) J. Harriss, K. Stokke & O. Törnquist. Basingstoke: Palgrave Macmillan.

UN 2006. *Water: A shared responsibility*. The UN World Water Development Report 2. New York: United Nations.

UNDP 2003. Human Development Report. *The Millennium Development Goals.* New York: United Nations Development Programme.

UNDP 2006. Human Development Report. *Beyond Scarcity: Power, Poverty and the Global Water Crisis.* Ch. 2 Water for Human consumption. New York: United Nations Development Programme.

UN Economic and Social Council 2003. Substantial Issues arising in the implementation of the International Covenant on Economic, Social and Cultural Rights. General Comment 15 (2002) The right to water. E/C. 12/2002/11 20 January 2003. New York.

WUP n.d. (late 1990s). *Water Utility Partnership for Capacity Building in Africa.* Strengthening the Capacity of Water Utilities to Deliver Water and Sanitation Services, Environmental Health and Hygiene to Low Income countries: Case Study for Kano (Town), Nigeria. Water Utilities Project 5. (as downloaded December 2007).

Watts, M. 1996. Islamic Modernities? Citizenship, Civil Society and Islamism in a Nigerian City. *Public Culture* 8 (2), 251-289.

"They Have Left Us in a Hole"

Democratisation and Political Power in a West African Village

Lars Rudebeck*

A conceptual distinction is made between minimal and substantial democracy, where the latter concept aims to integrate constitutional minimalistically defined democracy with a notion of political equality in actual practice. In this perspective, 'substantial democratisation' and 'development' are linked to each other. The argument is illustrated through a diachronic case study of a village in Northern Guinea-Bissau. Minimal democratisation through national multi-party elections since the early 1990s has resulted neither in substantial democratization, nor in development in the village. Some limit to people's patience is indicated by the opening in 2006 of a primary school in the village, run by the parents to substitute for the public school which closed in 1989. The initiative can be seen as an emergency attempt at self-empowerment by a local community in dire need of development. Whether sustainable or not, it concretises the core issue of horizontal self-organisation from below.

Une distinction conceptuelle est introduite entre démocratie minimale et démocratie substantielle. Le dernier concept intègre une démocratie minimaliste constitutionnellement définie, et une notion d'égalité politique dans la pratique. Selon cette perspective, la 'democratisation substantielle' et le 'developpement' sont liés. L'argument est illustré avec une étude de cas diachronique d'un village au nord de la Guinée-Bissau. Pour le village, la démocratisation minimale manifestée à travers des élections multi-partistes depuis le début des années 90 n'a abouti ni à la démocracie substantielle, ni au développement. Il y a néanmoins des limites à la patience des villageois, car en 2006 l'école du village, fermée depuis 1989, a été réouverte par les parents d'élèves. Cette initiative pourrait, en effet, être vue comme une tentative de prise de pouvoir (empowerment) *par une communauté locale en quête de développement. Durable ou non, cette intiative concrétise la question-clé de l'organisation horizontale par le bas.*

* Professor of Political Science, Centre for Sustainable Development, Uppsala University: Lars.Rudebeck@csd.uppsala.uu.se

Decentralisation and democratisation

The conceptual focus of this article is on *democratisation*. More concretely, its thematical focus is on power, livelihoods and cultural meaning, which were the interdisciplinary catchwords of the conference on *decentralisation* where an early version was presented in May 2004 (Rudebeck 2004).[1] The confluence of concepts and themes becomes logical and possible, as the overlap is considerable between the concepts of democratisation and decentralisation. But, the two are far from identical. All decentralisation is certainly not democratic, and some democratisation may well involve centralisation of democratic power in order to overcome local non-democratic power. Still, as said, the two are close.

We are concerned primarily with 'substantial democracy' and its links to 'development'.[2] The latter is conceptualised as a process of structural change whereby the gap is bridged between existing possibilities and general needs recognised as legitimate in a given society. In the analytical language employed here, 'substantial democracy' is a two-dimensional concept aiming to integrate constitutional minimalistically defined democracy with a notion of political equality in actual practice. 'Substantial democratisation', thus, is about political power becoming more equally/less unequally distributed between citizens in a process where constitutional rules and actual practice support each other. This is to say that more people than before begin to take charge as citizens, sharing in decision-making on issues of common concern at various levels of society, including the local level. The more of this, the more 'substantial democracy'.

In this perspective, substantial democratisation and development are linked to each other, at all levels, including the local level.[3] The following case

---

[1] This is a new version bringing in additional material and observations, as well as being marked by the author's continuous reflection on the issues under consideration.

[2] For the conceptual framework employed, see my previous work on democracy, democratisation and development (e.g. Rudebeck 2002a; 2003, 2008), with references. Using the term "substantial" for a non-minimalistic and two-dimensional view of democracy is by inspiration from OlleTörnquist: "Substantial democracy 'only' means that the conventional rules of the game... are both fair *and* applied in vital sectors of society..." (2002:29).

[3] The argument is in line for instance with Törnquist's theoretical analysis of post-tsunami development and democratisation in the autonomous province of Aceh in Indonesia. Recent develop-

study of a village in Northern Guinea-Bissau provides a mainly negative illustration of the linkage, in the sense that non-development stands out as linked to non-substantial democratisation. At the end, however, the possibility of a positive linkage is also suggested. First, a brief background is given on overall democratisation and development in the specific country where the case is situated.[4]

Brief background on democratisation and development in Guinea-Bissau

Guinea-Bissau is a West-African country, located between Senegal in the north and Guinea-Conakry in the south and east, living largely off agriculture and international assistance. Its surface covers 36,125 square kilometres and the population is a bit over 1.5 million. It is divided into nine administrative regions.

Like many other countries in Africa and the world, Guinea-Bissau has been going through a process of democratisation since around 1990. This process is shaky and vulnerable for being limited to the constitutional aspects of democracy at the expense of decentralised citizen sovereignty or autonomy in a substantial sense. Constitutionally and election-wise, this democratisation is nevertheless real.

Guinea-Bissau became a juridically sovereign state in 1974, after eleven years of decolonisation war against Portugal. The autocratic single-party system was legally abolished in 1991, and democratic parliamentary and presidential elections were held in 1994. The ruling party since independence and former liberation movement, PAIGC (*Partido Africano da Inde-*

---

ments in Aceh lead Törnquist to suggest (2009:1): "Peace and development in Aceh is due to more, not less, democracy."

[4] The writing of this article had largely been concluded by early November 2008, at the very moment Guinea-Bissau was entering a period of acute political violence and instability. For the sake of completeness, the dramatic key events of the period until early August 2009 have been added to the background description. Empirically these events serve furthermore to support the analytical argument of the article.

pendência da Guiné e Cabo Verde), managed to win both elections and remained in power. Still, a political multi-party system began to function, and some economic and civic progress began to take place.

The last few years of the 1990s turned violent, however. Although the regime had been democratically legal since 1994, it was hardly legitimate within its own society. A destructive civil and regional war erupted in June 1998, breaking the peace that had lasted since 1974 (Rudebeck 2001). In spite of being supported by several thousand neighbouring country soldiers sent in mainly by Senegal but also by Guinea-Conakry, the president João Bernardo 'Nino' Vieira, legendary fighter in the independence war turned autocratic ruler, was forced to abdicate in May 1999. He had by then been president of the country without interruption since 1980. His humiliating defeat marked the end of the civil war.

Under the leadership of a transitional government, Guinea-Bissau returned to constitutional democracy by way of general elections in November 1999 and January 2000. The opposition became the largest party in parliament and ousted PAIGC from the government. The presidential election was won by the populist opposition candidate Kumba Yalá who scored 69 per cent of the national vote in the second round, against the PAIGC candidate Malam Bacai Sanhá, interim president under the preceding transitional period. Kumba Yalá was installed as new president for a five-year period in February 2000, supported in parliament by his party PRS.

Because of its flagrant inability to deal with the country's developmental problems, Kumba Yalá's regime was deposed by way of a bloodless military putsch on 14 September 2003 – gradually and somewhat reluctantly accepted by the 'international community' as inevitable under the circumstances.[5] A transitional regime was set up, and after a period of quite peaceful constitutional transition, parliamentary elections were held on 28 March 2004, resulting in the return to parliamentary majority power of PAIGC, with Kumba Yalá's party PRS (*Partido da Renovação Social*) in the second place. The election of a new president was delayed but finally took place in two rounds, on 19 June and 24 July 2005. It resulted, paradoxically, in the

[5] The 2003 putsch and subsequent developments were given good coverage by *Lusa*.

return to presidential power of the very same 'Nino' Vieira who in 1999 had been chased into political asylum in Portugal by the rebellious forces of his own army and by popular revolt. In the second round of the 2005 presidential election, 'Nino' defeated Malam Bacai Sanhá, candidate for a second time of 'Nino's' earlier own party PAIGC, by a very narrow margin. The victory was juridically contested by the loser and by the ruling party that accused Vieira of having cheated. In a heated and paralysed political atmosphere, João Bernardo 'Nino' Vieira was nevertheless reinstated as President of the Republic on 1 October 2005.

Before, during and after the 2003-2005 interlude, governments continued to move in and out of office. Strong dissatisfaction among the military, who often do not receive their pay, is an important factor fostering political instability. Furthermore, the weakness and consequent vulnerability of state institutions in Guinea-Bissau is currently turning the country into a favourite place of transit for South American drug-trafficking to Europe (UN 2008). Large amounts of Colombian cocaine are re-loaded in Guinea-Bissau for further transport to European markets.

True enough, democratic institutions are in place, but civic and human rights are far from guaranteed and the level of life of the people is deteriorating in rural as well as urban areas. Power in society seems linked more closely to the possession of arms and illicit drug money than to popular support. Thus, the gap between state and society appears as wide as ever and perhaps even widening, in spite of constitutional democracy.

On 16 November 2008, parliamentary elections were held again in Guinea-Bissau. Initial reports were that election-day had passed off in peaceful and orderly fashion, resulting in a convincing two-thirds majority for PAIGC (Lusa 16-21.2008). At first glance, this kind of outcome might have seemed to forebode a measure of political stability. But less than one week after the election, during the early hours of the night of 23 November 2008, the President of the Republic barely survived an armed attack on his life mounted at his residence by a group of nine soldiers from his own navy (*Lusa*, 23-26.2008).

The following months were marked by fear and threats of violence between the various military and political factions. Finally, on 2 March 2009, before sunrise, President João Bernardo 'Nino' Vieira was murdered in his home by a group of soldiers, only hours after the death of the chief of the army, General Tagmé Na Waié, in a bomb attack.[6] No serious investigation, let alone trial by court of any suspects, has taken place so far.[7]

Under pressure from 'the international community' in various shapes (the United Nations, the organisation of West-African states, the organisation of Portuguese-speaking nations, the European Union, Portugal, and others), Guinea-Bissau did after the initial shock begin to prepare for the regular election of a new president. The campaign was partly violent. One presidential candidate and one other leading politician were murdered by soldiers in early June 2009 (*Lusa*, 5-8.6.2009), and others, such as former Prime Minister Francisco Fadul, brutally harassed. Still, presidential elections were held in two rounds on 28 June and 26 July 2009, resulting in the end in the reversal of the January 2000 result. The second round was held between the two of the original eleven candidates who had done best in the first round, none reaching 50 per cent. This time the PAIGC candidate Malam Bacai Sanhá did defeat his opponent Kumba Yalá by getting 63 per cent of the votes (*Lusa*, 29.7.2009). A great number of observers testified to the peacefulness and fairness of the election process as such. A more telling fact, however, is probably that on both election days as many as about 40 per cent of the registered voters simply did not turn out to vote (*Lusa*, 2.7.2009 and 30.7.2009). This is a much higher abstention rate than in previous elections in Guinea-Bissau, with for instance 25 per cent of registered voters abstaining in the parliamentary elections of 2004 and 12 and 21 per cent respectively in the first and second rounds of the 2005 presidential elections (Rudebeck 2009).

All through the period of democratisation now described, welfare conditions for ordinary people have been stagnating or worsening, regardless of some GDP-growth in the nineties as well as more recently in 2004-2007, due to good cashew harvests (World Bank 2008). In 1997, before the eruption of civil war, Guinea-Bissau had occupied place 168 among 174 in the UNDP's Human Development Index ranking (Human Development Report

[6] For facts and analyses, see *Lusa's* continuous and detailed reporting.
[7] At the moment of writing these lines in early August 2009.

1999:137). Ten years later, after seven years of democratic restauration, the equivalent ranking was 175 out of 177, thus even worse. This means, in the concrete, that in 2007 average life expectancy at birth was estimated to be 46 years (45 in 1997); adult literacy 45 per cent (34 in 1997); school attendance 37 per cent (36 in 1997); while average per capita purchasing power was estimated to be one sixth of the average for all 'developing countries' (one fourth in 1997) (Human Development Report 2007/2008:293).

At the same time, in a globalised world system, the country's dependence upon international aid continues to be extreme. This structural condition is not accurately reflected in aid statistics, as flows of aid have been slower to materialise after 1999 than before, due to low credibility of the regime in the eyes of 'international community' donors. Still, in 2005, official development aid received accounted for 26 per cent of gross domestic product (GDP), as compared with one per cent for all developing countries and 9 for the category labelled 'least developed' (Human Development Report 2007/2008:293). In a more qualitative sense, aid dependence as a political and ideological constant is distinctly reflected in the leadership's recurring references to aid as a key solution to the country's problems.[8] Vulnerability in the face of potential 'earnings' from drug trafficking is the other side of the same coin. Substantial dependence for development upon the democratically organised support of the people seems far away, in spite of constitutionally correct elections.

All of this, obviously, is in glaring contrast to hopes and expectations once raised by the successful 1963-1974 struggle for liberation from colonialism.

A village study

I have described and analysed the transition now summarised in several books and articles which will be drawn upon here (e.g. Rudebeck 1997,

[8] In December 2007, for instance, the Minister of Finance presented a budget in the National Assembly which added up to a deficit of 60 per cent. His comment was that the deficit "would easily be overcome with the approval of the Post-Conflict programme about to be negotiated with the International Monetary Fund and a subsequent donor conference" (*Lusa*, 6.12.2007).

2001, 2002b, 2008b). The special feature of the present article is that it selectively highlights one aspect of this work over the years by focusing upon the political repercussions in *one particular village* of the overall democratisation occurring in two phases in Guinea-Bissau: firstly, the introduction of democracy by way of multi-party elections in 1994; and, secondly, democracy's fragile re-birth without concurrent development since 1999-2000, after collapse in 1998.

As a result of multiparty elections generally, citizens at all levels of society are drawn into the democratisation process, if in no other way than by registration as voters. The practical preparations for elections and their implementation also activate many people at the local level. Whether this is decentralisation of political power or not is a completely different matter. From the point of view of substantial democratisation the decisive point is whether the elections do, in practice, empower citizens to jointly formulate their interests and wishes, appoint their representatives and demand accountability. Or, whether the principal significance of the elections is on the contrary to help the leaders mobilise their supporters to legitimise and promote these same leaders' own interests. In this respect Guinea-Bissau is not alone in the world in inclining significantly more to the latter than the former. But, in Guinea-Bissau as in other places, there are features of both. These features are difficult to capture in quantitative terms and therefore the method of using an illustrative case study can be of great assistance. Such a case study follows below, taking what I like to call a diachronic perspective.

Kandjadja – a village among thousands

There are almost four thousand villages of varying size in Guinea-Bissau. I have had the opportunity to follow one of them ever since 1976. We shall obtain our material from that village. The village is called Kandjadja. It is a normal Guinean village, similar to thousands and tens of thousands of other villages in rural Africa.[9] I have described it many times before (e.g. 1992,

[9] In Guinea-Bissau the name of the village is usually spelt Candjadja, which is the Portuguese spelling. When transcribing from Mandinga, however, which is the predominant language in the

1997, 2001, 2002:b). The directly visible changes take place slowly, but life and history do not stand still. With its thousand or so inhabitants Kandjadja is one of the larger villages in Guinea-Bissau. It is the main village in an administrative section that also includes twelve smaller villages spread out in the forest south of the river Farim, which flows westwards towards the Atlantic sea.[10] The whole section had somewhere around 4,500 inhabitants in 1999 and thus perhaps close to 6,000 in 2009, although I have no firm ground for judging population growth and out-migration against each other.[11] The area is situated in the administrative sector of Mansabá, in the Oio region, in the northern part of Guinea-Bissau. As the bird flies the distance is not more than twenty-five kilometres north-west to the border with Senegal and its politically unsettled Casamance province. From Kandjadja to the sleepy regional capital of Farim there is a bumpy road, twenty kilometres long, through the forest in a north-easterly direction. Bissau is some one hundred and ten kilometres to the south, including twelve initial kilometres of track road eastwards through the forest, before reaching the main road between Farim and Bissau. Cars make only rare apperances in the village.

The Muslim Mandinga people dominate in Kandjadja, but ethnicity-wise there are also 'Animist' Balanta and Muslim Fula in the section. The main village is entirely Mandinga and thus its religion is Islam. The livelihood and economy of the people are based upon agriculture in a wide sense of the term, pursued with simple techniques on the basis of proven methods and, in addition, certain handicrafts. There is also some inflow of money

---

area, as well as when writing in Guinean Creole, it is common to use the letter *K* for the k-sound. I therefore continue to use the *K*, as I have always done, although this is not the official usage.

[10] The villages in the section are (with official spelling): Candjadja, Dabocunda, Corinto, Sabalacunda, Ninjobaia, Colissari, Mandina, Breco-ba, Breco-rim, Salinto, Madina Saladala, Tambato, and Djebacunda.

[11] The point of departure for my population estimate is the number of persons entitled to vote and thus over 18 in the section in 1999, which was 2,209 voters, according to a local count made in 1999 (*Mansabá, sector, constituency no. 7*, 2000). I have then extrapolated from the proportion over 20 + 1/10 of those under 20 years found in the whole country according to population estimates by a group of Guinean social scientists (Imbali et al. 1995). My figure is thus based on the assumption that the age distribution is the same in Kandjadja as in the whole country. If so (and if Imbali et al. are right), then the population of the thirteen villages of the section would have been 4,536 inhabitants in September 1999, which is not unlikely.

from villagers employed in various occuptions in Bissau or abroad. The amount of this is unknown but hardly impressive.

In recent years cashew nuts have been the most important source of cash income. Previously it was groundnuts. Sometimes an enterprising villager takes other products, for example a sack of onions, all the way to the large Bandim market in Bissau. During the civil war in 1998-99 the area around Kandjadja was not directly affected by acts of warfare. Nevertheless, the war and the ensuing crisis of subsistence and survival were still felt harshly, not least through refugees coming from Bissau.[12]

Since the beginning of the 1980s the population has been left to itself, as far as development is concerned.[13] In an interview made in 1986, a villager told me that "they (the state) have left us in a hole". The same could just as well have been said at the time of my visit in 2007. The forest road leading to the village was then in worse condition than it had been in 1976, over thirty years earlier, at the time of my very first visit. The state-employed nurse of the village had already left before 1981. The former state-owned store passed into private ownership in 1986, as a result of the structural adjustment reforms sweeping over Africa at that time in accordance with World Bank and International Monetary Fund prescriptions. Simple consumer goods are found in the store, but the purchasing power in the village is limited. The state school was closed in 1989, as the government gave up its earlier ambitions in the field of public education.

A paradox

Politics in Kandjadja may seem paradoxical. The village and the whole area are, in practice, untouched by government development policies. Literally nothing has reached there in terms of benefits of national policy since the

[12] Just after the civil war, the large family I know best told me that, from time to time, they had had up to thirty different relatives staying with them as refugees in their simple houses. Now their supplies had been emptied, including the seed for sowing the following year.

[13] I have described this in some detail, including the far-reaching effects of economic liberalisation and structural adjustment, in earlier writings (see Rudebeck 1992, with full references to even earlier writings). I have also noted the lack of any change during the 1990s (2001:72 ff.)

last school teacher left in 1989. Still, for all that, PAIGC, and state power under PAIGC control, have always been able to count on political support from the area where Kandjadja is located. Even in the multi-party elections of 1994 – the first time ever that it was possible to vote against PAIGC – the outcome was quite distinct.[14]

The general explanation provided locally for such paradoxical loyalty is that "this is an '*antiga zona libertada*'/an old liberated area", i.e. an area controlled by the PAIGC as early as in the anti-colonial war between 1963 and 1974. This, today, is not a real explanation. It is rather an indirect way of saying that the only political contacts existing between the village (meaning: a few of the villagers) and the politicians in the capital go through PAIGC.

This does not mean that people are satisfied with being "left in a hole". The demand for change (*mudança*) is as strong in Kandjadja as in other places in the country. Still, in 1994, 1999, 2000, 2004 and 2005, there were as we shall see more votes in the village cast for PAIGC than for any of the other parties. Surely these outcomes may be traced largely to links established during the war of liberation, but in a more complex manner than indicated by mere reference to political tradition.[15]

What happened in the area in the 1960s was that the PAIGC political structure was grafted onto the local 'traditional' structure of extended families led by *homens grandes* (great men, singular: *homem grande*) of varying standing, the most prominent of whom were also recognised as leaders of villages and groups of villages. Through this structure, the area of Kandjadja was largely mobilised on the side of PAIGC during the liberation war. During the immediate post-war years, a centralised attempt was made to impose a 'revolutionary' political structure with a party committee headed by an outsider sent in by PAIGC to be in charge of the thirteen-village section of Kandjadja. With the resilience of the traditional political structure and fading revolutionary ardour, this reverted quite soon to a situation where the party/state simply maintained elementary political control by re-

[14] 59 per cent of the Kandjadja voters still supported PAIGC in 1994 as opposed to 38 per cent in the whole country (Rudebeck 2001:77).

[15] See Rudebeck 1992, in particular pp. 269-270, with full references to earlier works.

lying on the loyalty of locally more or less influential people – 'clients' in relation to regional and national levels. These persons in turn continued their co-existence with the rest of the villagers as weak local 'patrons', with nothing concrete and ever less hope to deliver in terms of development.[16]

We will soon return to more specific considerations of the Kandjadja paradox. Let us see first how democratic elections worked in the village – after a devastating civil war on top of ordinary hardship. How did the local voters rate the political parties, in particular their old favourite PAIGC? Did the promises made by the opposition seem to influence them? How did the opposition's leading presidential candidate, Kumba Yalá, fare, as the voters were facing his image on the voting bulletin?

The following account is based on observations and interviews made in connection with visits in May and December 1999, January 2000 and June 2007. To facilitate use of the tables presented, they have all been assembled in a special section at the end of the text.

Democratic elections at village level

Parliamentary elections 1999 and 2004

As in several other places in the country, voting was delayed in Kandjadja on Sunday, November 28, 1999.[17] According to the chairman of the section committee for Kandjadja, the ballot box had arrived late. He was also the chairman of the section's committee of support for PAIGC and had kept precise notes. According to those notes, voting in the village had started at 15.52 and, in agreement with the rules, had ended at 17.00. Since this was

[16] The *homem grande* of Kandjadja village took over more or less formally as the chairman of the section until his death in 1992. His son coninued in the same function which, however, seems to have become more and more nominal, except in connection with elections when he, as we shall see, continued to be very much in charge at the local level.

[17] In the section there were five other polling stations besides the one in Kandjadja (which included Kandjadja-Balanta), namely in the villages of Mandina, Djebacunda, Corinto, Madina Saladala and Salinto.

too little time for everyone to have had a chance to vote, the voting had been continued on Monday between 7.30 and 15.00.[18]

The reason for the delay in the arrival of the ballot box was most probably a nation-wide threat of strike by the voting officials. Demands for an increase in pay made by certain voting officials in the region had also caused problems the day before. It had therefore been impossible to have the polling equipment in place in the village on Sunday morning. Once the voting finally started, everything had proceeded very calmly and in orderly fashion. According to the chairman of the section, this was only "to a certain extent" due to civic awareness, since the political parties, in his view, had not taken the trouble to make it clear to the people what they represented.[19] Consequently the voters could not be expected to really know what they were voting for. Still the citizens had taken everything calmly and turned out strongly to vote, but apparently without great expectations, according to the section chairman.

Despite the fact that Kandjadja is situated off the beaten track in the forest, with very poor communications, several political parties had visited the village to mobilise voters before election-day. The constituency consisting of the administrative section of Mansabá, of which Kandjadja is a part, sends three members (deputies) to the People's National Assembly/parliament (*Assembleia Nacional Popular*/ANP). PAIGC's candidates were well known in the area and had as always promised to work for schools, health services and road construction if they were elected. Even "Helder Vaz's people" from 'Bafatá' (RGB/MB), the major former opposition party besides PRS, had visited the village, with their promises of similar kind, as

[18] Interviews on 4 and 11.12.1999. During the latter interview the chairman carefully consulted the notes he had made on election day.

[19] Guinea-Bissau's various political parties will not be presented here. See my book *On Democracy's Sustainability* (Rudebeck 2001:42-56) for a detailed such presentation. The following summarising characteristic is just as valid in 2008 as it was around 2000: "It is not possible to distinguish between the political parties in Guinea-Bissau by studying their party programmes. The slogans of all the parties are almost identical... all the parties claim to stand for democracy, justice and human rights, as well as a market economy that is socially accountable... Any discernible differences tended to concern social and cultural/ethnic roots, financing, historical ties between leaders and supporters, and the personal qualities of the leaders" (2001:42.) The full names of the parties are found in the list of abbreviations at the end of this article.

well as representatives of 'Abubacar' and 'Bubacar', leaders respectively of the two small parties UNDP and LIPE. But besides Malam Bacai Sanhá, PAIGC's presidential candidate as well as interim President of the Republic, there was only one other party leader and presidential candidate who had visited Kandjadja in person during the election campaign before 28November 2008. This was Victor Mandinga from AD. On the other hand Kumba Yalá's party, PRS, had not shown up at all in the village. This was generally explained by the fact that Kumba Yalá is 'Balanta', while Kandjadja is 'Mandinga', which is true although not necessarily the whole explanation.

The Kandjadja votes were counted on site under the close supervision of representatives of the various parties. They were then taken to Mansabá and included in the votes for the entire constituency. The results for the village, including Kandjadja-Balanta, are shown in tables 1 and 2 at the end of the text. The first table compares the results of the 1999 and 2004 parliamentary elections in Kandjadja with the results for the entire country. As seen, PAIGC was considerably stronger in the village than in the whole country. The difference is greater in 1999 and in 2004 than it had been in 1994 (cf. note 10 above). This is true for both years.

In 1999, immediately after the civil war, PAIGC was down to an all-time low of 15 per cent at the national level. But in Kandjadja, 40 per cent of the 432 voters still voted PAIGC, in spite of the defeat of the regime. Two specific explanations may be mentioned:

- PAIGC's candidates for Mansabá constituency's three mandates in parliament were well-known in the village.
- There was a direct personal link to the PAIGC presidential candidate Malam Bacai Sanhá's campaign office.

The upward link consisted of the fact that a "son of the village", who had been a teacher in the village school in the 1980s, worked in 1999/2000 for Malam Bacai Sanhá's wife in PAIGC's national campaign secretariat.

Furthermore, according to information from several sources that cannot be verified due to election secrecy, all, or almost all votes cast in favour of the opposition presidential candidate's party, PRS, originated from Kandjadja-Balanta, a small neighbouring village, administratively part of the main village and situated a couple of kilometres south of it. In that village, all the inhabitants are Balanta. Thus they are not Muslims, they do eat pork, and they like to drink palm wine. They also speak a completely different language from the Mandinga language spoken in the main village. For all these reasons, and others as well, they were tempted in 1999/2000 by the idea of asserting their cultural identity by voting for PRS and its presidential candidate of Balanta ethnic origin. As opposed to the nation-wide distribution of votes which was clearly influenced by a combination of non-ethnic and ethnic factors differing from place to place and between the national and local levels, we do seem here to have a very clear-cut example of ethnic voting.

In the 2004 election, PAIGC generally did considerably better than in 1999, due to the disastrous developmental and political performance of the regime that had been voted into power in 1999 and 2000 but forced out through the 2003 putsch. At the overall national level this recuperation of PAIGC reached 31 per cent,[20] while soaring to an overwhelming 67 per cent in Kandjadja.

Table 2 shows in detail how people actually voted in Kandjadja in the parliamentary elections of 1999 and 2004. To facilitate comparison between the parties and years, the table also gives percentages.

The distribution of party sympathies in Kandjadja was different from the whole country, not only with regard to PAIGC, but also in other ways. For example, UNDP, a new and very small party at the national level (3 per cent of the total vote) was the second largest party in Kandjadja in 1999 with 34 votes of the 432 votes cast – more than PRS and 'Bafata' (RGB) which both in that year outscored PAIGC at the national level. I was told that UNDP's success had been achieved by donating "a little medicine" and a new mat to the mosque.

It is notable in table 2, among other things, that as many as 11 of 13 national parties competing in 1999, and 12 of 15 in 2004, actually succeeded in obtaining at least a few votes even in an isolated village, such as Kand-

[20] Resulting in 45 out of 100 seats for PAIGC in parliament, enough to form a national majority coalition, given the system of distributing seats between the parties applied in Guinea-Bissau (the so-called d'Hondt system) which favours the largest party.

jadja. Those parties that failed to attract any votes whatsoever in the two parliamentary elections in the village are very small even at the national level. One of them is FCG/SD, the party of the only female presidential candidate, Antonieta Rosa Gomes, a lawyer who ran for president both in 1999–2000 and in 2005. Although her party scored zero in the village, Rosa Gomes still did obtain one (1) of the 436 votes counted in the Kandjadja ballot box for president in the first round of the 1999–2000 presidential election. We can only speculate about the driving forces behind that single, and singular, vote for a woman as President of the Republic.

It is, in any case, a significant observation about political democratisation in Kandjadja that several citizens do seem to make use of their new-won right to cast a vote of their own, freely and secretly. They value the relative civic freedom coming with democratisation. The same persons are sadly aware, though, that just spreading their individual votes among a dozen political parties quite alien to the village will hardly bring them any political influence, let alone power.[21] The majority who did continue to vote for PAIGC are also likely to have been disillusioned about the developmental outcome of their support, while a few of them may still have been hoping for some personal benefit in exchange for the vote delivered.

Presidential elections 1999/2000 and 2005

The pattern of the first round of presidential elections is similar to that of the parliamentary elections. On 28 November 1999, Kumba Yalá even received exactly the same number of votes for president as his party PRS did in the parliamentary election taking place simultaneously. On the other hand, Malam Bacai Sanhá received considerably more votes than PAIGC – as many as 313, which corresponded to 72 per cent of the total. This is much more than the 20 per cent he reached in the whole country. It is also the same pattern as in 1994, in the first multi-party election ever to have

[21] See Rudebeck (1997:38-44), on positive recognition in the village of greater civic freedom coupled with disillusionment over powerlessness in regard to development.

been held in independent Guinea-Bissau.[22] Thus, the impression that Kandjadja in 1999 stuck to old political habits, as opposed to the rest of the country, was even stronger in the presidential than in the parliamentary election. Table 3 at the end gives further detail.

The ethnic, cultural factor that seems, according to my sources, to explain why most voters from Kandjadja-Balanta voted for PRS and Kumba Yalá worked also in the opposite direction. Only very few people voting in the main village cast their votes for the "Balanta party" and for its leader in 1999–2000, according to the same sources.

A locally acute ethnic conflict, furthermore, influenced electoral behaviour in 1999/2000. Robbing cattle from neighbouring villages is a traditional test of manhood of young Balanta. In recent years several households in Kandjadja-Mandinga had suffered from that cultural tradition – or criminal habit, as some would say. Things had even gone far enough to cause some villagers to keep their cows locked up at night, for fear of cattle thieves from the neighbouring village. Anger at this insecurity fostered negative feelings for PRS and scepticism about its presidential candidate with his red Balanta cap. Regardless of how much they agreed with him on the need for *mudança*/change, many villagers feared a hidden ethnic agenda: "Perhaps Kumba Yalá doesn't like us?"

However, the conflicts over cattle and other material and cultural differences did not keep the inhabitants of Kandjadja-Mandinga and Kandjadja-Balanta from having normal social relations, which did, on the surface, appear uncomplicated and even friendly. For instance, people from the Balanta village do their shopping in the store in the main village; they vote there; and until 1989 their children went to school there with the Mandinga children.

The second rounds of the two presidential elections were straightforward. The choice was either for or against: Kumba versus Malam in 2000; 'Nino'

[22] For the 1994 presidential election in Kandjadja, I only have exact data on the second round. In that round 'Nino' scored 90 per cent in the village as compared with 49 in the country as a whole (Rudebeck 1997:31, 25).

versus the same in 2005. The inviting images of the candidates faced the voter from the ballot paper. In 1999 Kumba Yalá was wearing a red Balanta cap and Bacai Sanhá the same type of patterned West Africa knitted woollen cap as the historic leader of the anti-colonial liberation struggle, Amílcar Cabral, used to wear in his time, before he was murdered by a member of his own party in 1973. All that was required of the citizen was to step behind the screen and mark her or his preferred candidate. Table 4 shows the outcomes for both years, in absolute as well as relative terms. Table 5 adds the overall national comparison.

In statistical terms, as seen in the tables, the villagers' support for the PAIGC candidate Malam Bacai Sanhá was overwhelming in both years, around 90 per cent. This was very much above his national level scores. But in fact, as we know, he lost his bid for the presidency on both occasions: resoundingly in 1999 against the PRS candidate Kumba Yalá and narrowly in 2005 against his former party comrade João Bernardo 'Nino' Vieira. In Kandjadja, though, PAIGC prevailed as ever. Even 'Nino' himself running as a non-partisan 'independent' only got 33 votes in the village in 2005, as opposed to 328 eleven years earlier, in 1994, when he was still the leader of the country and of PAIGC (see note 18).

Electoral democratisation in the village

We have seen that the voters of Kandjadja do make use of their freedom to vote in the simple sense that they distribute their votes among many parties. But even after eleven years of electoral democracy, a large majority continued to vote the old (single-) party line in spite of being "left in a hole" as far as development is concerned. In this they are considerably more 'conservative' than the average voter in the country. A number of mutually reinforcing explanations have emerged from the foregoing presentation. Let us summarise them:

- Kandjadja is an "old liberated area", indicating a specific kind of historical tradition.
- There are few obvious differences between the parties' programmes, platforms, ideas or proposals, and therefore most voters have to rely on

personal impressions and authoritative persons in their local community.

- The people have very limited experience of any other 'upward' political channels than PAIGC.
- What matters in the PAIGC hierarchy is personal contacts, either directly or through local 'patrons', with PAIGC's representatives at regional and national level, for instance in parliament.
- There is an ethnic, cultural Mandinga versus Balanta factor working against PRS and Kumba Yalá, reinforced at the time of the studied elections by acute problems with cattle thefts.
- There was at the time of the studied elections a direct link between the village and Malam Bacai Sanhá by way of a respected "son of the village".

A special event had also impressed the villagers. On 10 January 2000, fairly late in the evening, after dark, on the last Monday before election Sunday, Malam Bacai Sanhá, the interim president of the country and presidential candidate for PAIGC had suddenly arrived in Kandjadja. Driving in from the north, from the regional capital Farim, with his campaign team, he had stopped for a public meeting in the middle of the village which was dramatically illuminated by the headlights of his cars. He spoke to the villagers and answered their questions for about half an hour. He had said, not surprisingly, among other things, that if he was elected president, he would help the people of Kandjadja section to get water, schools and health care. The message, I was told, had been received with a "certain amount of trust". Malam Bacai Sanhá had been wearing his woollen Amilcar Cabral cap, a symbol of 'revolutionary' legitimacy. A great deal of interest had been aroused. Once the meeting was over, the national leader had continued his journey southwards through the night to a larger town called Olossato. Darkness had returned to the village, broken up only by small fires in front of the houses where people gathered to discuss the singular event they had just experienced.

The chairman of the section emphasised to me that this was the first time ever in Kandjadja's history that a President of the Republic had visited the village. Kumba Yalá for his part, he added, had never visited the village.

Thus, on second thoughts, perhaps the voting behaviour of the people of Kandjadja is not so difficult to understand. On the contrary, in the concrete context of prevailing conditions, of which the villagers are well aware, there may well be a type of disillusioned rationality in it. If so, what are the implications for democratisation and democracy? And, what are the implications for 'civil society'?

Civil society

'Civil society' is a much-used concept. But for analytical purposes, it is diffuse and contested and therefore somewhat difficult to use. At a minimum, though, most of those who do try to use the concept for analytical purposes agree that it refers to people acting together in the social space existing in society between the state and the private sphere. This obviously makes it relevant to democracy theory.[23]

At the overall level there are in principle two ways of increasing the opportunities for citizens to assume responsibility in society, once single-party authoritarianism is done away with. One is that the state draws back, leaving space for citizens to act more independently of the state than before – in 'civil society'. The other way is that the institutions of the state are democratised and decentralised. At the end of 1995 the constitution of Guinea-Bissau was revised so as to allow for the establishment of elected local assemblies (Rudebeck 1997:44-46), but no further steps in that direction have been taken since. There is no reason to assume that such assemblies would have any effects in practice, unless provided with locally controlled financial resources, which are unavailable anyway.

[23] The theoretical and theoretically inspired literature on civil society, democratisation and development is huge. This is not the place to enter into it. For a useful introduction see Törnquist 1999. For an instructive survey of the history of the concept see Sjögren 2001. For a recent comment by myself on the closely related discourse on 'civic trust' see Rudebeck (2007:17-18). I point out there that trust between citizens is often assumed to reign high in 'civil society', which clearly could be positive for democracy – when or if it happens and, if so, depending on how. It is a significant research task to study the *if*, *when* and *how* of that possibility. Neither the correlation itself nor its democratising implications can be taken for granted.

The strategic issue for democracy is how the two approaches can supplement and support each other. In its political practice so far, as illustrated by the case of Kandjadja, the Guinean government has withdrawn far in favour of 'civil society' at the local level, except for the occasions of national elections. The question has been avoided or evaded, how far such practice can be carried without large groups in the population ending up completely without access to common resources. Rural Africans are known to be patient and resilient, but there may still be limits which cannot be transcended without breaking the bonds of society.

'Civil' and 'political' society

A distinction is sometimes made between 'civil' and 'political' society. It is a question of definition for political and other social scientists whether, for instance, political opposition parties should be included in 'civil' or in 'political' society. The parliament is part of the state, but the political parties also act in society at large, which could give them a place in 'civil' society. Törnquist (1999:50) suggests that 'political society' can be seen as a link between purely 'civil' society and the state. Then, obviously, the opposition parties will be crucial to that link.

Using the distinction between 'civil' and 'political society', it is of particular interest in our context to note that constitutional democratisation in the studied village affected the two in very different ways. Democratisation did indeed result in the politicisation of the villagers in the sense of getting them to participate actively and willingly in national multiparty elections – largely in support of the old regime. Thus, 'political' society was clearly activated and also democratised in the constitutional, minimalistically conceptualised sense. What happened in 'civil' society is however more difficult to pin-point. As we shall see, it was activated, too, and possibly also politicised, but not in a democratic way and not in a way involving the decentralisation of political power.

'Civil society' at village level

Before 1990, one-party rule had made it impossible in practice for voluntary organisations to participate in development work in the rural areas of Guinea-Bissau, unless they enjoyed the direct support of the state and the party PAIGC. But in 1990, the first year of democratisation, something very new happened in the village. Representatives of RADI (*Réseau Africain pour le Développement Intégré*) began to visit Kandjadja and to encourage the population to start programmes to develop local farming based on their own traditional forms of organisation.[24]

Since then, RADI has continued to function in the region of Oio where Kandjadja is located. Seventeen kilometres east of Kandjadja, in a neighbouring administrative section, the organisation has put up a training centre for farmers in the forest near the village of Djalicunda.

The centre is very ambitious. It is built with local materials, has its own source of fresh water, and even computers working with the aid of solar cells. Local varieties of seeds are cultivated in ways that take the environment into ecological consideration. Those working at the centre in Djalicunda are locally recruited Guineans. Various training courses are held there and the intention is that farmers in the area shall be inspired to integrate modern farming techniques with the use of local seeds and due respect paid to tradition and the environment.

According to a written report delivered in 1999, the key concept of RADI's theory is "cooperation with the people" (RADI 1999a:6-7[25]):

> In Guinea-Bissau there is real potential to develop the rural sector, since land is still available for further cultivation, and there are also possibilities to intensify cultivation, to diversify forestry, to extend local fishing and to increase the herds of cattle. But it is important to note that a strategy to exploit all these possibilities requires more than technical invest-

[24] RADI is an African NGO for culture-based development work in agriculture. The countries that are represented through their national organisations are Burkina Faso, Central African Republic, Guinea-Bissau, Guinea-Conakry, Mali, Mauritania, Senegal and Congo. (RADI, no date; Hellström 1995:36-37). Another document (RADI 1995) provides information on RADI's organisational structure in the Oio region. The Guinea-Bissau branch of RADI relies on funding by SWISSAID, a Swiss NGO.

[25] Translated from the French language original by Lars Rudebeck.

> ments. It is necessary to make great efforts to stimulate the interest of the rural population, to train, to organise and reorganise, to improve the motivation of the technicians – all with the aim of getting those involved in the rural areas to assume more responsibility and to strengthen the position of women. This is the focus of RADI/Guinea-Bissau's support for development.

Another report described food support provided through RADI to 27 villages in the region of Oio that received refugees during the civil war in 1998/99 (RADI 1999b:2, 4).

Although Mansabá sector was included in the food programme, Kandjadja, was *not* among the 27 villages listed in the report. This is possibly due to the fact that support for RADI's work seemed to have declined in Kandjadja during the second half of the 1990s. It is clear that opinions in the village on RADI are quite divided. Some villagers work actively with the organisation and have succeeded in benefitting from it. Others, however, express dissatisfaction with RADI's work and find that it focuses more on the organisation's own needs than on the needs of the local people (interviews, December 1999 and January 2000).

These observations indicate that in 1999 and 2000 the kind of politicisation of civil society in the village that the activities of this particular NGO had resulted in was more patron-client oriented than characterised by the emergence of autonomous grassroots citizenship. Civil society had been activated, but not democratised.

The shortcomings and even the absence of the state in developmental activities had created a vacuum, as well as deep popular disenchantment in Kandjadja. This in turn had opened up chances for an organisation such as RADI to strike a chord of strong response within civil society. Thanks to democratisation, alternatives had become legal. Still, the democratic vacuum had not been filled.

A 'civil society' initiative

Visiting Kandjadja on 29 June 2007, I was surprised by a novelty. In fact, I was told that in 2006, deep and growing frustration over the lack of any elementary education whatsoever in the village, except the Koranic school, had in the end caused a number of families to join forces to set up a school of their own.

Ever since 1989, when the state run school was closed, only the Koranic school had been available for the children of Kandjadja. The two finest houses in the village, the only ones with outer walls of white plaster, are in fact the mosque where the Koranic school is held and the house where the *imam* (the leader of the mosque) lives.

As I was told, the idea of the new school is simple. In 2007, it had one teacher and a little over one hundred pupils enrolled, divided between the first, second and third grades of elementary school. The teacher had been hired from outside the village.[26] The families pay him 350 CFA francs (0.53 euro) per child and month. They also provide him with food and a simple house. If some family is unable to pay, others help out.

In June 2009, my only further information on this grassroots educational project was that the school was still working, attended by about 70 children.[27] But whether it survives into the future or not, the fact of its existence in 2007, 2008 and 2009 does represent a departure from the patron-client pattern. It demonstrates, in practice, the idea of citizens getting together in ‘civil society’ to solve a problem they have in common. The problem in this case is due to the dismal failure of the very same state that those citizens were once prepared to trust. Their project can be interpreted as an acute emergency attempt at self-empowerment by a local community. The outcome remains of course to be seen.

The wider context of power, resources and culture

Understanding the politics of development is, at the very least, a three-dimensional task involving the integrated analysis, of not only power and resources, but also of cultural norms and patterns of behaviour. Let us end

[26] On the occasion of my visit, the teacher was on summer vacation.

[27] Information received in Uppsala by mobile phone call from the chairman of the section committee in Kandjadja, 26 October 2008, confirmed in another call in mid-June 2009.

this article by briefly setting our West African example in that wider context.

The problem of democratisation resulting in local civil society being activated rather than democratised is not unique to Guinea-Bissau. It has general relevance. When the local political process is focused upon and reaches into family and personal interests of survival and reproduction, it will very easily take the form of 'patron-client' relationships rather than democratic organisation. Both citizens and leaders take advantage of the few opportunities available to them to promote their short-term interests. As far as the citizens are concerned, in situations of harsh material poverty, this is principally a question of day-to-day survival; while for the politicians it is more a question of power resources. As long as the citizens cannot discern any concrete reasons to assume that public, collective, action might actually help them survive and improve their lives, the likelihood is great that they will continue to turn to their patrons, even under the guise of the constitutionally democratic system or through various civil society activities. This is probably not for trusting those patrons, but for not seeing any realistic alternatives. Such minimal democracy, thus, is likely to support political practices incapable of giving rise to development.

This looks like an impasse, at least in the short run. But in the somewhat longer run, such negative dynamics are not likely to be sustainable. Both the development necessary for people to survive in acceptable ways and their readiness, as well as capacity, to support their patrons' power is undermined.

The example of Kandjadja is instructive by clearly demonstrating how little the local people get in return for their political support. But it also suggests certain limits to their patience. Such limits are indicated by the decline in voting support for PAIGC between 1994 and 1999, however modest in comparison to national results, and more distinctly by the start of the new school in 2007. Still, so far, the self-perceived short-term interest of the villagers has not incited them to new forms of politicisation, beyond participating in multiparty elections.

It is a common view in modernisation school inspired development studies that particularistic political culture or codes of conduct marked by patron-client relations, as in Kandjadja, and corruption would somehow causally *explain* the facts of unequal resource control and lack of development in 'developing countries', and today most particularly in Africa.[28] That kind of argument, however, risks coming close to tautology or question-begging, by tending to explain political clientelism and corruption as caused by culture or codes of conduct marked by – clientelism and corruption. The same argument also tends to overlook that patron-client relations and corruption as such certainly have not prevented economic development in other parts of the world, whether, for instance, historically in the West or in modern Asia.

By concentrating – or appearing to concentrate – the explanatory effort to cultural variables, the question of *power* in society tends to be avoided. True enough, an inherited culture of client deference to patrons obviously supports unequal power and thus does not facilitate democratisation. But in accordance with Max Weber's classical sociological perspective, culture is more fruitfully analysed as the 'switchman' between interest and action than as an overall explanation of the functioning of society (cf. Rudebeck 1994, 1998). Culture provides values, images and frameworks for interpreting reality. Still, when necessary to daily survival, even democratically minded persons often bow to patrons or bosses, however reluctantly. Likewise, people whose cultural values are non-democratic may well accept to share inherited power if necessary to their political or perhaps even physical survival.

In describing the politics of Kandjadja and its links to national politics in this text, I have myself made use of the concepts of 'patrons' and 'clients' to grasp the hierachical structure obstructing substantial democratisation. I have not, however, designated client deference to patrons as a Guinean cultural norm or trait, causing the village to be "left in a hole". This is not to say that patron/client relationships do not mark human behaviour. They certainly do. But the decisive question on clientelism in regard to development

[28] To illustrate, Leys 1996 offers a critical analysis of such development studies, while Chabal & Daloz 1999 navigate close to it in their analyses. In an essay on 'modernisation thinking' found in a contribution to a volume on the theoretical heritage of Marx and Weber in development studies, I have myself attempted a critical deconstruction (Rudebeck 1994).

is about the power relations that determine clientelism rather than its existence as such, of which we are usually well aware.[29]

In the theoretical perspective applied here, therefore, the core of the conceptual theme of democracy and democratisation in relation to development is about material interests and relations of power. Culture is conceptualised as the Weberian 'switchman'. What material forces or interests and structures of power do actually obstruct democratisation? Can they be challenged? How do cultural norms, codes and patterns of behaviour intervene in this?

Horizontal self-organisation from below by people with similar developmental interests – across lines of ethnicity, gender and age – would thus be crucial to gradually breaking up vertical patron-client structures at all levels, including the local one. However simple or modest, and whether sustainable or not, the recent school project in Kandjadja concretises this core issue. Furthermore, the project may well come to contribute to cultural change in the village. Whether such change is likely or not to facilitate self-empowerment and *substantial democratisation* as referred to in the introductory part of this article, will in turn depend on the kind of teaching provided in the school.

This may seem like a tiny conclusion for a study aiming to grasp such a lofty abstraction as 'substantial democracy'. Though possibly tiny in a quantitative sense, it does nevertheless hold a grain of – substance.

[29] Cf. the following incisive remark by Mamdani (1996:295 note 2) on "the mode of domination" as an explanatory variable: "My point about clientelism is that it is more an effect of the form of power than an explanation of it".

Tables referred to in the text

Table 1. *Comparison of national assembly election results in Kandjadja and the country as a whole, 28 November 1999 and 28 March 2004 (results rounded to the nearest percentage point)*

	Kandjadja		*Whole country*	
	2004	*1999*	*2004*	*1999*
PAIGC	40	67	15	31
Other parties	42	29	68	62
Blank + invalid	18	4	17	7
Total percentages	*100*	*100*	*100*	*100*

Sources: The Kandjadja percentages are based on figures noted by the local voting official, filled in by the chairman of the section committee for Kandjadja on the basis of the voting official's own information received directly from the polling station, 28 and 29.11.1999 (*Kandjadja*, 1999 national assembly election), and 28.3.2004 (*Kandjadja*, 2004 national assembly election). The 1999 figures for Kandjadja were furthermore checked against hand-written material from the deputy elected in 1999 for PAIGC in constituency no. 7, Mansabá, to which Kandjadja belongs (*Mansabá sector, constituency no. 7,* 1999). The 1999 national level percentages are based on figures published by *Comissão Nacional de Eleições*, Bissau, 9.12.1999 and 25.1.2000. The 2004 national level percentages are based on figures published by *Nô Pintcha*, 8.4.2004 and *Lusa*, 4.4.2004.

Table 2. *Results of national assembly elections in Kandjadja, 28 November 1999 and 28 March 2004, total number of votes and rounded-off percentages*

	Number of votes 1999	2004	% 1999	% 2004
PAIGC	172	257	40	68
UNDP	34	13	8	3 (3.4)
PRS	30	38	7	10
RGB	30	3	7	1 (0.8)
UM	23	12	5	3 (3.2)
PSD	19	-	4	-
AD	16	-	4	-
LIPE	14	-	3	-
FDS	10	-	2	-
FLING	4	-	1	-
PRP	2	-	1 (0.5)	-
PUSD	-	15	-	4
APU	-	9	-	2 (2.4)
Frente para a Dem.	-	6	-	2 (1.6)
PU	-	4	-	1 (1.1)
PDS	-	3	-	1 (0.8)
PUN	-	2	-	1 (0.5)
UE	-	1	-	0 (0.3)
blank + invalid	78	-	18	-
blank	-	15	-	4
Total	*432*	*378*	*100*	*100*

Sources: The figures for 1999 (*Kandjadja*, 1999 national assembly election) were noted by the local voting official and then filled in by the chairman of the section committee for Kandjadja in a copy of the original form, on the basis of the voting official's own information received directly from the polling station, 28 and 29.11.1999. I also checked these data against hand-written material shown to me by the deputy elected in 1999 for PAIGC (*Mansabá sector, constituency no. 7*, 1999). The figures for 2004 were given to me directly by the chairman of the section committee on the occasion of my visit on 29 June 2007 (*Kandjadja*, 2004 national assembly election). The figures for total number of votes cast (381) do not quite match the sum arrived at (378) when the separate posts are added. I decided to put the latter figure in the table. There is also a small uncertainty in regard to PUSD, which appears twice in the data (2+13=15 = the figure found in the table). "Frente para a Democracía" is not found in the official statistics. It may refer to FDS (Frente Democrática Social). These minor inconsistencies and uncertainties do not in any way affect the credibility and validity of the data.

Table 3. *Results of the first round of presidential election in Kandjadja, 28 November 1999, number of votes and rounded-off percentages*

	Number of votes	*% of total*
Kumba Yalá (PRS)	34	8
Malam Bacai Sanhá (PAIGC)	313	72
Faustino Fudut Imbali (independent)	3	1 (0.7)
Fernando Gomes (independent)	2	0 (0.46)
João Tatis Sá (independent)	–	–
Abubacar Baldé (UNDP)	12	3
Bubacar Rachid Djaló (LIPE)	4	1 (0.9)
Joaquim Baldé (PSD)	1	0 (0.2)
Salvador Tchongo (independent)	3	1 (0.7)
José Catengul Mendes (FLING)	2	0 (0.46)
Mamadú Uri Baldé (PRP)	–	–
Antonieta Rosa Gomes (FCG/SD)	1	1 (0.7)
blank	23	5
invalid	29	7
protested	9	2
Total votes	*436*	*100*
abstained	*38*	*8 (of 474))*
Total registered votes	474	8 % (of 474)

Sources: The figures for 1999 (*Kandjadja*, 1999 presidential election, first round) were noted by the local voting official and then filled in by the chairman of the section committee for Kandjadja in a copy of the original form, on the basis of the voting official's own information received directly from the polling station, 28 and 29.11.1999. I also checked them against hand-written material shown to me by the deputy elected in 1999 for PAIGC (*Mansabá sector, constituency no. 7,*

1999). There were a few very minor inconsistencies between the two sets of data, in no way affecting their credibility and validity. The table is based on the local voting official's figures.

Table 4. *Results of the second rounds of presidential elections in Kandjadja, 16 January 2000 and 24 July 2005, number of votes and rounded-off percentages*

	Number of votes			
	2000	*2005*	*% 2000*	*% 2005*
Malam Bacai Sanhá (PAIGC)	352	423	86	93
Kumba Yalá (PRS)	39	-	10	-
'Nino' Vieira (independent)	-	33	-	7
Blank votes	18	*	4	*
Invalid votes	1	*	0 (0,2)	*
Total votes cast	*410*	*	*100*	*

* Information not available on blank and invalid votes and thus not on "total votes cast" for the 2005 election in Kandjadja. Thus, the percentages in the table are not quite comparable between the two years. Calculated on the basis of "votes for candidates", as for 2005, Malam Bacai Sanhá got 90 percent in 2000.

Sources: *The figures for 2000 are based on hand-written records shown to me by the deputy elected for PAIGC in 1999 (*Mansabá sector, constituency no. 7, *2000). This was based in turn on information received on election-day by the PAIGC parliamentarian directly from the 51 polling stations. The polling stations were under the supervision of the PAIGC supervisor for the whole constituency, who was also the chairman of the section committee for Kandjadja. The figures for 2005 were given to me in Bissau on 30.6.2007 by mobile phone from the village by the chairman of the section committee for Kandjadja* (Kandjadja, *24.7.2005 presidential election, second round*).

Table 5. *Comparison between Kandjadja and the country as a whole, second rounds of presidential elections in Kandjadja, 16 January 2000 and 24 July 2005, rounded-off percentages of votes for the two remaining candidates*

	% 2000		*% 2005*	
	Kandjadja	*Whole country*	*Kandjadja*	*Whole country*
Malam Bacai Sanhá	90	27	93	47
Kumba Yalá	10	69	-	-
'Nino' Vieira	-	-	7	51

Sources: For Kandjadja, same as table 4; for whole country 2000, *Comissão Nacional de Eleições*, 2000a; for whole country 2005, *Comissão Nacional de Eleições*, 2005.

References

Literature, reports and news material

Chabal, P. & J.-P. Daloz 1999. *Africa Works: Disorder as political instrument*, London: James Currey; Bloomington: Indiana University Press.

Hellström, E. 1995. *Non-Governmental Organizations and Their Role in Democratization*. A Minor Field Study of Guinea-Bissau. Unit of Development Studies, Uppsala University, Minor Field Study Series 9.

Human Development Report 1999. United Nations Development Programme (UNDP), Oxford University Press, Oxford.

Human Development Report 2007/2008. United Nations Development Programme (UNDP): http://hdr.undp.org/en/media/HDR_20072008_EN_Complete.pdf

Imbali, F., F. Koudawo, P.F. Gomes, C. Cardoso, P.K. Mendy *Guiné-Bissau. Uma retrospectiva. Síntese*, Instituto Nacional de Estudos e Pesquisa/National Institute for Studies and Research (INEP), Bissau.

Leys, C. 1996. The Crisis in Development Theory. *New Political Economy* 1 (1), 41-51.

Lusa: Agência de Notícias de Portugal, various issues, 2003-2009 : http://www.lusa.pt

Mamdani, M. 1996. *Citizen and Subject: Contemporary Africa and the legacy of late colonialism*. Princeton University Press, Princeton.

RADI (Réseau Africain pour le Développement Intégré/African network for integrated development), no date. *Le RADI. Ce qu'il est et ce qu'il veut*, presentation brochure, Dakar.

–. 1995. *Projet d'appui aux associations rurales de la Région d'Oio pour leur reconnnaissance légale-juridique*. RADI, Farim, April.

–. 1999a. *Rapport d'activités et d'exécution financière du projet de renforcement institutionnel GW006031 au profit de RADI/Guinée-Bissau, mai 1997 à avril 1999*. R.A.D.I., Farim, April.

–. 1999b. *Rapport d'exécution technique et financière du solde de projet GW006011, dans le cadre d'un programme d'appui d'urgence aux populations victimes du conflit armé en Guinée-Bissau, dans la région d'Oio*. RADI/Guinée-Bissau, Farim, 30.4.1999.

Rudebeck, L. 1992. Politics and Structural Adjustment in a West-African Village. In *When Democracy Makes Sense* (ed.) L. Rudebeck, AKUT, Uppsala.

–. 1994. Traditional/Modern in Modernised Modernisation Thinking: The development of a Weberian dichotomy. In *The Theoretical Heritage from Marx and Weber in Development Studies* (ed.) J. Martinussen. Occasional Papers 10, International Development Studies, Roskilde University, Roskilde.

–. 1997. *"Buscar a felicidade"* (To seek happiness) *na Guiné-Bissau,* Lala Kema, no. 1, INEP, Bissau, 1997. A condensed version is found under the title "'To Seek Happiness'. Development in a West-African Village in the Era of Democratisation". *Review of African Political Economy* 71, 1997, 75-86.

–. 1998. Popular Sovereignty and Constitutionalism. A historical and comparative perspective. In *Democratization in the Third World* (eds.) L. Rudebeck & O. Törnquist, with V. Rojas. London: Macmillan.

–. 2001. *On Democracy's Sustainability. Transition in Guinea-Bissau*, Sida Studies 4, Sida, Stockholm.

–. 2002a. Beyond Democratic Constitutionalism: on the twofold meaning of democracy and democratization. *African Sociological Review* 6 (1), 173-180.

–. 2002b. Multiparty Elections in Guinea-Bissau: viewed against late-colonial non-party and post-colonial single-party elections. In *Elections in Africa* (eds) M. Cowen & L. Laakso. London: James Currey.

–. 2003. Democracy as Actual Practice. In *Democracy as Actual Practice: What Does Democracy Really Bring?* (ed.) L. Rudebeck. Utsikt mot utveckling 20, Collegium for Development Studies, Uppsala University, Uppsala.

–. 2004. Democratisation and 'Civil Society' in a West-African Village. In *Decentralisation in Practice: Power, Livelihoods and Cultural Meaning in West Africa*, International Workshop Highlights, Uppsala, Sweden, May 4-6, 2004, IIED (International Institute for Environment and Development),

London and Department of Cultural Anthropology and Ethnology, Uppsala University, Uppsala (brochure + CD-ROM).

–. 2007. Building Civic Trust in Post-Conflict Societies. In *Reconciling Winners and Losers in Post-Conflict Elections in West Africa: Political and Policy Imperative* (eds) C. Norberg & C. Obi. Uppsala: Nordic Africa Institute: http://www.nai.uu.se/publications/books/book.xml?id=2524

–. 2008. Demokrati, utveckling och globalisering (Democracy, development and globalisation). In *Statsvetare ifrågasätter: Uppsalamiljön vid tiden för professorsskiftet den 31 mars 2008* (eds) S. Gustavsson, J. Hermansson & B. Holmström. Uppsala: Acta Universitatis Upsaliensis.

–. 2009, forthcoming. Electoral Democratisation in Post-Civil War Guinea-Bissau 1999–2006. Uppsala: Nordic Africa Institute.

Sjögren, A. 2001. State, Civil Society and Democratisation: Theoretical Debates Past and Present. In *Civil Society and Authoritarianism in the Third World* (eds) B. Beckman & A. Sjögren. PODSU (Politics of Development Group), Department of Political Science, Stockholm University, Stockholm.

Törnquist, O. 1999. *Politics and Development: A critical introduction*. London: Sage Publications.

–. 2009. Introduction and General Conclusions. In *Aceh: The Role of Democracy for Peace and Reconstruction* (eds) O. Törnquist, S. Adi Prasetyo & T. Birks. Jakarta: PCD Press and ISAI (Institute for the studies of the free flow of information).

UN 2008. Security Council warns drug trafficking, other crimes imperil Guinea-Bissau. *UN News Service*, 3.10.2008. http://www.un.org/apps/news/story.asp?NewsID=24349&Cr=guinea&Cr1=bissau

World Bank 2008. *Country Brief, Guinea-Bissau.*

http://web.worldbank.org/WBSITE/EXTERNAL/COUNTRIES/AFRICAEXT/GUINEABISEXTN/0,,menuPK:356680~pagePK:141132~piPK:141107~theSitePK:356669,00.html

Election documentation

Comissão Nacional de Eleições (National Election Commission), 2000a. Official record of national assembly elections held on 28 November 1999, Bissau, 9.12.1999 and 25.1.2000.

–. 2000b. Official record of presidential elections held on 16 January 2000, Bissau, 21.1.2000.

–. 2005. Official record of second round of presidential elections held on 24 July 2005, Bissau, 10.8.2005.

Kandjadja, 1999 national assembly election. Copy of the form (white) to be completed for the first round of the parliamentary election by the local voting officials at each voting station, completed in this case by the chairman of the section committee for Kandjadja, based on the returning officers' figures, 28 and 29.11.1999.

–. 1999 presidential election, first round. Copy of the form (brown-yellow) to be completed for the first round of the presidential election by the local voing officials at each voting station, completed in this case by the chairman of the section committee for Kandjadja, based on the returning officers' figures, 28.11.1999.

–. 2004 national assembly election. Figures provided 29.6.2007 by the chairman of the section committee for Kandjadja, based on his own preserved notes from 28.3.2004.

–. 24.7.2005 presidential election, second round. Figures received in Bissau 30.6.2007 by mobile phone call from the chairman of the section committee for Kandjadja consulting his notes.

Mansabá sector, constituency 7, 1999. Detailed record, shown to me in Bissau, of the results of the national assembly election and the first round of the presidential election 28.11.1999 for the voting station in Kandjadja (no. 81), in Mansabá sector/constituency 7, Oio region. The record is hand-written, based on reports from the returning officers and drawn up during the days after election day by the PAIGC deputy (member of paliament) for Mansabá then elected,

–. 2000. Detailed record, shown to me in Bissau, of the results of the second round of the presidential election 16.1.2000 for 51 polling stations, including

Kandjadja, in Mansabá sector/constituency 7, Oio region. The record is hand-written, based on reports from the returning officers and drawn up during the days after election day by the PAIGC deputy (member of paliament) for Mansabá elected 28.11.1999,

Nô Pintcha, 8.4.2004. Local newspaper report on results of national assembly election 28.3.2004, based on data from *Comissão Nacional de Eleições* (National Election Commission),

Lusa, 4.4.2004. Portuguese news agency report on results of national assembly election 28.3.2004, based on data from *Comissão Nacional de Eleições* (National Election Commission).

http://www.lusa.pt

Abbreviations

AD, *Acção Democrática*/Democratic Action

ANP, *Assembleia Nacional Popular*/National Assembly, i.e. parliament

APU, *Aliança Popular Unida*/Popular United Alliance

CFA, *Communautée Financière Africaine*

CNE, *Comissão Nacional das Eleicões*/National Election Commission

FCG-SD, *Fórum Cívico Guineense - Social Democracia*/Guinean Civic Forum - Social Democracy

FDS, *Frente Democrática Social*/Democratic Social Front

FLING, *Frente da Libertacão Nacional da Guiné*/Guinea's National Liberation Front

GDP, *Gross Domestic Product*

LIPE, *Liga Guinense de Protecção e Desenvolvimento Ecológico*/Guinean League for Ecological Protection and Development

NGO, *Non-Governmental Organisation*, i.e. voluntary organisation – ONG in Portuguese, French, etc.

PAIGC, *Partido Africano da Independência da Guiné e Cabo Verde*/African Party for the Independence of Guinea and Cape Verde

PDS, *Partido Democrático Socialista*/Democratic Socialist Party

PRGB/MB, *Partido da Resistência da Guiné-Bissau - Movimento Bâ-Fatá* /Guinea-Bissau's Resistance Party – Bâ-Fatá-Movement

PRP, *Partido da Renovação e Progresso*/Party for Renewal and Progress

PRS, *Partido da Renovação Social*/Party for Social Renewal

PSD, *Partido Social Democrata*/Social Democratic Party

PU, *Plataforma Unida*/United Platform

PUN, *Partido da União Nacional*/Party of National Union

PUSD, *Partido Unido Social Democrata*/United Social Democratic Party

RADI, *Résau Africain pour le Développement Intégré*/African Network For Integrated Development

RGB/MB, the same as PRGB/MB, often merely RGB

UE, *União Eleitoral*/Electoral Union

UM, *União para a Mudança*/Union for Change

UNDP, *União Nacional para o Desenvolvimento e Progresso*/National Union for Development and Progress

UNDP, *United Nations Development Programme*

Foncier, pouvoirs locaux et décentralisation dans le département de Dakoro (Niger)

Abdoulaye Mohamadou[1]

In this article we show that the decentralisation initiated in Niger since the early 1990s has led to the strengthening of local chieftaincy (of cantons, villages and groupements), to the primacy of sedentary settlement over mobility, and to the marginalisation of pastoralists left with no other choice than to apply settlement logics to 'obtain' chieftaincies and community 'territories'. This development towards territorialisation could threaten the survial of the pastoral mode of life in pastoral and agropastroal zones.

Dans cet article nous montrons que la décentralisation amorcée au Niger depuis le début des années 90 a eu pour conséquence le renforcement des chefferies locales (cantonales, villageoises et de groupements), la confirmation du primat de la sédentarité sur la mobilité et la marginalisation des éleveurs qui n'ont eu d'autres choix que de s'inscrire dans une logique de sédentarisation pour « obtenir » des chefferies et des « territoires » communaux. Cette évolution vers la territorialisation pourrait constituer une menace pour la survie du mode de vie pastoral dans les régions agricoles et agropastorales au Niger.

Le processus de démocratisation amorcé au Niger depuis le début des années 90 s'est traduit, au plan politique par la mise en route d'un projet de décentralisation. Après un début laborieux lié en partie à l'instabilité politique du pays, la décentralisation est devenue effective avec le découpage territorial de 2001 et les élections locales de juillet 2004. Il s'agit d'une avancée démocratique majeure pour un pays longtemps dirigé par une dictature militaire.

Mais comme nous allons tenter de le montrer dans ce texte la décentralisation a eu pour conséquence le renforcement des chefferies locales (cantonales, villageoises et de groupements), la confirmation du primat de la sédentarité sur la mobilité et la marginalisation des éleveurs qui

[1] Enseignant-chercheur Faculté d'Agronomie, Université Abdou Moumouni de Niamey, chercheur au LASDEL : azawagh@yahoo.fr

n'ont eu d'autres choix que de s'inscrire dans une logique de sédentarisation pour « obtenir » des chefferies et des « territoires » communaux. A long terme, cette évolution vers la territorialisation pourrait constituer une menace pour la survie du mode de vie pastoral dans les régions agricoles et agropastorales.

Contexte

La loi n°60 du 30 avril 2002 portant création des communes et fixant le nom de leurs chefs lieux a découpé le territoire de la République du Niger en 265 communes (urbaines et rurales). L'Etat a décidé au nom d'une démarche progressive et prudente de ne rendre opérationnel que le niveau communal. Rappelons que les communes sont le dernier niveau de découpage qui comprend aussi dans l'ordre ascendant des départements et des régions. Ces collectivités territoriales administratives sont venues se superposer aux territoires coutumiers qui comprennent des sultanats, des provinces, des cantons et des zones pastorales.

L'Etat a longtemps hésité sur le schéma de découpage à adopter craignant surtout que la décentralisation ne soit une source de velléité d'autonomie ou de sécession de certaines régions (Hahonou 2006). Finalement, c'est un découpage, basé sur les cantons et certains groupements, qui sera retenu. Les cantons sont de petites chefferies sédentaires créées par l'administration coloniale et qui regroupent quelques villages et tribus. Pour l'administration des nomades, ce sont des groupements qui ont été créés. Les cantons ont des territoires avec des frontières plus ou moins connues alors que les groupements n'en ont pas. Certaines chefferies cantonales ou de groupements ont une légitimité précoloniale mais la plupart sont des entités administratives mises en place pour les besoins du contrôle des populations (Olivier de Sardan 1998). Mais la question du découpage n'était pas la seule inquiétude, il y avait aussi la place que devrait avoir les chefs traditionnels dans la future configuration des pouvoirs locaux.

Le Niger est l'un des rares pays de l'Afrique de l'Ouest a avoir maintenu la chefferie traditionnelle comme un pilier de l'Etat poursuivant ainsi une pratique de l'Etat colonial. Au Mali et au Bénin par exemple où les chefferies ont été affaiblies par les régimes socialistes de Modibo Keita et de Mathieu Kérékou, la décentralisation est présentée comme une manière de « réconcilier le pays légal avec le pays réel » dans le cas du Mali et un moyen de revalorisation de la chefferie traditionnelle dans le cas du Bénin (Blundo 1998 ; Fay 2000).

La chefferie traditionnelle en particulier cantonale était au Niger en l'absence d'une expérience municipale, l'acteur politique dominant des arènes locales nigériennes. Mais cette situation a évolué au cours des vingt dernières années. La chefferie elle-même ne parle pas d'une seule voix. Elle comporte plusieurs lignages avec certains au pouvoir et d'autres dans l'opposition (Olivier de Sardan 1998). Depuis le début des années 80 avec la généralisation de l'approche projet, de nombreux comités villageois ont été mis en œuvre par les projets et ONG. Les dirigeants de ces projets sont devenus au fil des ans des notabilités locales qui tirent leur légitimité des liens avec les projets et ONG et des ressources matérielles et financières qu'ils contrôlent localement. Il peut s'agir d'anciens leaders des coopératives et de jeunes (*samarias*), organisations affiliées aux anciens régimes (du PPN-RDA et des militaires) ou de nouveaux acteurs souvent opposés aux chefferies.

La libéralisation politique amorcée depuis le début des années 90 a enfanté les partis[2] politiques qui se sont implantés aussi dans les villages avec des leaders plus au moins importants en fonction des ressources (économiques, capital social, capital symbolique) qu'ils peuvent mobiliser. Ces leaders d'origines diverses peuvent être basés au niveau local, régional et national. Dans les deux derniers cas, ils agissent en tant que ressortissants, courtiers en développement et/ ou entrepreneurs politiques (Hahonou 2006).

Les pouvoirs locaux sont donc le produit de plusieurs processus interdépendants, comme la recomposition des espaces politiques précoloniaux suite à la pénétration française, et la superposition de nouvelles formes politiques mises en place pour assoir un pouvoir centralisé

[2] Le Niger a connu une première expérience des partis politiques à la veille de l'indépendance mais ils seront interdits juste après la proclamation de celle-ci

symbolisé par l'Etat colonial et l'Etat postcolonial (Bourmaud 1997, cité par Olivier de Sardan 2007).

La décentralisation démarre donc dans des paysages socio-historiques variés (Fay 2000) et des arènes complexes (Bierschenk & Olivier de Sardan 1998). C'est pour cette raison que Blundo (1998:17) nous rappelle que « L'absence de terrains institutionnels 'vierges' est donc une donne essentielle pour comprendre la manière dont la décentralisation – qui vise à implanter de nouveaux modes de gestion, de nouvelles formes de légitimité et d'autorité et de nouvelles règles juridiques –, fonctionnera concrètement ».

Le processus de décentralisation a suscité un intérêt certain pour le local tant de la part de ses promoteurs (Etat et bailleurs de fonds) que des acteurs locaux et des chercheurs en sciences sociales. Au Niger l'Etat avait mis en place une administration de mission, le Haut Commissariat à la Reforme Administrative et à la Décentralisation (HCRAD) chargé de l'opérationnalisation du projet de décentralisation. Cette institution avait pour mission d'animer le processus en relation avec les différents acteurs concernés. Le choix d'un schéma de découpage basé sur les cantons et certains groupements a mis au devant de la scène les chefs traditionnels. Ces derniers étaient les principaux interlocuteurs du HCRAD au niveau local. Les administrateurs locaux et les services techniques ont été peu impliqués dans le processus.

Les bailleurs de fonds quant à eux s'étaient investis dans la décentralisation avant 2004 à travers les projets de développement local dont l'un des axes principaux était la bonne gouvernance déclinée par la mise en place d'institutions locales de concertation et de gestion des activités de développement.

Au niveau local, le projet de décentralisation a suscité beaucoup d'appréhensions (Mohamadou 2003) avant que sa réalisation ne mobilise les différents acteurs du pouvoir local. Les chefs traditionnels voyaient d'un mauvais œil l'arrivée des conseils municipaux avec lesquels ils auraient à partager leurs anciennes prérogatives et responsabilités : collecte des impôts, justice civile, développement local, gestion des marchés, gestion du foncier, etc.

La question foncière est certainement la problématique la plus délicate car son traitement ait toujours été un sujet éminemment politique au Niger. C'est une chasse gardée des chefferies traditionnelles sous le contrôle de l'Etat. Il était par exemple conseillé aux projets de ne pas intervenir là où il y a des problèmes fonciers. Les chefs traditionnels ont réussi à renforcer leur pouvoir sur le foncier à travers les textes de loi notamment l'ordonnance n° 93-28 du 30 mars 1993 portant statut de la chefferie traditionnelle arrachée le dernier jour du régime de transition de l'après conférence nationale. Les textes du Code rural reconnaissent aussi le pouvoir des chefs sur le foncier et ils sont membres des commissions foncières.

La décentralisation apparaissait dès lors pour les chefs comme un risque de remise en cause de leurs privilèges en matière foncière mais le non transfert aux nouvelles communes de compétences dans le domaine foncier profite aux chefferies traditionnelles dont les prérogatives et attributions n'ont pas été abrogées. Les conseils municipaux vont se contenter de la compétence générale qui ne clarifie ni les pouvoirs, ni les responsabilités des uns et des autres. Fay (2000 : 123) résume bien le contexte dans lequel intervient la décentralisation marqué par une forte prégnance et imbrication du foncier et du politique.

> « [...] du point de vue du paysan, tout s'inscrit dans des paysages socio-historiques variés, où coexistent des formes concrètes très différentes de solidarité d'une part (notamment autour des 'propriétés' possédées et/ou gérées à différents niveaux au nom d'appartenances ethniques, lignagères, villageoises ou historico-politiques), de pouvoir d'autre part (de la chefferie lignagère à la chefferie de village, à des rémanences de chefferies d'origine précoloniale ou coloniale, et aux pouvoirs administratifs et politiques de différentes natures) ».

Ici se trouve posée la question de la réappropriation de la décentralisation par les acteurs locaux. La décentralisation qu'elle soit imposée ou produite de la nécessité historique a suscité des inquiétudes, des attentes, des stratégies d'anticipation, des négociations, etc. Le découpage des cantons, le choix des groupements nomades éligibles, le rattachement des villages et des tribus, le choix des chefs lieux des communes, le choix des noms des communes, etc. ont été l'objet de négociations, oppositions et compromis entre acteurs locaux et acteurs nationaux.

Dans cette première phase du processus, ce sont les chefs traditionnels, les ressortissants et les leaders associatifs qui ont joué un rôle important. La longue durée de gestation du projet (1994-2004) a permis aux différents acteurs d'élaborer des stratégies d'anticipation pour leur positionnement.

Nous menons des recherches[3] à Dakoro depuis 2002, ce qui constitue une assez longue période d'observation des processus sociaux autour de la décentralisation. Notre approche s'inscrit dans une perspective historique et interactionniste pour comprendre les transformations et les permanences de l'arène politique locale. L'analyse va s'orienter sur deux axes. Dans un premier temps nous allons faire une genèse de la mise en ordre foncière dans le département en montrant que l'accès à la chefferie cantonale ou de groupement a toujours été pour les différents groupes le moyen privilégié de contrôle des populations dans une zone dont l'occupation massive de l'espace date de la période coloniale. Dans un second temps, nous analyserons le processus de construction des communes à travers les stratégies des différents acteurs dans le canton de Birnin Lallé et sa zone restante.

La territorialisation/ appropriation de l'espace: des frontières aux usages

La collectivité de Dakoro a été créée dans ses frontières actuelles en 1947 comme subdivision administrative rattachée au cercle de Maradi. Elle est née d'un redécoupage des subdivisions et cercles voisins et comprenaient quatre cantons (Kornaka, Birnin Lallé, Bader Goula et Soli Tagriss) et 3 tribus nomades (Serkin Rafi, Kel Gress et Kel Ferwan).

Nous allons faire l'historique de l'appropriation du « foncier-territorial » selon le mot de Fay (2000) depuis la création de la subdivision. Dans la nouvelle collectivité où la chefferie est peu institutionnalisée, le contrôle des populations et de l'espace vont de paire. Les nouveaux cantons créés

[3] Ces recherches ont donné lieu à des publications dans la série Etudes et Travaux du LASDEL : www.lasdel.net Un article sur les pouvoirs locaux à Birnin Lallé est à paraître dans un ouvrage collectif chez Karthala

n'avaient pas d'assise territoriale et n'ont pas de limites précises. Il fallait donc chercher le rattachement des entités villageoises qui disposaient de propriétés foncières. Les villages eux-mêmes, venus d'horizons divers s'étaient récemment installés et étaient très mobiles. Dans une étude sur la région de Gao, Grémont (2007) souligne que dans les zones peu peuplées, les groupes qui se disputent le pouvoir politique cherchaient d'abord à contrôler les populations. Le contrôle des hommes déterminait le contrôle de l'espace. C'est une situation très proche de celle de Dakoro.

Apres les rattachements des villages et tribus qui ont donné aux cantons et aux groupements leurs configurations territoriales actuelles, l'enjeu était devenu la mise en valeur des terres. La croissance démographique, les sécheresses récurrentes et les politiques foncières ont été les déterminants des pratiques et stratégies foncières.

Le découpage de 1947 : « la zone restante », un espace de non droit

Apres la délimitation de l'espace de la nouvelle subdivision, son territoire a été découpé en deux parties : au sud, la zone agricole sur laquelle s'exercent l'autorité de chefs de cantons et, au nord une zone appelée zone restante qui correspond à la zone pastorale peuplée de nomades. Ces nomades étaient rattachés aux tribus indépendantes de la subdivision. Mais pour bien marquer les frontières de la nouvelle subdivision, ses limites septentrionales avec les cercles d'Agadès et de Tahoua correspondaient aussi aux limites nord des cantons de Birnin Lallé, Bader Goula et Soli Tagriss. Autrement dit, les territoires des cantons englobent la zone restante mais sans droit d'appropriation.

Les agriculteurs et les nomades avaient des chefferies distinctes mais les nomades n'avaient pas de territoires juridiquement reconnus. L'élevage n'est pas considéré comme une mise en valeur et les éleveurs trop mobiles pour posséder un territoire au nom d'une conception qui est toujours d'actualité. Mais les éleveurs ont toujours considéré la zone comme leur appartenant au nom du droit du premier occupant.

A la logique « civiliste » du droit positif selon le mot d'Etienne Le Roy s'oppose une légitimité historique d'occupation de l'espace. Cette maltraitance du foncier pastoral, liée à une lecture à partir du primat de la sédentarité ou d'une lecture politique et moderne de la territorialité (Le Roy, 1999) est à l'origine de malentendus entre Etats coloniaux et postcoloniaux, d'une part, et éleveurs nomades, de l'autre.

En 1953, pour empêcher l'extension de l'agriculture dans la zone pastorale de la colonie du Niger, l'administration coloniale avait tracé une limite nord des cultures qui correspondait à la ligne de démarcation entre la zone agricole et la zone d'élevage des nomades du nord.

Pour bien marquer la ligne de partage entre les deux activités dans le département de Dakoro, des couloirs de passage ont été tracés de la frontière nigériane au sud jusqu'à la vallée de la Tarka, considérée comme la limite naturelle entre les zones agricole et pastorale. Ils permettaient aussi la circulation des éleveurs transhumants entre les deux zones.

La zone restante de Dakoro est demeurée un point de discorde entre chefferies cantonales et chefferies nomades, entre éleveurs et agriculteurs. Alors que théoriquement, c'est un domaine public de l'Etat, diverses pratiques d'appropriation s'y sont développées. Les agriculteurs ont longtemps profité du flou juridique et du soutien tacite de l'Etat avant que les éleveurs ne se mobilisent à partir des années 90 pour une prise en compte du foncier pastoral dans la législation foncière nationale.

De la limite nord aux terroirs d'attache : vers une reconnaissance du foncier pastoral

En 1961, un an après les indépendances, le gouvernement du Niger a modifié le tracé de la limite des cultures en la repoussant plus au nord au profit des agriculteurs. C'est la loi No 61-05 du 26 mai 1961 (Journal officiel spécial 3 du 15/07/61) qui divise le pays en deux zones distinctes : une zone agricole au sud et une zone pastorale au nord. Au-delà de cette limite légale, l'agriculture est interdite et les dégâts commis sur des champs ne sont pas susceptibles de dédommagement. Seule l'agriculture oasienne et une agriculture de subsistance sont autorisées pour les nomades. Dans le département de Dakoro, cette limite se situe désormais au nord de la vallée de la Tarka à une vingtaine de kilomètres au nord du chef lieu du département. Mais la forte croissance démographique chez les sédentaires et les sécheresses des années 70 et 80 ont poussé à une colonisation des espaces pastoraux par les agriculteurs et des nomades qui ont perdu leur capital bétail. Le front agricole a franchi la Tarka et a pénétré dans la zone pastorale. Les couloirs de passage sont occupés et de nombreux conflits opposent agriculteurs et éleveurs autour des itinéraires de transhumance.

L'Etat a encouragé cette avancée du front agricole dans la mesure où le président de l'époque, Seyni Kountché a proclamé que « la terre appartient à celui qui l'exploite ». Or, l'élevage n'étant pas considéré comme une mise en valeur, le front agricole a progressé au nord au détriment de l'espace pastoral. Même l'adoption en 1993 d'une loi d'orientation sur les textes du code rural n'a pas corrigé cette lacune et les éleveurs se sont vus dépossédés de leur espace.

Dans la foulée de la libéralisation politique des années 90, les éleveurs ont réagi avec la création de plusieurs associations pastorales dont l'un des objectifs majeurs était la défense des intérêts des éleveurs. Les affrontements meurtriers (une centaine de morts) de 1990 entre agriculteurs et éleveurs peuls dans le département de Guidan Roumji (frontalier de celui de Dakoro et par lequel passent plusieurs axes de transhumance en direction de la vallée de la Tarka) ont ému l'opinion nationale et ont servi à une prise de conscience de l'ampleur de la compétition autour du foncier.

La lutte menée par la société civile pastorale a abouti à l'adoption en 1997 d'une loi sur le Statut des Terroirs d'attache des Pasteurs. Cette loi stipule que les éleveurs ont des droits d'usage prioritaires sur leurs terroirs d'attache. Le terroir d'attache est défini comme une unité territoriale déterminée et reconnue par les coutumes et/ou les textes en vigueur, à l'intérieur de laquelle vivent, habituellement pendant la majeure partie de l'année, des pasteurs ; unité territoriale à laquelle ils restent attachés lorsqu'ils se déplacent que ce soit à l'occasion de la transhumance, du nomadisme ou des migrations. Elle s'inspire fortement des droits coutumiers mais elle ne donne pas un droit de gestion et de négociation avec les tiers. Sa remise en cause par les associations des éleveurs est à l'origine du processus d'élaboration en cours d'une loi sur l'élevage et le pastoralisme. Mais ce texte constitue une avancée significative puisque la zone pastorale est désormais considérée comme un ensemble de terroirs d'attache des pasteurs et non plus comme des terres vacantes et sans maîtres. Les procédures administratives pour faire reconnaitre leurs droits sur les terroirs d'attache étaient lourdes, les éleveurs ont développé d'autres stratégies de marquage de l'espace.

Les stratégies de marquage de l'espace des éleveurs

L'objectif commun à tous les éleveurs (Peuls et Touaregs), c'est d'arrêter le front agricole. Plusieurs stratégies ont été observées dans la zone. Elles sont portées par les chefferies et le mouvement associatif pastoral. L'une des toutes premières stratégies a été de créer des ceintures agricoles autour des terroirs pastoraux. Les éleveurs eux-mêmes se mettent à l'agriculture pour empêcher aux agriculteurs de défricher de nouveaux espaces. Ainsi un espace vital est préservé pour l'élevage. Certains villages d'agriculteurs sont rattachés aux chefferies nomades, ce qui permet à ces dernières de contrôler leur accès à la terre.

Avec l'intervention des projets de développement de l'élevage dans la zone, les associations pastorales de concert avec les chefferies ont opté pour la création d'infrastructures socio-économiques (puits, écoles, banques céréalières, banques d'aliments du bétail, cases de santé, etc.). Il s'agit de créer des sites d'ancrage ou sites de fixation sur le modèle des villages d'agriculteurs pour marquer l'espace. Avec ces sites, une partie des familles ne vont pas en transhumance avec les animaux. Il y a donc une permanence d'occupation pour éviter l'arrivée de nouvelles populations. Par le passé la mobilité des éleveurs a favorisé l'installation de populations hausa qui ont fini par s'approprier l'espace en le cultivant. Ces deux stratégies combinées (ceintures de champs et viabilisation des sites d'ancrage) ont permis de stabiliser le front agricole autour de la vallée de la Tarka.

Avec le PASEL (Programme d'appui au secteur de l'élevage) financé par la coopération suisse, une action d'identification et de balisage des couloirs de passage et des aires de pâturage a été initiée. Elle a été conduite en concertation avec l'administration, les chefferies cantonales et nomades des départements de Dakoro et Guidan Roumji. Elle a permis de faire baisser les conflits entre agriculteurs et éleveurs. La commission foncière départementale

(COFODEP), cheville institutionnelle du code rural nigérien a été maître d'œuvre du processus. La COFODEP dont la mission est de vulgariser les textes du code rural et sécuriser les opérateurs ruraux est composée de l'ensemble des acteurs du pouvoir local (Préfecture, services techniques, chefferies traditionnelles, société civile, éleveurs, agriculteurs, femmes et jeunes). Elle a joué un rôle important dans la prévention des conflits et la promotion d'une culture de concertation entre les différents acteurs. Le projet PASEL a aussi apporté un soutien aux associations pastorales qui se sont fédérées en 2001 en Collectif des Associations Pastorales du département de Dakoro (CAPONG). Il compte une dizaine d'associations animées principalement par des cadres et leaders peuls et touaregs. Ce collectif s'est distingué dans la défense des intérêts des éleveurs et s'était investi dans la mobilisation des fonds au profit des communautés pastorales. Il a réussi à s'imposer comme un acteur incontournable dans l'arène locale[4].

Les investissements réalisés ont permis de doter les sites des principales tribus d'infrastructures sociales et hydrauliques. Le collectif s'est employé à défendre les intérêts des éleveurs dans le cadre du processus de décentralisation. Il a mené plusieurs campagnes de sensibilisation pour prévenir la marginalisation des éleveurs. Plusieurs de ses membres se sont impliqués et se sont fait élire conseillers municipaux.

Les positions institutionnelles jouent un rôle important dans le jeu politique local. Ainsi, nous verrons comment la quête de reconnaissance politique par les différents groupes sociaux a été une constante dans l'émergence des chefferies traditionnelles de Dakoro. La particularité de Dakoro par rapport à de nombreuses régions du pays, c'est l'absence avant la colonisation de chefferies coutumières. C'est à l'administration coloniale et à l'Etat postcolonial qu'il était revenu la responsabilité de créer des chefferies au sein de groupes récemment installés.

[4] Il s'est distingue pendant la famine de 2005 par la mobilisation de plusieurs financements au profit des sinistrés.

Emergence des chefferies sur des « terres vacantes »

Les populations actuelles de Dakoro appartiennent à divers groupes socio-linguistiques du pays et se sont installées au début du XXème siècle. La colonisation a joué un rôle majeur dans l'occupation progressive de l'espace de la nouvelle subdivision.

> « A l'époque pré-coloniale, ce fut un 'no man's land', avec peu de ressources en eau, situé entre les territoires de plusieurs confédérations : en particulier Kel Gress, Kel Ferwan et Iwellemenden.[...] Le creusement de puits jusqu'à une profondeur de 30 à 40 mètres, à partir de cette époque, a permis durant toute l'année l'occupation de ces terres qui auparavant n'avaient été habitées qu'en saison des pluies. Des familles appartenant à différentes confédérations touarègues et à d'autres groupes ethniques – Arabes, Peuls (Fulani), Hausa – ont progressivement migré vers cette région durant les années trente et quarante, encouragées par une administration qui souhaitait démanteler les groupements politiquement les plus importants ». (Oxby 1996)

Avant la création de la subdivision, la région était une zone refuge pour les populations fuyant les exactions coloniales et l'arbitraire des chefs locaux. Mais il y a eu surtout une migration économique massive des populations hausa, touareg et peul à la recherche des terres des cultures et des pâturages. La majorité des villages au sud de la Tarka ont été créés entre 1930 et 1950 (Rey 1989).

Les populations étaient venues de toutes les zones limitrophes :

- les Hausa, groupe majoritaire est composé de deux groupes : les Gobirawa venus du sud et du sud ouest (du Gobir et de Madaoua) et les Aderawa venus de l'ouest (de Bouza principalement) ;
- les Touaregs étaient venus de l'ouest pour les Kel Gress (de Madoua), de l'est pour les Tagamaoua et les Kel Ferwan (de l'Aîr), du nord et nord ouest pour les Iwellemenden (de l'Azawagh) ;
- Les Peuls viennent du sud pour les deux groupes « Farfaru » et Wodaabé (de Sokoto).

Ces différentes populations se sont séparées des chefferies auxquelles elles appartenaient pour aller fonder de nouveaux villages et de nouvelles entités politiques. Le contexte de la colonisation a accéléré les processus de fractionnement des grands ensembles politiques.

Les chefferies coloniales : s'assurer le contrôle des populations

La création de la subdivision de Dakoro et de son chef lieu fut l'oeuvre de l'administrateur colonial Maurice Vilmin. Quand on parle localement de Dakoro, on ajoute souvent « Garin Maïbougé » c'est-à-dire village de Maïboué pour signifier qu'il en est le fondateur. Il était réputé pour ses méthodes arbitraires et la figure de commandant autoritaire qu'il a incarnée est restée vivace dans la mémoire collective.

Pour s'assurer le contrôle des populations de la nouvelle subdivision, l'administration coloniale met en place de nouvelles chefferies en détachant progressivement les populations des anciennes tutelles chefferiales précoloniales ou coloniales.

<u>La chefferie cantonale de Birnin Lallé</u>

La région nord de Maradi qui englobe une bonne partie du département actuel de Dakoro était pendant les premières années de l'occupation coloniale administrée depuis Kornaka, Maradi et Tanout. Le secteur de Dakoro actuel en particulier dans sa partie septentrionale qui nous intéresse était une zone excentrée et peu peuplée. Birnin Lallé était le seul gros village de la zone, avec un marché et une mare semi-permanente. Le village était devenu un lieu d'escale pour les convois de l'administration coloniale sur la route Maradi-Tanout. Mais le village de Birnin Lallé doit sa renommée aussi à son passé. En effet, Birnin Lallé est une ancienne capitale du Gobir historique (Hama 1967). Les vestiges de l'ancienne cité sont encore visibles à quelques mètres de l'actuel village. Elle a été abandonnée lors de la pénétration des Gobirawa vers le Sud. Dans les années 20, quelques familles venues de la région de Tibiri (fief actuel du Gobir) se sont installées dans le village[5].

En 1931, Birnin Lallé est érigé en subdivision englobant les villages situés au nord de Birnin Lallé et de Dakoro mais l'administration coloniale n'installa pas de poste administratif. Quand en 1947, il fut décidé enfin de créer un poste administratif, on l'implanta à Dakoro qui devint le chef lieu de la subdivision.

---

[5] Entretien avec le chef de canton et Sanoussi Jackou, économiste et homme politique du Kornaka.

L'administration coloniale réorganisa les chefferies et trois nouveaux cantons ont été créés :

- le canton de Birnin Lallé avec comme chef lieu Birnin Lallé créé le 5 novembre 1947 ;
- le canton de Bader Goula avec comme chef lieu Goula ;
- le canton de Soli Tagriss avec comme chef lieu Soli.

Les Kel Gress d'Azagor et les Kel Ferwan de Gadabeji deviennent des tribus indépendantes. Ces nouvelles chefferies viennent s'ajouter à celle déjà existante du canton de Kornaka qui administrait le sud mais aussi les nomades de la zone dont la tribu peule Serkin Rafi. Le canton de Kornaka a été détaché de Maradi pour être administré par Dakoro.

Au cours de la même année 1947, les premiers chefs de cantons sont nommés après des élections. A Birnin Lallé, les élcctions du 3 novembre 1947 donnent la victoire à Boubakar Garandam. Il a été élu avec 32 voix sur 54 chefs de villages consultés. Son concurrent le plus sérieux était Haido Tambari Jackou, fils du chef de canton de Kornaka qui a recueilli 16 voix. Boubakar Garandam a été désigné chef de canton de Birnin Lallé le 12 décembre 1947 par le Gouverneur Toby lors de la visite de ce dernier dans la subdivision (Vilmin 1947).

La décision est confirmée le 2 janvier 1948 (Journal Officiel de la colonie du Niger, 1er février 1948, 203 :23). Par la même décision, Tambari Djako, chef du Kornaka assurera le commandement supérieur de l'ensemble des cantons de Kornaka et Birnin Lalle. Malgré la création du canton de Birnin Lalle, celui-ci reste sous la domination du canton de Kornaka qu'on appellera d'ailleurs province de Kornaka et de Birnin Lalle. Les autres chefs de canton de la subdivision ont également été nommés Tankari Dan Maika et Aghali Abambacho deviennent respectivement chefs des cantons de Soli Tagriss et de Bader Goula. Mouloul est nommé chef de la tribu des Kel Gress d'Azagor.

Le premier chef de canton de Birnin Lalle, Boubakar Garadam est originaire de l'Ader dans la région de Tahoua. C'est un Hausa Aderawa. Il était un *dilali* (courtier), commerçant et féticheur très influent, qui s'était lié d'amitié avec les agents de l'administration coloniale qu'il hébergeait lors de leurs escales à Birnin Lallé. Ses liens privilégiés avec l'administration coloniale et son capital économique ont probablement joué un rôle important dans son élection-nomination. Boubakar Garandam règnera de 1947 à 1972. A sa mort, il sera remplacé par Maydabo, du groupe Gobirawa de Birnin Lallé, issu de l'une des premières familles à s'installer dans le village. C'est un ancien goumier (les goumiers constituaient le corps d'auxiliaires indigènes méharistes mis en place par l'administration coloniale, chargés entre autres de la collecte des impôts). Il doit sa nomination, selon les descendants de Garandam, à son amitié avec un ancien administrateur civil du cercle de Tanout sous les ordres duquel il a servi. A la mort de Garandam, cet administrateur était préfet de Maradi sous le régime du Rassemblent Démocratique Africain (RDA). Après sa nomination, Maydabo quitta Birnin Lallé et s'installa à Dakoro.

La chefferie passe donc des mains du groupe des Aderawa à celui des Gobirawa. Maydabo meurt en 1981 et son fils Issoufou Maydabo, actuel chef de canton, est nommé par arrêté du président Seyni Kountché en sa qualité de ministre de l'intérieur. Il appartient au corps de la garde républicaine (nouvelle appellation du corps des méharistes) comme son père. Depuis que la chefferie est passée aux mains des Gobirawa, elle a progressivement réintégré le giron du Gobir en se rapprochant politiquement et symboliquement de la chefferie de province de Tibiri, qui assure la tutelle des chefferies des cantons du Gobir, et en s'appropriant les attributs et les rites des chefferies du Gobir, notamment la nomination d'une « *Inna* » ou « mère » (associée aux cultes de possession) et la présence d'un may *raya, intronisateur* (« celui qui passe le turban au chef ») désigné par le chef de province du Gobir.

Olivier de Sardan (1998 : 67) explique comment les chefferies administratives coloniales essayent d'asseoir leur légitimité en se parant des attributs des chefferies précoloniales : « Tout un apparat et toute une idéologie produisent et reproduisent cette légitimité soi-disant 'traditionnelle', avec diverses 'inventions' de la tradition (ou néo-traditions) et le recyclage de certains éléments des rituels politiques précoloniaux, insérés dans un contexte tout différent ».

En se donnant une légitimité de chefferie du Gobir, les deux chefs de canton successifs visent surtout à disqualifier les autres groupes sociaux qui revendiquent la chefferie (les Aderawa et les Touaregs). Les candidatures aux premières élections de 1947 montrent que c'était un fauteuil ouvert.

La chefferie de Birnin Lallé est donc une chefferie administrative avec une faible profondeur historique. L'actuel chef est seulement le 3ème. Mais le symbole historique (ancienne cité du Gobir), le rattachement du village au canton de Kornaka au début de la colonisation et les origines de son premier chef de canton en font une chefferie disputée par plusieurs chefferies et groupes socio-linguistiques: la chefferie de Sabon Birni au Nigéria, qui était avant sa conquête par Ousman Dan Fodio la capitale du Gobir ; la chefferie du canton de Tibiri, actuelle capitale politique du Gobir nigérien, la chefferie de Kornaka, ancien chef lieu de la province de Kornaka et de Birnin Lallé et les descendants du premier chef de canton. Après la mort du second chef de canton en 1972, toutes ces chefferies avaient manifesté leur intention de présenter des candidats avant que le président Seyni Kountché ne décide de nommer par arrêté le nouveau chef de canton.

L'opposition à la chefferie est constituée par la famille de Garandam. Une grande partie de ses descendants et sympathisants est regroupée dans le quartier Kourmi à Dakoro. Ils sont propriétaires fonciers mais n'ont pas d'ancrage dans les zones rurales. Le groupe des Aderawa auquel ils appartiennent est surtout présent dans la ville de Dakoro, où il contrôle une grande partie de l'activité économique et investit de plus en plus dans la politique locale.

Mais les appréhensions du chef de canton s'orientent surtout vers l'émergence de nouveaux pouvoirs et de nouveaux acteurs avec la décentralisation. Dans ces conditions, son souci est de contrôler le processus de découpage pour amoindrir les effets de la territorialisation sur son pouvoir.

Le Serkin Rafi de Korahane

La migration des Peuls « Farfaru », les Peuls blancs en hausa (pour les distinguer des Wodaabé de couleur noire) au nord de leur fief de Sokoto dans l'actuel territoire du Niger a accompagné le processus de pacification et d'installation de l'administration coloniale. Ils fondèrent les actuelles chefferies peules de Konni, Tahoua, Bangui et Madaoua. Une partie du groupe, après être passé par Tahoua et Keita, s'installa à Kornaka. Il était conduit par Amadou, le fils d'un grand marabout. C'est à la suite d'une querelle de succession qu'ils auraient quitté leur village de Guelbadi, au sud de Guidan Roumji, dans l'actuel Nigeria.

Le groupe fut bien accueilli à Kornaka. Le chef de canton Jackou donna sa fille en mariage à Amadou et plus tard le nomma Serkin Rafi, c'est-à-dire le titre hausa dans le Gobir, qui veut dire « chef d'escorte ». En période de guerre, les populations en déplacement sont souvent escortées de guerriers pour les protéger d'éventuels assaillants.

Avant l'arrivée des Peuls de Sokoto, il y avait déjà d'autres Peuls, notamment les Peuls Wodaabé (grands transhumants) et les Peuls Katsinawa (animistes et hausaphones). Les nouveaux venus avaient surtout la particularité d'être d'obédience islamique et auréolés du prestige politique de Sokoto. Il faut dire aussi que les Peuls de Sokoto et les Touaregs Kel Gress de Kornaka entretenaient de vieilles relations politiques. Les Tambari de Kornaka étaient intronisés pendant les premières années du XIXème siècle à Sokoto (Jackou 1970).

Au début des années 20, avec la dislocation par l'administration coloniale de la chefferie peule de Mahaman Assao qui assurait le commandement des Peuls de Maradi, ces derniers ont été subdivisés en trois chefferies dans les trois cantons sédentaires de Maradi, du Gobir et du Kornaka.

> « En 1924, le chef de canton de Kornaka reçut le commandement des 11 fractions peules nomadisant dans son canton. Il laisse peu à peu le commandement de ce groupement à un de ses Ardo Serkin Rafi Amadou, originaire du Nigeria et ayant séjourné vers Madaoua en 1925 » (Jackou 1970).

Les Peuls resteront à Kornaka pendant une vingtaine d'années avant de se déplacer en 1946 plus au nord à Korahane, leur fief actuel, à la suite de malentendus entre Amadou Serkin Rafi et Tambari Jackou.

La tribu a été érigée en 1956 en Groupement Peul de Kornaka et Amadou Serkin Rafi devient chef de groupement. Il mourut en 1984 et son fils Mahé (actuel chef) lui succéda. Celui-ci a deux résidences, une à Korahane, chef lieu du groupement, et une seconde à Dakoro. Le groupement était jusqu'en 1980 à la tête de plus d'une centaine de tribus peules et touaregs. La création dans les années 80 de trois nouveaux groupements, le groupement Wodaabe de Bermo, le groupement Kel Gress d'Azagor et le groupement Kel Ferwan de Gadébéji, l'a amputé de la plus grande partie des tribus qui lui étaient rattachées. Il ne dirige aujourd'hui que 18 tribus.

Le Serkin Rafi a acquis une reconnaissance politique en se faisant nommer chef de groupement. Mais la zone presque vierge dans laquelle le groupe s'est installé dans les années 30 est aujourd'hui à la lisière du front cultural. Elle est sous l'autorité du canton de Birnin Lalle. Les conflits entre agriculteurs et éleveurs se multiplient.

La stabilisation du front agricole et la préservation d'un espace vital pour l'élevage et le groupement sont un nouvel enjeu pour le Serkin Rafi. La communalisation apparaît comme une opportunité pour soustraire le secteur de la tutelle politique du canton de Birnin Lallé.

Les chefferies postcoloniales

A l'indépendance en 1960, le canton de Birnin Lallé et « la zone restante » comptaient trois chefferies principales : le canton de Birnin Lallé, le groupement Serkin Rafi et la tribu indépendante Kel Gress Mouloul.

Le groupement Kel Gress d'Azagor

Les Touaregs de ce groupement ont émigré pour la grande majorité d'entre eux de la région de Madaoua au début du siècle. Ils appartiennent à la confédération touareg des Kel Gress, mais se sont métissés au cours des années avec les populations locales et l'autre groupe touareg du departement, les Kel Ferwan, venus de la région d'Agadez.

A l'arrivée des Français, ils nomadisaient déjà dans la région. Un village symbolise leur présence, Maylafia, situé à une vingtaine de kilomètres au nord-est de Dakoro. C'est ce village qui a accueilli en 1947 la première école nomade de la région, qui a formé les premiers cadres[6] touaregs et peuls de la région dont trois dirigent des partis politiques à Niamey. Dans le cadre de la politique de recensement et de contrôle de la population par

[6] Hamid Algabit, président du RDP-Jamaa, Sanoussi Jackou, président du PNA-Alouma, Cheiffou Amadou, president du RSD-Gaskiya

l'administration coloniale, les Kel Gress devinrent une tribu indépendante. Cette tribu que dirigeait le père de l'actuel chef de groupement au moment de la création de la subdivision de Dakoro a entretenu des relations sans histoires avec l'administration coloniale (Vilmin 1947).

Elle a été érigée en groupement en 1984 sous le régime militaire de Seyni Kountche en même temps que celles des Kel Ferwan et des Peuls Wodaabe. Ces promotions ont été possibles grâce à la mobilisation des réseaux sociaux et politiques au sein du régime militaire notamment les préfets militaires successifs de Maradi et des cadres ressortissants évoluant dans les hautes sphères de l'Etat, car le népotisme ethnique est une pratique constante des régimes nigériens successifs.

La plus grande partie des membres du groupement Kel Gress sont sédentarisés dans des villages appelés localement Zongo. Certains de ces Zongo sont situés sur le territoire d'autres cantons et groupements du département. Mais la plupart des chefs de tribu sont installés autour du chef lieu du groupement, le campement d'Azagor.

Le chef de groupement ne considère pas que le groupement soit situé sur le territoire du canton de Birnin Lallé. Il est selon lui dans la zone restante. Il défend la spécificité pastorale de son fief, dans la vallée de la Tarka. Tout comme le Serkin Rafi, l'enjeu principal pour le groupement d'Azagor est le contrôle de l'accès au foncier et aux ressources naturelles. Le contrôle d'une commune rurale, au-delà de l'enjeu politique, est perçu surtout comme un moyen d'obtenir un droit de gestion sur les ressources pastorales.

Lorsque la tribu voulait devenir groupement, le premier chef avait autorisé l'installation des agriculteurs qu'il faisait recenser pour augmenter le nombre de ses administrés. Cette stratégie se retourne aujourd'hui contre le groupement, les agriculteurs ayant colonisé une bonne partie de l'espace pastoral du groupement et ont fondé des villages dont certains sont administrativement rattachés au canton de Birnin Lallé.

Compte tenu du caractère récent de l'occupation de l'espace et de la création des chefferies, on observe qu'il y a un enchevêtrement des populations, une instabilité et une pluralité de tutelles administratives. Les chefs des villages passent d'une chefferie à une autre au gré de leurs intérêts. Certains sont affiliés à deux ou trois chefferies à la fois.

La faible profondeur historique des chefferies et la mobilité des populations aussi bien nomades que sédentaires engagées dans une compétition d'occupation d'un espace « vacant » explique ce phénomène. Le plus souvent, ce sont plusieurs familles avec leurs chefs qui se déplacent à la recherche de nouvelles terres.

La création des trois groupements a renforcé le poids politique des nomades et leurs assises territoriales dans le département de Dakoro. Même si les ressources pastorales demeurent ouvertes, dans la pratique les groupements exercent un contrôle sur des portions de la zone pastorale.

Les chefferies de l'après communalisation

La zone pastorale de Dakoro est occupée par plusieurs sous-groupes Peuls et Touaregs. La création des premiers groupements a permis aux tribus Kel Gress et Kel Ferwan de mettre sous tutelle les autres tribus touaregs et au clan peul du premier chef de prendre de l'ascendant sur les autres lignages des Wodaabé.

La politique de création de groupements remise à l'ordre du jour sous la 5ème république (depuis 2000) a offert une opportunité à d'autres groupes de nomades du département de Dakoro de revendiquer des groupements. L'option de création de nouveaux groupements s'inscrit dans une politique visant à donner un cadre d'expression politique et une assise territoriale aux éleveurs peuls. Ces derniers, pour la plupart, transhumants n'avaient pas de chefferies de nouveau groupement, ce qui les excluait de la gestion politique locale. Par la suite, cette politique a été étendue aux autres groupes nomades (Touaregs, Toubous et Arabes) souvent pour des raisons clientélistes et électoralistes.

Dans le nord Dakoro, deux nouveaux groupements ont été créés :

- Le groupement touareg des Kel Temerkest. Les Kel Temerkest viennent de l'Azawagh au nord et appartenaient à la confédération des Iwellemenden. Ils étaient rattachés au 2ème groupement d'Abalak avant de migrer dans le nord de Dakoro. Ils se sont rattachés au Serkin Rafi d'abord, et au groupement Kel Gress, ensuite ;
- Le groupement Peul Kassassawa. C'est un important lignage des Woddabé qui s'est autonomisé de la première chefferie.

Ces deux groupements sont localisés dans l'actuelle commune de Bermo avec des administrés disséminés dans l'ensemble de la zone pastorale dite restante. Leur création est la conséquence des conflits autour de l'occupation de l'espace entre différents groupes d'éleveurs et la volonté de certaines tribus ou lignages de participer au jeu politique local. Au cours des dernières années de nombreux conflits ont opposé Peuls et Touaregs mais aussi sous groupes peuls entre eux et sous groupes Touaregs entre eux autour du fonçage de points d'eau (Mohamadou 2004).

L'émergence des deux chefferies a fragilisé les premières chefferies nomades qui ont perdu une partie des tribus qui leur étaient rattachées. Comme les premières, les nouvelles chefferies ont opté pour une politique de marquage de l'espace (villagisation, fonçage de puits, courtage, etc.) qui préfigurent une tendance à la territorialisation. On peut faire l'hypothèse qu'elles finiront par réclamer dans les années à venir des communes à elles.

La construction des communes : entre critères officiels et logiques sociales

La popularisation du projet de décentralisation a été faite dans le cadre de missions ministérielles et parlementaires. Elles ont surtout concerné les leaders d'opinion au niveau des chefs lieux des départements. A la suite de la promulgation du projet de loi sur la décentralisation, il a été demandé aux chefs de cantons et de groupements de faire des propositions de communalisation de leurs territoires. Les propositions sont envoyées au Haut Commissariat à la réforme administrative et à la décentralisation qui les examine, les amende et envoie des missions sur le terrain pour en discuter avec les acteurs locaux.

Il n'existait pas au niveau local un cadre de concertation autour du projet de décentralisation, ce que dénonçaient à Dakoro le sous-préfet et les responsables des services techniques qui considéraient que le découpage obéissait plus à des logiques politiques que techniques. Pour eux, les critères techniques et économiques ne sont pas encore pris en compte alors qu'ils déterminent la viabilité économique et financière des futures communes. La symbolique du pouvoir a pris le pas sur les enjeux économiques.

Le principe de la communalisation des cantons et de certains groupements a laissé la porte ouverte à toutes les interprétations, aux négociations et compromis. Pour les chefs des cantons et groupements, le découpage, c'est leur affaire puisque les territoires et les populations sont sous leur responsabilité. Il y a derrière cette perception, la volonté des chefs de mettre sous tutelle cantonale les futures communes rurales. La loi leur a du reste ouvert le chemin puisqu'ils sont membres de droit avec voix consultative de tous les conseils municipaux des communes créés sur leurs entités territoriales ou administratives. Les chefs lieux des cantons et de groupement doivent naturellement devenir des chefs lieux des communes. Dans l'ensemble du département de Dakoro, tous les sièges de chefferies de rang cantonal sont devenus chefs lieux de communes à l'exception du canton de Soli Tagriss où un puissant leader politique national a transféré le chef lieu de la commune dans son village. Les critères technico-administratifs[7] du HCRAD apparaissent comme des possibilités de légitimation parmi plusieurs autres mobilisées localement : légitimités historiques, capital social, légitimité politique, etc.

---

[7] Parmi lesquels les infrastructures, une position excentrée, les distances entre chefs lieux, l'accord des communautés, etc.

Le découpage du canton de Birnin Lalle

Le canton de Birnin Lalle compte 4 grands secteurs avec comme épicentre la ville de Dakoro. Un secteur ouest autour du village de Korahane, un secteur nord avec comme village principal, Intuila, un secteur nord-est autour du marché de Sakkabal, un secteur sud-est avec Birnin Lalle comme centre politique. Les secteurs sont organises autour de villages centres abritant soit une importante chefferie villageoise, soit un marché hebdomadaire, soit des infrastructures scolaires ou sanitaires.

La première proposition du chef de canton était de 12 communes. Tous les gros villages du canton ont demandé à être érigés en communes. C'est cette proposition qui a été transmise au HCRAD qui n'a retenu que trois communes avant que l'Assemblée Nationale n'en rajoute une quatrième. Voyons le cas des communes retenues et quelles sont les logiques qui ont prévalu.

<u>La commune rurale de Birnin Lallé : le poids du symbole</u>
Sa création a été surtout dictée par des considérations historiques et politiques car elle ne satisfait à aucun des critères officiels. Elle a pour elle la légitimité historique en tant qu'ancienne cité historique du Gobir. Pour le chef de canton, c'est pour la charge symbolique qu'il fallait la créer. Mais, de son passé glorieux, il ne reste plus que les vestiges, au point où le village ne compte comme infrastructures qu'une école. Le marché ne s'anime plus ; le chef de canton a installé son palais depuis 1972 à Dakoro, ville qui n'est distante que d'une dizaine de kilomètres qui abrite le chef lieu de la commune urbaine.

D'autres gros villages de la commune ont contesté le choix de Birnin Lallé comme chef lieu de la commune rurale à cause de sa position géographique et de son faible équipement. Les ressortissants d'Intuila ont vivement protesté parce que leur secteur satisfaisait aux critères officiels. Finalement, leur secteur a été éclaté entre la commune rurale de Birnin Lalle qui voulait l'englober et la commune urbaine de Dakoro dont le siège est plus proche et qui a la préférence des communautés. Cinq villages sont actuellement en litige entre les deux communes mais, tout porte à croire qu'ils seront intégrés dans la commune urbaine de Dakoro. L'absorption par cette dernière commune du marché de Intuila et par la commune de Roumboul de celui de Sakkabal a privé la commune de Birnin Lallé de gisements fiscaux. La commune de Birnin Lalle apparaît comme la commune du fief premier du canton sur lequel la chefferie exerce un contrôle en raison de la proximité sociale de ses habitants.

La commune rurale de Korahane : un espace très disputé

Le village de Korahane est situé à 23 km à l'ouest de Dakoro en bordure de la Tarka sur la route latéritique Dakoro-Keita. Il a été fondé par un chasseur hausa du nom de Nahantchi. Avant la création du village, des nomades peuls wodaabé et touaregs nomadisaient dans la région. Le fonçage du premier puits a été l'œuvre de Peuls Wodaabé, ce qui constitue une forme de marquage de l'espace chez les nomades.

Quatre chefferies sont installées dans le village :

- la chefferie du village de Korahane I, qui regroupe les descendants du fondateur du village;
- la chefferie du village de Korahane II, dont le chef Chipkao est arrivé avec sa population de Sourakane, un village situé à 4 km plus à l'Ouest, suite à une dispute avec des Peuls. Bien que d'un groupe social casté, sa forte personnalité lui a permis de supplanter le premier chef,
- la chefferie du groupement peul Serkin Rafi qui s'est installé aux abords du village,
- la chefferie du village peul, *ardo* Dodo, nommé par le Serkin Rafi, dont les administrés viennent d'un fractionnement des populations des deux premiers villages. C'est un épisode dans la rivalité entre les chefferies sédentaires et la chefferie nomade.

Le choix du village de Korahane comme chef lieu de la commune n'a pas posé des problèmes, puisqu'il a une bonne position géographique et dispose d'infrastructures : un marché, un forage même s'il est en panne, une petite mini-adduction, un puits cimenté, une école, un centre intégré de santé, une grande mosquée, etc. A cela, il faut ajouter qu'il abrite le siège d'un groupement dont les ressortissants sont puissants au niveau national.

La particularité de ce village, c'est que la plupart de ses infrastructures ont été financées totalement ou en partie par des ressortissants, tous du groupement peul. Cheiffou Amadou, ancien premier ministre, jeune frère du chef de groupement, a financé ou facilité la réalisation de la mini-adduction d'eau et le centre de santé intégré (CSI). En outre, il possède là une grande résidence qui pourrait selon ses proches abriter les services municipaux. Un officier supérieur, neveu du chef de groupement, a fait forer le puits cimenté et a financé la construction de la mosquée. Ces réalisations sont diversement appréciées : pour les ressortissants du groupement, c'est une contribution au développement du village et de ses environs ; pour les Hausa c'est une volonté de faire main basse sur le village. L'enjeu autour de cette commune est à la fois politique et économique : au plan politique, il y a le contrôle de la future commune qui se joue entre chefferies villageoises sous les auspices de celle du canton et la chefferie du groupement peul. Cette lutte pour le leadership n'est pas récente et les rapports sont très conflictuels entre les deux communautés comme on a pu le constater au cours de notre enquête. Chaque groupe défend l'antériorité de son installation par rapport à l'autre.

Au plan économique, c'est le contrôle des ressources naturelles de la Tarka qui est l'enjeu principal. La rivalité politique se double d'une compétition entre l'agriculture et l'élevage. La question semble être : quel mode d'exploitation demain pour la Tarka ? Pour les éleveurs, il ne fait aucun doute que si la majorité municipale est détenue par les agriculteurs, la Tarka sera défrichée et l'activité d'élevage aura du mal à se maintenir. Pour les agriculteurs, le groupement veut faire de Korahane son lieu d'ancrage et une réserve fourragère.

La compétition entre les deux communautés a été transposée au niveau des partis politiques. Le frère du chef du groupement qui fut fonctionnaire international et premier ministre de la transition civile de 1991-1993 est actuellement président d'un parti politique, le RSD-Gaskiya[8] qui est né d'une scission de la CDS-RAHMA[9]. Il est président du Conseil économique social et culturel, une institution de la république qui conseille le gouvernement. Korahane est un fief du parti. Il recrute principalement dans la communauté peule alors que les Hausa gobirawa, l'autre groupe du

[8] Rassemblement social démocratique.
[9] Convention démocratique et sociale.

village votent massivement pour le MNSD-Nassara[10]. Aux élections locales du 24 juillet, les deux partis ont obtenu chacun 5 conseillers (soit 10) sur les 11 postes en jeu.

La rivalité autour des ressources naturelles se double donc d'un duel politique animé par les ressortissants. Le MNSD est porté localement par un technicien en télécommunication, petit-fils du premier chef de village qui a du reste été élu maire de la commune.

La commune rurale de Roumbou I : la revanche des Touaregs Ibroubak

Elle faisait partie des 12 premières communes proposées au titre du canton mais elle ne figurait pas sur la liste des communes transmises à l'Assemblée Nationale. Ce secteur du canton situé en zone agropastorale autour du grand marché de Sakkabal est occupé par des touaregs Ibroubak agropasteurs et des agriculteurs hausa. Toutes les deux communautés sont administrées par le chef de canton de Birnin Lallé. Ici les Touaregs se sont sédentarisés très tôt et détiennent des droits fonciers sur les terres au même titre que les agriculteurs hausa.

Lorsque que les ressortissants touaregs de l'aristocratie villageoise ont appris que leur secteur n'avait pas été retenu comme commune, ils ont adressé une lettre de protestation au HCRAD. Ils accusent indirectement le chef de canton d'avoir enlevé le nom de leur secteur dans les propositions. Pour eux, c'est une manière d'affaiblir la chefferie villageoise.

Un ressortissant de la chefferie villageoise de Roumbou qui était à l'époque député a négocié pour ajouter la commune de Roumbou avant l'adoption de loi déterminant le nombre et les noms des chefs lieux des communes. De nombreuses communes ont été créées sur l'initiative des membres du gouvernement et des députés. Le nombre proposé par le HCRAD a été pratiquement multiplié par deux.

Le gros village de Sakkabal avec son marché n'a pas été choisi comme chef lieu de la commune. Le député a préféré donné le nom du village de sa famille à la commune. Il est distant de quelques mètres de Sakkabal.

[10] Mouvement National pour la Société du Développement.

La création de la commune de Roumbou I est considérée par ses ressortissants comme une reconnaissance politique des Touaregs Ibroubak. Ces derniers estiment avoir été spoliés par l'administration coloniale de leur pouvoir politique au profit des autres groupes Touaregs et Hausa du département. Au-delà de la légitimité historique retrouvée, les Touaregs Ibroubak de Roumbou ont mis fin à leur façon à la rivalité entre le chef de canton de Birnin Lallé et le chef de groupement Kel Gress d'Azagor. Ces deux notabilités convoitaient les villages de ce secteur et surtout le marché de Sakkabal. La création de la commune de Roumbou montre aussi le rôle des ressortissants dans les liens entre le national et le local.

La commune urbaine de Dakoro

Le chef lieu de l'arrondissement de Dakoro (devenu département en 2004) a été érigé en commune urbaine par la loi n° 096/98 mais il n'y a jamais eu d'élection pour élire le conseil municipal. Il a fallu attendre 2004 pour que la commune urbaine soit dotée d'un territoire et d'un conseil municipal élu. Bien que située sur son territoire et abritant son siège, la chefferie cantonale a une faible emprise sur la ville de Dakoro. Son statut de centre administratif abritant le pouvoir d'Etat, le cosmopolitisme de son peuplement et la présence de l'élite économique et intellectuelle du département aux origines diverses en font un espace presque autonome.

La ville est constituée de plusieurs quartiers-villages regroupant tous les groupes sociaux du département : les Hausa gobirawa, les Hausa aderawa, les Touaregs Kel Gress, les Touaregs Roumboukawa, les Peuls, etc. Une partie des chefs de quartiers ne dépend pas du chef du canton. Mais ce dernier a tenté de circonscrire la zone rurale de la commune urbaine. Il s'est heurté à l'opposition des communautés de la zone périurbaine qui ont préféré se rattacher à la commune urbaine plus proche et qui offre plus de services.

La fondation des communes du canton s'est faite selon des critères différents. Le chef de canton a réussi à faire du siège historique de la chefferie un chef lieu de commune contre les critères officiels. Sa tentative de créer une grande commune rurale regroupant deux autres secteurs (Intuila et Sakkabal) qui allaient assurer la viabilité économique de la commune a échoué. Il pourrait ainsi perdre le contrôle politique sur une partie de la population du canton. La création de la commune de Roumbou ressuscite un lignage aristocratique touareg longtemps mis aux marges de la politique locale. Quant à la commune de Korahane, son émergence pourrait renforcer la chefferie du groupement peul.

La commune du groupement Kel Gress d'Azagor
Le village d'Azagor est situé à une vingtaine de kilomètres au nord de Dakoro. C'est le chef lieu du groupement Kel Gress. Le village dispose d'infrastructures dont la réalisation a été financée par le Projet de développement de la zone pastorale (PROZOPAS) initié dans le cadre des accords de paix de 1995 entre l'Etat du Niger et la rébellion touareg. Il s'agit d'une école et sa cantine, d'une case de santé, d'une banque céréalière et d'un parc de vaccination. Il existe deux puits cimentés l'un construit par l'Etat et l'autre par le projet « Hydraulique villageoise ».

Le choix du chef lieu du groupement comme chef lieu de la commune n'a pas posé problème. Le village est le seul à répondre aux critères officiels sans compter le leadership du chef de groupement. Mais le chef de groupement n'a pas réussi son projet de fédérer les Touaregs de la Tarka de Dakoro dans une seule commune. Une partie des tribus et Zongo du groupement a choisi de se rattacher à la commune urbaine de Dakoro. La création de la commune de Roumbou dont le chef lieu est à 13 km d'Azagor a été mal ressentie. Elle prive Azagor de plusieurs villages qui étaient prêts à se rattacher et du marché de Sakkabal. Des vieilles mésententes entre les deux groupes touaregs autour de l'implantation des infrastructures socio économiques seraient à l'origine de l'échec du projet de création d'une commune unique.

Conclusion

Le choix de l'Etat du Niger d'un découpage basé sur les cantons et certains groupements a cristallisé les enjeux politiques autour du local. La superposition de territoires administratifs et de territoires coutumiers a réveillé de vieilles rivalités entre les notabilités locales et entre les agriculteurs et les éleveurs. Ces derniers tentent de profiter de la décentralisation pour baliser les frontières de leurs territoires dans une zone agropastorale très disputée aux agriculteurs. La décentralisation au-delà du découpage territorial pose aussi le problème de la construction de l'Etat. Ce dernier était absent des zones rurales et la fourniture des services et biens publics a fortement régressé ces dernières années du fait des difficultés économiques. L'Etat avait délégué aux chefferies la gestion des affaires politiques et économiques locales mais celles-ci gouvernent selon un mode patrimonial et « extractif » et ne sont pas porteuses de projet de société. Elles sont surtout préoccupées par la préservation de leurs privilèges. Avec l'émergence des communes, le maillage administratif s'améliore et il faut s'attendre à de fortes rivalités entre les élus locaux et les chefs traditionnels sous l'arbitrage de l'Etat central et des partis politiques. Au Benin et au Mali, la décentralisation a réhabilité et renforcé les chefferies. Au Niger, les chefferies ont des appréhensions sur leur avenir, ce qui explique leur opposition à la décentralisation et leur tentative d'influencer le jeu politique au niveau national.

Bibliographie

Blundo, G. 2000. Décentralisation et pouvoirs locaux : Registres traditionnels du pouvoir et nouvelles formes locales de légitimité (Atelier : II), *Le bulletin de l'APAD* 16, 147-150 : « Décentralisation, pouvoirs locaux et réseaux sociaux » (eds) G. Blundo & R. Mongbo.

Bierschenk T., J.-P. Olivier de Sardan 1998. Les arènes locales face à la décentralisation et à la démocratisation : Analyses comparatives en milieu rural béninois. In *Les pouvoirs au village : le Bénin rural entre démocratisation et décentralisation* (eds) T. Bierschenk & J.-P. Olivier de Sardan. Paris : Karthala.

Fay, C. 2000. La décentralisation dans un cercle (Tenenkou, Mali). *Autrepart* 14, 121-142.

Grémont, C. 2007. Du contrôle des hommes et du contrôle de l'espace : Nouvelles formes de pouvoir et décentralisation dans la région de Gao (Nord Mali). Communication présentée au colloque international sur les pouvoirs locaux, LASDEL, Niamey, octobre 2006.

Hama, B. 1967. *Histoire du Gober et de Sokoto*. Paris : Présence africaine.

Jackou, S. 1970. *Intégration économique et sédentarisation des populations nomades : cas du Niger*. Thèse, Université Paris I. Institut d'études pour le développement économique et social.

Le Roy, E. 1999. A la recherche du paradigme perdu : Le foncier pastoral dans les sociétés sahéliennes. In *Horizons nomades en Afrique Sahélienne : Sociétés, développement et démocratie* (ed.) A. Bourgeot. Paris : Karthala.

Mohamadou, A. 2003. Les pouvoirs locaux à Birnin Lalle. *Etudes et travaux du LASDEL 16.*

Mohamadou, A. 2004. Foncier agropastoral, conflits et gestion des ressources naturelles au Niger : cas de Dakoro et Abalak. *Etudes et Travaux du LASDEL 26.*

Olivier de Sardan, J-P. 1998. Chefs et projets au village. *Le bulletin de l'APAD* 15, 65-89 : « Les dimensions sociales et économiques du développement local et la décentralisation en Afrique au Sud du Sahara » (eds) Nassirou Bako-Arifari & Pierre-Joseph Laurent.

Olivier de Sardan, J-P & M. Tijani Alou (eds) A paraître. *Introduction : Pouvoirs locaux, espace public et politiques publiques*. Paris : Karthala.

Oxby, C. 1989. Les allégeances d'une tribu touarègue entre deux confédérations (Kel Ferwan, Dakoro, Niger). *Cahiers de l'IREMAM* 7-8. « Touaregs et autres sahariens entre plusieurs mondes : Définitions et redéfinitions de soi et d'autres ».

Rapport établi par le chef de la subdivision centrale de Maradi sur le recensement des Peuls de cette subdivision. 1953, 1 E 434, 12 pages.

Rey, M.C. 1989. *Limite nord des cultures pluviales : occupation et dégradation d'un environnement sahélien marginal (Dakoro, Niger)*. Mémoire, Université de Lausanne, Institut de géographie.

Vilmin, M. 1947. Journal de bord. Archives de la Préfecture de Dakoro.

The mobilization of the local in a public primary school in peri-urban Niamey, Niger

Gabriella Körling[1]

In Niger the decentralization of the education system and the implication of local communities in the management and financing of education services is the dominant logic of national education policy promoted by international donors. In the article I examine the mobilization of local actors in public education provision. I do this using an ethnographic study of the daily management of a newly established public primary school in peri-urban Niamey. The case study illustrates the diversity of actors, from traditional chiefs to district advisors and international development projects that are implicated in the provision of public education as well as the different logics and stakes at play. It is also revelatory of the limited room for manoeuvre of the 'local community' organized in school committees in ensuring the day-to-day functioning of the school. Finally it is argued that at the same time as education provision is in part taken over by local actors the idea of the state as the ideal provider of public education remains strong.

Au Niger la décentralisation du système éducatif et l'implication des communautés locales dans la gestion et le financement des services éducatifs constitue la logique dominante des politiques publiques de l'éducation nationale promues par les bailleurs de fonds internationaux. Dans cet article, j'examine la mobilisation des acteurs locaux dans l'éducation publique nigérienne à travers une étude sur la gestion quotidienne d'une école nouvellement créée dans une zone périurbaine de Niamey. Cette étude de cas décrit la diversité des acteurs : des chefs traditionnels, des conseillers municipaux, des projets de développement, etc. Elle include des logiques et enjeux différents. L'étude démontre que la marge de manoeuvre du comité de gestion local reste limitée en ce qui concerne le fonctionnement de l'école. En conclusion, l'article propose qu'en même temps que la provision de l'éducation est prise en charge par des acteurs locaux, l'idée de l'État en tant que fournisseur idéal de l'éducation publique reste forte.

Introduction

In this article I will address the theme of decentralization and the mobilization of the local through an analysis of public education provision in peri-

[1] PhD-candidate in Cultural Anthropology at Uppsala University: gabriella.korling@antro.uu.se

urban Niamey. Anthropological studies of public services in West Africa have illustrated the value of studying public service delivery and state administrations. These studies focus on everyday practices, interactions and social logics within these institutions, as a constitutive aspect of the state (Olivier de Sardan, 2004, 2005) addressing themes such as public health care (Jaffré & Olivier de Sardan 2003) and corruption (Blundo & Olivier de Sardan 2006). In a context in which the state is no longer the sole provider of public services, analytical attention should be paid not only to the production of public services by state administrations, but also to the "new spaces in which public services are produced" (Blundo & Le Meur 2009:14). Public service delivery is continuously reconfigured at the local level following the intervention of development actors, community organizations and private operators alongside that of the state administration (Blundo & Le Meur 2009). This is not to assume that the state has ever been the sole provider of public services. However, the role of the state as public service provider has been challenged by the turn in international development discourse and policies from a state centered approach pushing for the importance of a strong state as the promoter of development, to a neoliberal ideology pushing for the withdrawal of the state in many public sectors in favour of privatization and an increasing role of civil society. This shift has consequences for the policies promoted in domains such as education and healthcare. Reforms geared towards decentralization and privatization, are a case in point. These tendencies are reinforced by the inability of the state to provide such public services on its own.

The overall aim of this article is to analyze the changing role of the state and the diversification of actors and institutions involved in public education provision. This is achieved using a case study of a newly established public primary school in peri-urban Niamey, Niger, that was created with next to nothing in the way of infrastructure, furnishings and pedagogical material. The article will follow the daily 'management' of the public primary school, from its construction at the beginning of the school year to its literal dismantling at the end of the school year. As will be illustrated, this daily management – which often appeared as a struggle to make ends meet and to create a sense of certainty – opened up a space for the intervention of 'non state' actors such as neighborhood chiefs, elected district advisors, and international development projects. On the basis of the case study I will argue that the mobilization of the local in education provision involves a multiplicity of logics, strategies and interests on the part of different actors. And that the 'local community' so celebrated in development parlance, is difficult to locate on the ground. Moreover, the community structures assumed to represent the 'local community' – accorded a central place in education reform in both the financing and the management of schools – have little power and influence, and subsequently a very limited room for maneuver in carrying out the tasks they have been assigned in the name of decentralization and community participation. In addition to illustrating the changing configuration of public education provision at the local level, the case study is also revelatory of perceptions of the state. In a concluding reflection on the relation between the state and public education, I will suggest that despite the partial undoing of the role of the state in public service provision, the ideal of the state as service provider remains strong.

The article is based on 12 months of fieldwork in Niamey divided into two periods, between 2006 and 2008 conducted within the framework of a PhD thesis on public services, urbanization and the local state in urban Niger. Interviews as well as informal conversations with parents, pupils, teachers, traditional chiefs, NGO representatives, district and school inspection officials, and civil servants at the ministry of education, together with participant observation in schools form the core of the fieldwork material presented in this article.[2]

The reconfiguration of public education provision

Public education is traditionally an important sector of the state and considered as a state activity "in the standard image of the state" (Migdal & Schilchte 2005:33). In sub-Saharan Africa during the post independence period education was deemed as being central to the construction of the nation state and to economic development (Bierschenk 2007:268). According to

[2] During the fieldwork I was assisted by Fatimata Moussa during the first period of fieldwork and Amadou Boubacar during the second period of fieldwork, both of whom provided invaluable input. My stay in Niamey was also greatly facilitated by LASDEL (*Laboratoire d'Etudes et de Recherches sur les Dynamiques Sociales et le Développement Local*). The research was generously funded by Swedish International Development Cooperation Agency (Sida).

Bierschenk the definition of education as the exclusive domain of the state – a public good – was especially pervasive in Francophone Africa, both during the colonial period and after independence (Bierschenk 2007:262). The post independence period saw the rapid development of education as enrolment rates increased dramatically (Lange 2003:145). However, the economic crisis of the 1980s put a halt to the development of the education sector. Meanwhile, the imposition of structural adjustment programs led to drastic cuts in public spending, education and health care, with the latter being especially hard hit (Henaff 2003:167; Lange 2003:145). The period of crisis led to an increase in donor funding for education and to an increasing influence of financial institutions such as the World Bank over national education policies (Lange 2003:146). Donor influence increased yet again during the 1990s, a period which analysts of education policy have referred to as a period of consolidation of a 'global agenda on education' led by multilateral agencies such as the UNDP, UNICEF, UNESCO and the World Bank (King 2007). In a series of international conferences on education – in Jomtien in 1990, in Amman in 1996 and in Dakar in 2000 – the international community committed to ensuring basic education for all (EFA). This commitment was reiterated in the United Nations Millennium Declaration and the Millennium Development Goals (MDGs)[3] in which "education became part of the global development agenda" (King 2007:378). The subsequent intensification of international intervention in national education systems and the homogenization of education policies has been referred to as the imposition of a new 'world school order' (*ordre scolaire mondial*) (Lange 2003) and as the transformation of education from a 'public good' (*bien public*), under national state responsibility, into a 'global good' or possession (*bien global*) (Bierschenk 2007).

Regarding the actual contents of education policy promoted by international agencies, the neoliberal paradigm that prevailed encouraged the retreat of the state, the increasing role of civil society and the introduction of market logics in the education sector. The restructuring of the education sector en-

[3] Of the eight MDGs two directly address education. Goal 2 is to 'achieve universal primary education' and the target is to "ensure that by 2015 children everywhere, boys and girls alike, will be able to complete a full course of primary schooling". Goal 3 is to "promote gender equality and empower women" and the target is to "eliminate gender disparity in primary and secondary education preferably by 2005 and in all levels of education no later than 2015".

dorsed by international donors also included the promotion of decentralization. The most common argument for decentralization being that it will lead to a greater efficacy and a more parsimonious use of resources as administrative responsibilities are transferred from central authorities to the local level (Henaff 2003:178; Maclure 1994:240). It is also assumed to lead to an increased participation of local communities in education provision, a participation which it is argued will make schools more "attuned to community life" (Maclure 1994:240) improving or re-establishing the links between school and local populations (Charlier & Pierrard 2000:31).

In Niger the decentralization of the education sector was inscribed in the *Losen* (*Loi 98-12 1 Juin 1998, loi d'orientation du système éducatif*), presented as the first all encompassing juridical or legal framework and orientation of the education system since independence (Daouda et al. 2001:172). In addition to declaring education a national priority and a right of all Nigerien citizens, the Losen stipulated the decentralization of the management of the education system and the increased implication of local communities, the beneficiaries of education services, in the management and financing of education.[4] The PDDE (*Programme Décennal de Développement de l'Education*), the national education program for the period 2003-2013, implemented in cooperation with international donors follows along the same lines as the Losen.[5] The PDDE which is meant to harmonize all interventions in the education sector is divided into three components: access, quality and institutional development. Significantly, institutional development refers to the decentralization of the education system and includes the reorganization and reinforcement of the capacities of the Ministry of Education, of central and regional administrations and the creation of school committees (COGES) in all schools. In sum, education policy in Niger has been aligned to international directives encouraging the partial withdrawal of the central state from education services through the decentralization of the education sector. In the rest of this article I will focus on the effects of the reconfiguration of public education provision at the local

[4] Similar reforms aimed at introducing a rational and effective management of resources in the education sector had already been introduced in the 'Education Projects' of the 1980s and early 1990s backed by the World Bank and the IMF (Meunier, 2000:166).

[5] The donors include the World Bank, the African Development Bank, the Islamic Development Bank, Canada, France, Japan, Luxemburg, Belgium and the European Union.

level through an analysis of the practices and meanings that emerge in the daily 'management' of a public primary school in peri-urban Niamey.

Uncertain beginnings: the creation of a public primary school

Saga is situated on the eastern outskirts of Niamey on the bank of the river Niger that traverses the capital. Originally a village, it has attracted an ethnically and socio-economically heterogeneous urban population that has bought land or rented housing. Saga is today the home of approximately 30,000 people,[6] as well as the administrative capital of the canton of Saga that was created during the colonial period. Thirteen neighborhoods and villages are linked to the cantonal chieftaincy. Following the latest division of the urban municipality, the canton of Saga is completely contained by District Four of the urban municipality of Niamey. Although Saga is expanding, the industrial zone of Niamey physically separates it from the urban agglomeration and Saga is being overshadowed by recently established, faster growing and more dynamic neighbourhoods. From the city centre Saga is reached via a road which is frequented by taxis, minibuses, buses, trucks, bicycles and people on foot, and continues to the town of Kollo. The older parts of Saga – the quarters Saga Fondobon, Saga Gassia Kwara, Saga Sambou Kwara and Saga Gongou and the adjoining quarter Saga Kourtey – are located between the main road and the river. In these neighbourhoods the streets are crooked and narrow and extended family compounds in *banco* dominate. On the other side of the road more recently formed extensions of the older quarters stretch out, with wider and straighter streets and houses of concrete as well as *banco*. The edge of the river is lined with rice paddies. In the past Saga was known for the production of rice, however the productivity of the rice fields has started to dwindle. Agriculture is a traditionally dominant economic activity, however it is increasingly circumscribed to the rice fields and to market gardening along the river as customary land owners have sold farming land. Other economic activities have

[6] Figure based on the estimates of population growth of the district for the year 2007 (29,556). This includes the population of the neighbourhoods Saga Fandobon, Saga Gassia Kwara, Saga Gongou, Saga Sambou Kwara, Saga Kourté (and Pays Bas) and Saga Dababanda.

gained in importance due to the proximity of the city, including commerce and industrial work in the nearby industrial zone.

The first public primary school in Saga, called Saga 1, was created in the early 1960s. The school is located between a Friday mosque and a community library, near the residence of the canton chief. It is used for community meetings convened by the traditional chiefs. In 2007 there were four public primary schools as well as a public *medersa* (Franco Arabic school) and a public secondary school. Children could thus follow a full primary and secondary education cycle without having to go to the city centre. There were also one private primary school and two private secondary schools; however the overwhelming majority of children enrolled in school attended public schools. During the school year 2006-2007 4,717 children were enrolled in public schools in Saga and only 317 in private schools.

The creation of the fourth public primary school coincided with my stay in the field in the autumn of 2006. The plans for the construction of the new school were announced to me by the neighborhood chief. The school was to be built on one of the rare un-constructed plots of land in an otherwise fairly densely inhabited group of neighborhoods. Located behind the public dispensary and maternity and the confessional catholic dispensary which lay wall to wall, the site was prone to collecting stagnating water during the rainy season and had been used as a household waste site. Although the creation of the school had been announced, the transfer lists had been completed, teachers had been transferred and the new principal had been appointed, at the start of the school year in October the area was still empty. Two months into the term, six classrooms were built of straw, two with the contribution of the district and the remaining four by the financial contribution of the parents whose children had been transferred to the school. Thus at the beginning of December 2006, the school was ready to receive the pupils and teaching could start. The blackboards, the few school benches placed in the classrooms and a small number of school books had been borrowed from neighboring schools. As the fourth public primary school in Saga, the newly established school was given the name ‘Saga 4’. On what had been an empty piece of land there were now six straw classrooms which formed a semi circle. A wooden pole on which the Nigerien flag was hoisted and descended at the start and the end of the school day was placed in the middle of the semi circle, a seeming reminder of the status of the makeshift school as a public, or state, institution.

On my return to the field in 2007 the school had taken on a more permanent appearance. The six straw classrooms had become thirteen as student numbers had increased. Fine grained sand filled the school yard, a small house in *banco* housed the guard, and young trees had been planted at the edges of the school yard. A water tap and waste bins had been installed by a Canadian project which had also constructed four latrines and a garbage incinerator at the extremity of the school yard. The intervention of the project was announced by a placard, one of the ubiquitous signs of development interventions.

Community structures: making ends meet

During its first two years of existence and in the absence of (material) state support, the makeshift school became the arena of intervention of different actors, including the traditional chieftaincy, the local government, elected officials and international development aid. However, the greatest responsibility in ensuring the daily functioning was shouldered by the two community structures in the school, the school committee and the parents' association who also served as intermediaries in the relations with actors external to the school.

The establishment of school committees – COGES (*comité de gestion des établissements scolaires*) – in all schools is posited as a central component of the decentralization of the education system. The importance attached to these committees by the Ministry of Education and international donors is evident in the vast administrative organization from the national to the district level that has accompanied the implementation of the system of school committees.[7] Made up of representatives from the school administration,

[7] A national coordinating unit – *Cellule de Promotion des COGES* – was established and every regional direction of primary education and alphabetization was accorded a *point focal* (PF) and every primary school inspection an *observateur relais* (OR), responsible for the supervision of activities related to the COGES.

parents and the student body, the school committees were added to the already existing parents associations (APE – *associations des parents d'élèves*) as the 'steering committee' of the school. The responsibilities attributed to the school committees ranges from practically and administratively oriented tasks such as the acquisition or reception and management of school books and other teaching materials, the management of school funds including state subventions and community funds, and the maintenance of school infrastructure, to more community oriented tasks such as the promotion of schooling, especially the schooling of girls. In a context of scarce state resources the school committees are also a means of mobilizing local resources and are encouraged to raise resources through parental contributions in money or in kind, contributions from local NGOs, associations, or private benefactors.

In Saga 4 the members of the school committee and the parents' association had been elected and a handwritten list of members of the school committee and the parents' association was posted on the wall of the straw classroom that served as the office of the principal. Among the most active members of the school committee and the parents' association was the principal, a woman in her forties who had moved to Saga in the early 1990s, who occupied the post of secretary general of the school committee in her capacity as principal. Another active member was the president of the parents association who also occupied the post as president of the school committee; a quiet and soft spoken man in his sixties from Saga Fondobon, according to the other committee members he was elected on the basis of his wisdom and availability. Given the lack of infrastructure, raising resources to meet the most basic needs of the school, such as the construction of classrooms in straw, became the most important role of the school committee. The 'action plan', which the school committee had been instructed to put together, was recorded in a notebook and kept by the principal. It included the construction of four straw classrooms, the acquisition of 25 school benches, the purchasing of textbooks, notebooks and crayons and a pharmaceutical box. In the end the contributions raised allowed for the construction of straw classrooms. Despite attempts to solicit the support of local 'big men' and politicians, the money raised came exclusively from the parents' financial contributions. The ability of the school committee to guarantee the daily functioning of the school thus depended on their ability to convince the parents to finance daily costs and investments in the school. In addition to the collection at the start of the school year, initiatives to collect money were also made during the course of the school year.

However, many parents criticized the frequent demands for money which added onto other expenses related to schooling (school material, notebooks, pens, clothes etc.). Overall interest in the activities of the school committee and the parents association was lukewarm. Placed in the larger context of the situation of public education this is not surprising. During my fieldwork, conversations about school and education – with pupils, parents and teachers – often ended in discussions about the deterioration of the public school and the poor quality of education. People pointed to the poor knowledge level of the pupils, unqualified teachers, frequent teacher strikes and lack of infrastructure. Moreover, whereas in the past a diploma or school leaving certificate might have held the promise of employment, this was no longer the case. The widespread unemployment of school graduates and the example of older children or siblings with high school and university diplomas but who were unemployed and struggled to make a living, caused people to question the advantage or use of education. All of these factors provided a shaky base for community participation and engagement. This point has been made by Maclure who, on the basis of a study in rural Burkina Faso, argues that the promotion of decentralization and local participation is based on "misplaced assumptions about continuing popular interest in formal education" when in fact increasing demand for time and resources for schooling coupled with diminishing prospects of private gain (employment) from education has lead to a dissatisfaction with public education (Maclure 1994:240, 245).

School committees are presented by the Ministry of Education, international donors and NGOs as key components in the increased implication of parents in schools which in its turn will lead to a local appropriation of the school, the local community taking responsibility for its daily functioning, fostering local initiatives and better management of resources etc. Discourses about the school committee also assume a causal link between the active involvement of the beneficiaries (parents) and improved equity and quality. The promotion of school committees is clearly inscribed in the logic of community participation popular in development circles. The resolute promotion of community participation has been criticized for the underlying assumption that a community is homogenous or shares the same interests.

In Niger similar forms of community participation in the management of public services or goods through the creation of community committees have been introduced in domains such as public health care and water provision. In localities with a history of development interventions and public investments, these community committees were added onto already existing structures such as co-operatives and associations (Tidjani Alou 2009:323). Studies of community management have pointed to the sometimes unexpected outcomes of such initiatives. In the case of village water pumps community management introduced by development projects was often transformed into informal, semi-private or private forms of management (Olivier de Sardan & Dagobi 2000:167). And, attempts at sidelining the chieftaincy, in order to encourage transparency, democracy and the responsibility of the whole community, were unsuccessful (Olivier de Sardan & Dagobi 2000:153, 163). However, Tidjani Alou has illustrated that community management (in this case of mini AEPs – *mini adduction d'eau potable*) can lead to the emergence of new social practices and "a notion of 'public goods'" (Tidjani Alou 2009:320).

Like these studies, the situation in Saga 4 also lends little support to the assumption that community management automatically leads to collective mobilization and appropriation. The much heralded participation of the local community was more or less limited to monetary contributions. Interest to get involved in the management of the makeshift school was limited and was perceived as a burden. However, the school committee was functioning. And, although it had not succeeded in mobilizing the 'local community,' neither had it been appropriated for personal profit. In fact there were few resources in the school to compete for – to privatize or to monopolize. The school committee was headed by a couple of individuals, notably the principal and the president, who displayed a marked determination that 'their' school succeed. Having worked as a teacher in another primary school in Saga before being appointed principal of Saga 4, the principal was anxious to show that she could shoulder the responsibility. Moreover for her it was an opportunity that was made possible because of the lack of infrastructure and resources etc. making the position unattractive to candidates who were better placed with personal contacts in the administrative echelons of the school inspection. The president, on the other hand, with no previous experience in local associations seemed to take the challenge in stride. His efforts in the school committee were acclaimed by other members of the parents' association and the school committee as well as by teachers and the principal. He was also backed by the neighborhood chief who, as I will describe in the next section, had taken on an active role in the school.

The legitimization of the traditional chieftaincy

Saga 4 is situated in Saga Fondobon, one of the older quarters of Saga. The chief of Saga Fondobon, a tall, calm man in his seventies who was also the neighborhood imam, was implicated in the school from its creation. Chiefs in Niger have an officially recognized administrative status.[8] Integrated into the local administration during the colonial period, the administrative role of chiefs was maintained after independence. The responsibilities accorded to the chiefs ranges from the collection of taxes, acting as the representative of the community in relations with the administration and third parties, 'conciliating' in the case of conflict to acting as a development agent, actor and partner. Before the implementation of the decentralization reform in 2004, chiefs were the sole representatives of the state in many rural areas in Niger (Olivier de Sardan 1999). However, in Niamey with the early creation of a local urban government, the role of chiefs was reduced early on. As pointed out by Bernus: "Rapidly, this title [neighborhood chief] designated, without anything else, the one responsible for the collection of taxes" (Bernus 1965:22, my translation). Today the key administrative role of chiefs in Niamey is still the collection of taxes[9] as well as the role of neighbourhood representative. This role is mobilised in contacts with the local administration, most frequently the district, for instance in organising community meetings, sensitisation sessions, etc. Motcho describes the role

[8] The role of chiefs is established in an ordinance on the 'status of the traditional chieftaincy in Niger' passed in 1993 (Ordonnance No 93-28 du 30 mars 1993 portant statut de la chefferie traditionnelle du Niger).

[9] The *taxe de voirie*, a 'council tax' used for the maintenance of infrastructure, roads etc. which are collected on the behalf of the district. The chiefs receive 10% of the amount collected.

of traditional chiefs in Niamey as being ambiguous. While the chiefs are perceived as increasingly irrelevant, both by the population and by the local administration (municipality), they hold a continuing influence on the territorial division of the capital (Motcho 2005).

In the case of Saga 4 the precarious situation of the school opened up a space for intervention for the neighbourhood chief. The chief frequently visited the school, often in the company of the president of the school committee. He also made trips to the district to solicit support for the school and contributed to the construction of the guard's one room house on the school grounds. Moreover a number of factors tied the school to the traditional chieftaincy or, rather, to the person of the neighborhood chief. Many of the key members in the community structures of the school, in particular the president and the vice president of the parents' association were close friends of the neighborhood chief. And the school was located in one of the founding quarters of Saga in which the neighborhood chief already maintained a visibility in neighborhood affairs which is not the case in all neighborhoods. The chief was widely respected both as a religious leader, as the neighborhood imam, and as a community leader. He had also played an important and active role in the health committee in the nearby health centre.

The neighborhood chief passed away in 2008. In conversations with parents, members of the school committee and the school administration, many recalled his dedication to the school. Following the death of the neighborhood chief, his son, who was later elected neighborhood chief, handled questions related to the school. The implication of the neighbourhood chief in the daily running of the school in a sense contributed to the legitimization of the traditional chieftaincy. Through his involvement in the school the chief fulfilled part of the official attributions of the traditional chieftaincy as an 'agent of development' (Motcho 2005). This implication was made possible, or at least reinforced, due to the absence of state support for the school. The support of the neighbourhood chief was also welcomed by the school committee and the principal, who felt that they had been left to fend for themselves. The interests of the school committee and the neighbourhood chief thus converged. Moreover the chief was an important ally in convincing the parents to involve themselves in the daily management of the school.

Of all of the actors that were to intervene in the school, the chief, who at times acted as an extension of the school committee, was the closest in terms of 'social proximity'. This was a result of both his relation with the members of the school committee, and his role as neighborhood representative. In the next section of the article I will describe the intervention of the district and a development project in the school, situations in which the school committee – though assigned the role of intermediary between different partners of the education system at the local level – had little influence or room for manoeuvre.

The district and the construction of straw classrooms

The district intervened in the school mainly through the construction of straw classrooms, which as I will describe below came to involve political and economic stakes. Saga is part of District Four of the urban municipality of Niamey. The district covers the eastern part of the capital and is made up of mostly peri-urban neighborhoods, a few villages and a couple of residential neighborhoods. The district office, a somewhat derelict two story building which is shared between District Three and District Four, is situated near the boundary between the two districts, a taxi ride away from Saga. Following a slate of different proposals during the late 1990s and early 2000 aiming to decentralize the management of the capital – to valorise local resources and to increase the implication of the population (Motcho 2004) – Niamey was finally divided into five districts. In the past the mayors of the districts were nominated. However, with the municipal elections in July 2004, the mayors were elected.

The district is responsible for giving material support to the primary schools and kindergartens in its constituency[10], a considerable responsibility given the number of pupils (Charlier & Pierrard 2000:41). The district struggled

[10] Examples include the construction of classrooms in straw, the provision of furniture for the schools (school desks, desks, chairs, blackboards, storage cabinets...), the renovation of classrooms and of school furniture, support to the primary school inspection in the organization of the end of the year exams and the transportation of students from villages/peripheries to the examination centers, etc.

to fulfil its responsibilities vis-à-vis the schools due to financial problems attributed by district officials to the difficulty of collecting taxes and to the unreliable financial support of the central government. The construction of classrooms in straw makes up approximately one third of the total education budget. It is also the most visible action of the district given the constantly increasing number of straw classrooms in the capital. According to the district official responsible for the education sector, at the beginning of the school year 2006-2007 the district had received requests via the school inspection for the construction of over a hundred classrooms. As the district was unable to build all classrooms needed, the final responsibility for the construction of classrooms was placed on the shoulders of the individual schools and ultimately on the parents.

For schools such as Saga 4 the preparation of the start of each school year was marked with uncertainty about the number of classrooms that would be provided by the district. However the organization of the construction of classrooms at the local level seemed to open up a space for negotiation as district advisors (elected members of the district council) were frequently given the contract for the construction of straw classrooms. According to one advisor in Saga this allowed the district to reduce the cost of the construction and to postpone the payment as the advisors constructed the classrooms on credit. However the members of the school committee in Saga 4 claimed that they would be able to construct a classroom for even less, and thus argued that they could build more classrooms if they were to be granted the contract instead of the district advisors. One of the members of the school committee recounted their unsuccessful attempts at negotiating with the district advisor who had been given the contract for the construction of classrooms. The following year they tried to bypass the advisor by approaching a district official who lived in Saga. However, this attempt was also unsuccessful as the contracts had already been divided up between two district advisors, both from Saga.

The rivalry over the construction of classrooms is illustrative of the monetary and political stakes involved. The granting of contracts to the district advisors benefited the district advisors as they, through the construction of classrooms, contributed something to the neighbourhood. This evidence of their political action gave them a certain visibility for their ability to direct investments to the neighbourhood (even if only temporary classrooms in straw). At the same time, the budgeted cost of the construction and the real costs also left a possibility (margin) for monetary benefits.

The arrangement was also beneficial for the district. First, the classrooms were sometimes constructed on credit guaranteeing the district that the classrooms would be in place at the beginning of the school year. This was important for the credibility of the district which still had a long way to go in convincing people to pay taxes. Second, it allowed the district or the mayor to keep the district advisors who had voted him into office on his side. In this context the school had little chance of accessing the contract despite their attempts to negotiate through local contacts from the district advisors to a district official.

An elusive development project

In the face of faltering state support and an uncertain support from the district, hope was placed on the possibility that a development project might support the school, a common ambition in many localities in Niger. On my return to the field for a second period of fieldwork, members of the school committee told me with exaltation and relief about the promised construction of thirteen furnished classrooms. A delegation had come to the school to take the measurements of the area and plans had been made of where to relocate the school during the period of the construction. The customary owners of the land including the canton chief among others had signed a paper as a guarantee that the land had been ceded to the school. I tried to inquire more about the project but people had little information and it was simply referred to as 'the Chinese' (*'les chinois'*). According to staff at the school inspection, the contacts with the project always passed through the Ministry of Education. Following the first flurry of activities months passed and the project was nowhere in site. Responses to questions, if there was any news about the construction, became increasingly dejected. It was only during a visit to the district's primary school inspection in another errand that the principal of Saga 4 was told that the project had in fact been transferred to another school.

The explanation given for this turn of events was that 'the Chinese' had wanted a completely empty space on which to build the school. However, a Canadian project had already installed a water tap, waste bins, a garbage incinerator and four latrines on the school grounds. The latrines built by 'the Canadians' would thus have to be destroyed for the project to go ahead. In Saga the news seemed to confirm the already creeping suspicions that the project had been co-opted to benefit another locality. Nonetheless the principal contacted an influential resident, originally from Saga with a long career in international development cooperation and the state administration, who promised to meet personally with the Minister of Education to plead the case of Saga 4. Once again the district official living in Saga was contacted but he claimed that it was out of his range of action as the district had not been involved in the discussions with the project. Finally, the efforts were unsuccessful to the great disappointment of the principal, teachers and members of the school committee.

For the second year in a row, a couple of weeks before the end of the school year and in anticipation of arrival of the rainy period, the classrooms were once again taken down. The president dismantled the straw classrooms with the help of a couple of young recruits. The wooden supports and straw mats along with the few school benches and blackboards were transported by the guard on a donkey cart to Saga 1 where they were stored in a padlocked classroom to be reused the following school year. Only the latrines, the tap, the wastebaskets and the guard's one room house remained, as well as the placard raised by the Canadian project with the arrow painted below the name of the primary school pointing into a seeming void.

This episode is illustrative of the hopes that were attached to the promised intervention of the development project and construction of classrooms which would create certainty and permanence. It is also revelatory of the school committee's limited room for negotiation or influence. Both the Chinese and the Canadian projects had come 'from above' channelled as they were through the Ministry of Education and with barely any contact with the school committee or the district. However, although they had been left out of the process and seemed to have been the last to be informed about the suspension of the project people in Saga involved in the school did everything in their power to alter the decision.

Discussion

> [...] our differentiation between image and practices facilitates bringing the ambiguities and contradictions of state domination to the fore. For example, it is possible that the image of the state can persist through long periods in which practices contradict that image (Migdal & Schilchte 2005:35)

This article has attempted to analyse practices and representations surrounding public education provision in the case of a public primary school. What emerges from these episodes and descriptions of the daily life – filled with ups and downs, hope and disappointment – of one particular primary school is the sense of uncertainty and impermanence that characterises the daily management of the school. In the case of Saga 4 the combination of a policy of decentralization and community participation, and the lack of infrastructure opened up for the intervention of a number of different actors in the school. The case is revelatory of the logics that motivate these actors such as the legitimization of the traditional chieftaincy and the political and financial stakes surrounding the construction of straw classrooms. It is also illustrative of the difficult mobilization of the so-called 'local community' and of the limited influence of community structures such as the school committee despite the emphasis that is placed on local participation in current education policy.

The case study also says something about the relation between education and the state. Education is an important sector of the state. A basic public service, it generally absorbs a significant part of the national budget and teachers are the largest group of state employees. School is also important as a means for the production of the idea of the state. First, schools through their physical presence demarcate the territory or space of the state (Wilson 2001:313). As pointed out by Bierschenk, in many African villages the state is embodied by the school – "...which distinguishes itself from neighboring constructions by its localization and its appearance, if not by the presence of a flag in the school yard and the uniforms of the pupils" (Bierschenk, 2007:269, my translation). Second, the school is "an institution that relays ideas about state, nation and citizen" (Wilson 2001:313). Although this article has focused on the 'practical' aspects of public education provision and school management at the local level I want to suggest that it is still possible to say something about the relation between education and the state.[11]

In an article on a public dispensary in rural Niger, Masquelier has evocatively linked people's experiences of constant medicine shortages, inefficiency, expensive prescriptions and corruption with experiences of the post colonial state (Masquelier 2001). She argues that the views of the dispensary as an empty and inefficient institution are part of the discursive construction and deconstruction of the state by rural dwellers (Masquelier 2001:270). In Saga people talked about the "disengagement of the state" when it comes to education. They found evidence for these claims among the increasing personal costs of education for school books, school material, uniforms etc., inadequate infrastructure, frequent teacher strikes and a worsening quality of education, etc. They compared the current state of affairs to the past when the majority of costs related to education were taken care of by the state. Statements, such as "the state has abandoned school" and "we have done everything and the state has done nothing", abounded in discussions about school and especially in relation to Saga 4. Such comments could be interpreted as an indication that the school is less obviously '*la chose de l'État*' (Lange 2003:147) – thought of as belonging to the state – as education provision is ensured by a diversity of 'non state' actors.

However, I want to suggest that despite, or maybe because of, the perception that the state is disengaging from education, people continue to bring forth the idea of the state as the ideal provider of social or public services, which is why it makes sense to talk about or decry the disengagement of the state. As Nielsen has argued in the case of a relocation process in Maputo, people continue to invest themselves in the idea of the state even in the relative absence of the state and the failure of the authorities to regularize and to equip the neighborhood (Nielsen 2007). Thus at the same time as public education provision is being reconfigured or decentralized to include a

---

[11] For an in-depth analysis of the relation between the state and education and the role of schools in state formation in Niger from the colonial to the post colonial period, see Tidjani Alou (1992).

number of non state actors – from parents, to the traditional chieftaincy to district advisors and international development aid – the idea of the state as the ideal provider of public education remains strong.

References

Bernus, S. 1969. *Particularismes Ethniques en Milieu Urbain: L'Exemple de Niamey*. Paris: Memoires de l'Institut d'Ethnologie.

Bierschenk, T. 2007. L'éducation de base en Afrique de l'Ouest francophone : Bien privé, bien public, bien global. In *Une anthropologie entre rigueur et engagement: Essais autour de l'oeuvre de Jean-Pierre Olivier de Sardan* (eds) T. Biershenk, G. Blundo, Y. Jaffré & M. Tidjani Alou. Paris: Karthala.

Blundo, G. & J.-P. Olivier de Sardan (eds) 2006. *Everyday Corruption and the State: Citizens and Public Officials in Africa*. London and New York: Zed Books.

Blundo, G. & P.-Y. Le Meur 2009. Introduction: An Anthropology of Everyday Governance: Collective Service Delivery and Subject Making. In *The Governance of Daily Life in Africa: Ethnograpic Explorations of Public and Collective Services* (eds) G. Blundo & P.-Y. Le Meur. Leiden & Boston: Brill.

Charlier, J.-E. & J.-F. Pierrard 2000. Systèmes décentralisés dans l'éducation sénégalaise, burkinabé et malienne. *Autrepart* 17, 29-48.

Daouda, A, A.A.I. Daouda & H Souley 2001. Le Niger: Politiques éducatives et système éducatif actuel. In *La Demade d'éducation en Afrique : Etat des connaissances et perspectives de recherche* (eds) M. Pilon & Y, Yaro.

Henaff, N. 2003. Quel financement pour l'Ecole en Afrique ? *Cahiers d'Études africaines* 169-170, XLIII (1-2), 167-188.

Jaffré, Y. & J.-P. Olivier de Sardan (eds) 2003. *Une médecine inhospitalière: Les difficiles relations entre soignants et soignés dans cinq capitales d'Afrique de l'Ouest*. Paris: Karthala.

King, K. 2007. Multilateral agencies in the construction of the global agenda on education. *Comparative Education* 43 (3), 377-391.

Lange, M.-F. 2003. Ecole et mondialisation. Vers un nouvel ordre scolaire? *Cahiers d'Études africaines* 169-170, XLIII (1-2), 143-166.

Maclure, R. 1994. Misplaced Assumptions of Decentralization and Participation in Rural Communities: Primary school reform in Burkina Faso. *Comparative Education* 30 (3), 239- 254.

Masquelier, A. 2001. Behind the Dispensary's Prosperous Façade: Imagining the State in Rural Niger. *Public Culture* 13 (2), 267-291.

Meunier, O. 2000. *Bilan d'un siècle de politique éducative au Niger*. Paris: L'Harmattan.

Migdal, J. & K. Schlichte. 2005. Rethinking the State. In *The Dynamics of States: The Formation and Crisis of State Domination* (ed.) K. Schilchte. Aldershot: Ashgate.

Motcho, K.H. 2004. La réforme communale de la communauté urbaine de Niamey (Niger). *Revue de géographie alpine* 92 (1), 111-124.

Motcho, K.H. 2005. Urbanisation et rôle de la chefferie traditionnelle dans la communauté urbaine de Niamey. *Les Cahiers d'Outre Mer* 229, 73-88.

Nielsen, M. 2007. Filling in the Blanks: The Potency of Fragmented Imageries of the State. *Review of African Political Economy* 34 (114), 695-708.

Olivier de Sardan, J.-P. 1999. L'espace public introuvable: Chefs et projets dans les villages nigériens. *Tiers-Monde* 40 (157), 139-167.

Olivier de Sardan, J-P. 2004. Etat, bureaucratie et gouvernance en Afrique de l'ouest francophone. *Politique Africaine* 96, 139-162.

Olivier de Sardan, J.-P. 2005. Classic ethnology and the socio-anthropology of public spaces: New themes and old methods in European African Studies. *Africa spectrum* 40 (3), 485- 497.

Olivier de Sardan, J.-P. & A. Dagobi 2002. La gestion communautaire sert-elle l'intérêt public ? Le cas de l'hydraulique villageoise au Niger. *Politique Africaine* 80, 153-168.

Tidjani Alou, M. 1992. *Les Politiques de Formation en Afrique Francophone : Ecole, Etat et Sociétés au Niger*. Thèse de doctorat, Bordeaux.

Tidjani Alou, M. 2009. Public goods and the management of collective infrastructure: the case of the drinking-water supply systems in the Maradi region of Niger. In *The Governance of Daily Life in Africa: Ethnograpic Explorations of Public and Collective Services* (eds) G. Blundo & P.-Y. Le Meur. Leiden and Boston: Brill.

Wilson, F. 2001. In the Name of the State? Schools and Teachers in an Andean Province. In *States of Imagination: Ethnographic Explorations of the Post-colonial State* (eds) T.B. Hansen & F. Stepputat. Durham and London: Duke University Press.

APAD KEY NOTE ADDRESS IN DECEMBER 2007
CONFÉRENCE PLENIÈRE DE L'APAD EN DÉCEMBRE 2007

Anthropologie et développement

Historiciser et localiser les approches[1]

Thomas Bierschenk[2]

Je souhaite saisir l'occasion qui m'est offerte par les organisateurs de ce colloque pour revenir sur le projet de l'APAD auquel j'ai été intimement associé, et ce pratiquement depuis les débuts de cette entreprise. Une réflexion de ce type me semble particulièrement opportune dans le cadre de ce colloque qui a été conçu dans une logique d'état des lieux et de discussion de nouvelles perspectives.

Mon objectif est de situer l'approche de l'APAD dans le champ plus large de l'anthropologie du développement, ce que je ferai en me tournant vers le passé, puis en regardant de côté, « à gauche et à droite » si je puis dire. Je me demanderai avant toute chose si nous pouvons tirer des leçons d'autres tentatives de réflexion sur les relations entre anthropologie et développement, tentatives qui ont précédé de beaucoup la naissance de

---

[1] Ce texte est une version légèrement modifiée du discours d'ouverture du colloque de l'APAD sur « Développement, libéralisme et modernité : trajectoires pour une anthropologie du changement social », 13-15 décembre 2007, Tervuren/Bruxelles. L'APAD (Association euro-africaine pour l'anthropologie du changement social et du développement) est à présent basée à Uppsala (Suède) et Leiden (Pays-Bas) ; cf. www.association-apad.org. Je souhaite remercier Nassirou Bako-Arifari, Pierre-Yves Le Meur et Eva Spies pour leurs commentaires productifs sur une première mouture de ce texte. Ma réflexion sur le sujet s'est également beaucoup inspirée des remarques perspicaces d'Ejima Baker, Jacob Doherty et Summer Wood lors du cours que j'ai donné à la New School for Social Research de New York à l'automne 2007.

[2] Professeur, Département d'Anthropologie et d'Études africaines, Université Johannes Gutenberg de Mayence, Allemagne. Contact : biersche@uni-mainz.de

l'APAD, et qui se sont poursuivies parallèlement à son existence. L'anthropologie du développement a commencé bien avant la fondation de l'APAD au début des années 1990 – nous n'en étions que faiblement conscient à l'époque – et avec le recul, il apparaît évident que la naissance de notre association s'inscrivait dans un mouvement plus global dans ce domaine. Observer ce qui s'y passait à ce moment là et ce qui s'y passe actuellement, également en dehors de, et en parallèle à l'APAD nous aide à mieux comprendre comment ses conditions particulières de création ont conféré à l'APAD ses caractéristiques spécifiques, durables, dont certaines valent indiscutablement d'être conservées, alors que d'autres mériteraient d'être revues. En d'autres termes, les quatre mots clés de l'acronyme APAD – Europe, Afrique, anthropologie, développement – doivent faire l'objet d'un examen attentif. Ainsi, après avoir regardé en arrière, puis à gauche et à droite, je terminerai cet exposé par un regard vers l'avant.

Mes propositions reposent bien sûr sur une prémisse qu'il faudra discuter préalablement. Cette prémisse est qu'il existe quelque chose comme une « approche APAD » de l'anthropologie du développement. Cette approche a évolué depuis ses premières définitions initialement formulées par Jean-Pierre Dozon (1978) et Jean-Pierre Chauveau (1985), puis plus largement et à plusieurs occasions par Jean-Pierre Olivier de Sardan (pour une évaluation, voir Bierschenk 2007a ; parmi ses nombreux écrits sur le sujet, voir Olivier de Sardan 1983, 1985, 1995, 2005a). On peut repérer cinq postulats fondant l'approche « apadienne ». Le premier de ces postulats consiste à séparer les réflexions normatives sur le développement de l'analyse empirique pour se concentrer sur cette dernière : sur les « faits du développement ». Le développement est tout simplement ce que les acteurs dans le champ désignent comme tel, et le monde social dans lequel ils évoluent. Ou, pour suivre Jean-Pierre Chauveau qui écrivait dès 1985 dans un style concis (Chauveau 1985 : 164) : « Il y a tout simplement 'développement' là ou il y a des 'développeurs', là où l'un des groupes se réclamant de la mise en œuvre du développement, organise un dispositif d'intervention sur d'autres groupes sociaux ». Si l'anthropologie du développement est empirique (second postulat), ce n'est pas par positivisme naïf, mais au sens de toute bonne anthropologie, dont le projet s'enracine dans les mondes de vie, les pratiques sociales et les expériences quotidiennes des acteurs. Le développement en tant que champ social (troisième postulat) est un objet légitime pour l'anthropologie, aussi

« noble » que les objets plus classiques de la parenté ou de la religion par exemple. En fait, le développement en tant que champ social est composé de réalités multiples pour l'étude desquelles l'anthropologie, grâce à son outillage méthodologique, est particulièrement bien équipée. Quatrième postulat : cette anthropologie du développement empirique et non normative a des ambitions théoriques. Sa contribution à l'anthropologie générale est non seulement faite de nouveaux objets, mais aussi, et plus encore peut-être, de nouvelles méthodes et d'approches théoriques innovantes. Dans le même temps (cinquième postulat), cette anthropologie du développement ambitieuse au plan théorique est aussi une anthropologie du développement appliquée. La recherche appliquée et la recherche fondamentale sont indissociables. Par conséquent, lorsque l'anthropologie néglige le développement, ou que le monde du développement néglige l'anthropologie, c'est à leurs propres dépens, au risque de leur appauvrissement à tous deux.

À ces cinq postulats essentiels, on doit ajouter le style particulier du travail anthropologique de l'APAD : une coproduction de savoirs anthropologiques sur le développement qui est l'œuvre de chercheurs européens et africains. La structure de la participation à ce colloque de l'APAD est une belle illustration de ce style – et c'était déjà le cas des précédentes.

Toutefois, si la description d'une approche propre à l'APAD se veut correcte (même si succincte) – une approche née dans les années 1980 dans un esprit de forte confiance en soi et de rupture historique –, comment la situer dans les champs plus larges de la production du savoir et de l'intervention pratique ?

Il existe diverses manières de structurer ce champ de savoir. Une typologie classique différencie la recherche anthropologique fondamentale sur le développement, et l'application des savoirs anthropologiques au développement ; une autre distingue les approches centrées sur les acteurs, les institutions, les politiques et les discours.

La première distinction (entre recherche appliquée et recherche fondamentale) s'exprime souvent en anglais via l'opposition (intraduisible) entre *development anthropology* et *anthropology of development* (cette dernière formulation au sens où l'on parle d'anthropologie du droit, de la religion, etc.). Nous avons vu que l'approche de l'APAD, tout en ne niant pas cette différence, tente sciemment de la réduire. Elle postule que la recherche appliquée ne peut exister par elle-même. Toute bonne anthropologie appliquée doit s'appuyer sur une bonne anthropologie fondamentale, bénéficiant de tous les garde-fous méthodologiques et de la réflexivité théorique de cette dernière. Il faut en même temps rappeler au passage, et par anticipation de ma revue à suivre de l'anthropologie appliquée américaine, que l'anthropologie du développement et l'anthropologie appliquée (ou pratique) se chevauchent mais ne se confondent pas : alors qu'il existe une anthropologie du développement non appliquée, il existe aussi une anthropologie appliquée non orientée vers le développement, ou alors seulement dans un sens très large.

En ce qui concerne la seconde typologie basée sur la distinction entre approches centrées sur les acteurs, les institutions, les politiques et les discours, il est probablement juste de dire que la manière apadienne de faire de l'anthropologie est essentiellement centrée sur les acteurs – conséquence quasi inéluctable de la priorité donnée à l'ethnographie. Mais si l'approche centrée sur les acteurs était innovante dans les années 1980 au plan théorique, elle est récemment devenue la cible de critiques venues d'autres points de vue, et en particulier de l'approche dite discursive. Si l'on analyse le programme de notre colloque, nous notons que l'approche même de l'APAD tend à évoluer en direction d'approches plus centrées sur les politiques.

Je souhaite aborder ces différences en opérant un détour via une troisième distinction partant de la localisation des approches, distinction qui me semble avoir été indûment négligée. L'idée de « localisation » peut porter tant sur l'écriture anthropologique que sur ses terrains. À propos de ceux-ci, on a pu décrire les évolutions de la théorie anthropologique en lien avec les sites à partir desquels celle-ci s'est développée (Fardon 1990). L'approche holistique de la culture de Bronislaw Malinowski, par exemple, aurait fondé sa plausibilité dans la nature insulaire des sociétés océaniennes et l'approche en réseau de l'École de Manchester dans le caractère fluide des relations sociales en Afrique Centrale et Australe. Une réflexion de ce genre appliquée à l'anthropologie du développement est toujours en quête d'auteurs : une anthropologie du développement dont l'inspiration empirique vient d'Inde, d'Indonésie ou d'Amérique latine est-elle différente d'une anthropologie du développement centrée sur l'Afrique ? C'est très probable, mais ce sont précisément les frontières géographiques de l'APAD qui nous ont empêchés d'identifier les éventuelles spécificités des situations de développement africaines[3].

Ma proposition est la suivante : si l'on veut mieux comprendre l'essentiel du débat actuel dans le champ de l'anthropologie du développement, en particulier concernant les positionnements et étiquetages mutuels, il faut prendre conscience de l'existence de deux grands sites d'écriture de l'anthropologie du développement – l'Europe et les USA – qui ont développé des caractéristiques propres qui les distinguent nettement. Cette idée de « sites d'écriture » n'est pas à prendre dans un simple sens spatial, même si la localisation géographique n'en est pas complètement absente, et elle n'a bien entendu aucun rapport avec l'origine nationale des auteurs. Je pense surtout en termes de communautés épistémiques, de traditions discursives et de références intellectuelles dominantes au sein desquelles s'écrit l'anthropologie du développement, ainsi qu'en fonction du marché du livre et des revues scientifiques pour lesquels elle s'écrit. Les fossés linguistiques jouent un rôle capital dans le découpage de ces sites.

En d'autres termes, j'émets l'hypothèse qu'il existe quelque chose comme un style européen et un style états-uniens d'anthropologie du développement, et que certaines positions et certains débats actuels deviennent plus lisibles si nous prenons ce facteur en compte. Je reconnais qu'en procédant de la sorte, je propose une perspective très « nord-atlantiste », faisant sans doute ainsi l'impasse sur d'autres discours « périphériques », ceux qui par exemple ont trait à la branche latino-américaine ou indienne de l'anthropologie du développement. Dans le cadre du présent texte – et aussi par simple ignorance… – je mettrai cette question entre parenthèses. Je passe aussi sur l'un des traits les plus caractéristiques

[3] Le degré d'extraversion des États et sociétés, en particulier vis-à-vis des agences de développement étrangères, lui-même lié aux forces et faiblesses relatives des États et à leur capacité stratégique différentielle – leur « ruse » (Randeria 2007) – la force relative des mouvements sociaux, et bien sûr les différents processus d'émergence des classes sociales constitueraient certaines des dimensions comparatives à analyser. Il est impossible de développer ce point ici.

de l'APAD : la coproduction euro-africaine de savoirs anthropologiques. D'ailleurs, si l'on prête attention aux trajectoires et réseaux professionnels de nos collègues africains, il est difficile de nier leur caractère européocentré.

J'avance ici que l'APAD incarne un style d'anthropologie du développement typiquement européen, tout comme l'École de Wageningen (Long 2001, 1989 ; Long & Long 1992) et le réseau EIDOS (Hobart 1993 ; Lewis & Mosse 2005, 2006 ; Quarles van Ufford 1993 ; Quarles van Ufford et al. 1988). Il existe en fait des chevauchements de personnes entre ces réseaux qui, avec la présence occasionnelle des uns aux réunions et conférences des autres, a généré des influences mutuelles, conscientes (Lewis & Mosse 2006 ; Olivier de Sardan 1988, 2001) ou implicites. Alors qu'une observation plus fine révélerait certainement d'importantes nuances, les traits communs à ce style européen sont plus faciles à repérer si on les observe de l'extérieur, des États-Unis en l'occurrence. Je me propose de mettra au jour ces différences intercontinentales en recourant à une perspective historique.

Pour le sens commun apadien mis en forme dans les textes fondateurs de l'association, l'anthropologie du développement a pris tournure dans les années 1970, même si l'existence de précurseurs (par exemple Bastide 1971) est reconnue en passant (Olivier de Sardan 1988). Cette façon d'écrire l'histoire du champ me semble refléter une perspective très européenne, voire euro-continentale. Elle néglige largement deux traditions : la très riche tradition nord-américaine d'anthropologie appliquée qui remonte quasiment aux débuts de l'anthropologie comme science empirique dans les premières décennies du 20ème siècle, et l'intérêt soutenu pour les applications pratiques de l'anthropologie en Grande-Bretagne pendant la même période. Dans le cas des États-Unis, l'intérêt pratique était plutôt tourné vers l'intérieur, en direction de la société américaine elle-même, et – fait unique dans la tradition anthropologique jusque dans les années 1970 – une littérature conséquente a été produite durant cette période visant à l'identification d'un champ distinct (pour un aperçu utile, voir Bennett 1996). Pour ce qui est de l'anthropologie britannique, elle accompagnait déjà les mouvements humanitaristes – en l'occurrence anti-esclavagistes – du début du 19ème siècle (Reining 1996, commentaire sur Bennett) ; elle est plus tard devenue une science auxiliaire de la colonisation, avec un intérêt pratique dirigé vers l'extérieur, les colonies tout d'abord, les pays indépendants par la suite (Gardner & Lewis 1996, ch. 2). En Allemagne et en France en revanche, l'anthropologie n'a développé aucun intérêt pratique avant les années 1970, bien que pour des raisons historiques différentes. En France, l'intérêt pour les sociétés coloniales contemporaines s'est surtout exprimé chez les auteurs qui travaillaient en dehors du champ de l'anthropologie académique (Delafosse 1941 ; Delavignette 1931 ; cf. Sibeud 2002), tandis que les thèmes des universitaires se limitaient jusque dans les années 1980 aux formes sociales « traditionnelles » et/ou en voie de disparition[4]. La situation fut pire encore pour l'anthropologie allemande qui, après 1918, a rompu avec l'empirie pour se perdre dans la spéculation historique – ce qui n'a pas empêché certains de ses praticiens de proposer (en vain) une version appliquée de leur discipline aux dirigeants nazis pour l'administration des futures colonies (Hauschild 1995 ; Streck 2000). Dans les deux cas, c'est l'intérêt qu'une nouvelle génération d'anthropologues a porté sur le développement qui est à l'origine du tournant empirique pris par la discipline à la fin des années 1970 et au début des années 1980 (Allemagne), parallèlement à la légitimité croissante des études empiriques des sociétés contemporaines (Allemagne, France).

Il faut admettre qu'il est très facile d'oublier cette tradition pratique, appliquée, qui perdure dans l'anthropologie américaine et britannique, car elle est habituellement omise dans les histoires standard de la discipline ou, au mieux, reléguée sur les marges, comme quelque chose que les fondateurs de la discipline « faisaient aussi », en plus de produire des textes canoniques[5]. Par conséquent, cette tradition appliquée n'est pas enseignée aux débutants en anthropologie, et dans le cas où elle l'est, elle est réservée aux cours de spécialisation. Le versant appliqué de l'anthropologie est toutefois parfois « critiqué » par des anthropologues généralistes, mais dans

[4] Et ce, malgré l'influence de George Balandier (1951, 1967) qui n'a pas ménagé ses efforts pour faire des études africaines modernes un sujet respectable.

[5] Dans Barth et al. (2005) par exemple, aucun des auteurs ne traite de manière autre que très superficielle de l'anthropologie appliquée, pratique ou de l'anthropologie du développement. De nombreux auteurs classiques ont écrit sur l'application pratique de l'anthropologie ; voir entre autres Malinowski (1929), Radcliffe-Brown (1980 [1930]), Herskovits (1936), Evans-Pritchard (1946), Mead (1977), Firth (1981).

ce cas, c'est le plus souvent pour le réduire à la question de l'anthropologie dans le contexte colonial (Asad 1973)[6]. En outre, l'histoire de l'anthropologie du développement est habituellement traitée par les spécialistes sur un mode très sélectif, et ils se focalisent sur une seule tradition nationale, même si les titres respectifs des contributions suggèrent une perspective plus générale : l'important article de Bennet (1996) par exemple traite exclusivement des États-Unis (sans que jamais le titre le dévoile)[7] ; Gardner & Lewis (1996, ch. 2) n'évoquent finalement que le cas britannique et, de manière très sélective, la situation des USA, et leurs références sporadiques à la France ne sont pas étayées. Spittler (1994) quant à lui ne donne aucune référence bibliographique et ne parle apparemment que de l'École allemande d'anthropologie appliquée du développement (qu'il critique pour son manque de réflexion théorique)[8]. Ces perceptions fragmentaires s'expliquent pour partie par une compétence linguistique limitée, et il n'est probablement pas injuste de dire qu'il existe un gradient dans la conscience de ce qui se passe au-delà des frontières nationales ou linguistiques spécifiques. Si les anthropologues allemands lisent au moins certains anthropologues américains, britanniques et français, la réciproque est loin d'être certaine[9].

Par conséquent, lorsque James Ferguson (1997) parle du développement comme de « l'âme damnée (*evil twin*) » de l'anthropologie – damnée car non reconnue – son intuition est juste, mais son argument souffre de simplisme car il ne prend pas en compte les différences entre traditions nationales. Il voit dans ce lien occulte un effet de l'épistémologie – il s'agit pour lui du lien inextinguible mais caché de l'anthropologie à

---

[6] Il est important de noter que la référence empirique de ce livre majeur est le colonialisme britannique – pas ses homologues français ou américain.

[7] Ainsi que le font Gow (1993), Hoben (1982) et Nolan (2002).

[8] Cette école est étudiée dans Schönhuth & Bliss (2004).

[9] Il n'existe aucun compte-rendu satisfaisant en anglais – ou en allemand – sur l'histoire récente de l'anthropologie allemande ; le traitement que fait Gingrich (2005) des développements post-1970 est extrêmement sommaire et biaisé. Pour un bon aperçu récent des études africaines en allemand, voir Probst (2005). Il faut noter que la compétence linguistique ne garantit pas la justesse de perception : la plupart des anthropologues allemands sous-estiment probablement l'étendue, la diversité intellectuelle et institutionnelle de l'anthropologie américaine ainsi que son factionnalisme (Silverman 2005 : 330ff.), alors que c'est cette situation qui permet aux « renégats de survivre » et explique « qu'aucun paradigme ne peut dominer très longtemps ».

l'évolutionnisme – et oublie qu'il résulte aussi de préoccupations pratiques pour le monde moderne qui sont tout autant constitutives de la discipline. Ces questions ont suivi un autre chemin aux États-Unis où, en l'absence d'un empire colonial formel, mais aussi pour des raisons prosaïques (difficulté à obtenir des bourses de voyage, faibles compétences linguistiques de la plupart des étudiants), les préoccupations pratiques de l'anthropologie sont plutôt restées d'ordre intérieur, alors que Grande-Bretagne est le seul endroit où l'anthropologie a été intégrée au dispositif colonial. Par comparaison, l'anthropologie en France et en Allemagne, nous l'avons dit, n'a connu ni application pratique, ni aspiration dans ce sens[10].

Aux États-Unis, les années 1930 ont constitué un moment clef pour le développement d'une anthropologie appliquée (Bennett 1996). Seule une partie de ce travail était centrée sur les réserves des Amérindiens. Les thématiques de l'anthropologie américaine appliquée étaient diversifiées, et celle-ci était également centrée sur l'Amérique « blanche », à l'exemple des études d'Harvard sur les fondements socioculturels de l'organisation industrielle, à l'origine du concept « d'ingénierie anthropologique » (Chapple 1943, cité dans Bennett 1996), et des études de communautés rurales américaines sponsorisées par le Bureau d'économie agricole et de santé rurale du Département de l'Agriculture du gouvernement Roosevelt. De toute évidence, le moteur de ce développement était le *New Deal* porté par la croyance dans la possibilité d'une ingénierie sociale. Les traits méthodologiques de cette recherche anthropologique appliquée étaient la pluridisciplinarité, le comparatisme et l'utilisation réflexive d'une palette de méthodes de recherche qui allait bien au-delà de la désormais classique

[10] Il ne s'agit pas de nier le profit qu'ont tiré les anthropologues universitaires français de l'infrastructure du régime colonial, lorsqu'ils travaillaient de manière empirique, comme pendant l'expédition de Dakar à Djibouti au début des années 1930 (Griaule 1975 ; Leiris 1999). À la différence de leurs homologues britanniques (Evans-Pritchard et plus généralement l'Institut Rhodes Livingston viennent ici à l'esprit), ils n'avaient pas néanmoins l'ambition de réformer ou d'être autrement utiles au régime colonial. À côté de la relation intrinsèque mais occultée à l'évolutionnisme et des préoccupations pratiques pour le monde moderne, il existe un troisième lien au développement omis par les anthropologues : ces derniers sont en fait étonnamment nombreux à s'enorgueillir d'être des purs représentants du style académique (i.e. non appliqué), tout en étant – eux ou leurs époux/ses – activement impliqué(e)s dans des entreprises de développement, en général sur leurs propres terrains. Dans ce cas, qui est loin d'être rare, cette activité parallèle dans le développement n'est soumise à aucune réflexion théorique.

observation participante, approche canonisée par Malinowski (1984 [1922], introduction) et rituellement invoquée mais bien peu réfléchie. À ces caractéristiques s'ajoutait une critique implicite de l'hégémonie culturaliste (*whole-culturalism* ; Bennet 1996 : 26) de l'anthropologie alors dominante. Ces orientations méthodologiques et théoriques hétérodoxes expliquent probablement pour une bonne part l'hostilité suscitée par ce travail appliqué chez de nombreux anthropologues universitaires. En d'autres termes, nombre des avancées récentes en anthropologie générale, mais aussi les disputes récurrentes qui les accompagnent entre anthropologie « fondamentale » et anthropologie « appliquée », étaient déjà présentes dans cette tradition américaine méconnue de l'anthropologie appliquée. Celle-ci a longtemps été, à l'instar de son homologue britannique pourtant plus nettement paternaliste, « le foyer exclusif des anthropologues intéressés par la société contemporaine » (Bennett 1996 : 25, note 5) – foyer revendiqué aujourd'hui par l'anthropologie générale.

Néanmoins, au-delà de ces approches appliquées, la conviction que l'anthropologie avait un rôle public à jouer, qu'elle pouvait être amenée à s'impliquer dans des questions d'intérêt pratique, a marqué l'anthropologie américaine en tant que telle, et elle était partagée par des figures tutélaires, Mead, Benedict ou encore Herskovits, qui s'étaient activement engagées dans l'effort de guerre et dans la création d'un nouvel ordre mondial après 1945. Les anthropologues américains partageaient l'optimisme humaniste-libéral et le populisme égalitaire qui avaient marqué les sciences sociales américaines depuis leurs origines au 19ème siècle et étaient liés à un élan moral visant à améliorer le monde (Anderson 2003). Dans ce sens, le *New Deal*, avec son intérêt pour l'ingénierie sociale, apparaît comme l'actualisation d'idées plus anciennes, et la Seconde Guerre Mondiale a ranimé ces convictions. Pour beaucoup de ses praticiens, l'anthropologie constituait une forme de « service public » (Lantis 1945, cité par Bennett 1996 : 30) défini comme une combinaison de professionnalisme et d'ingénierie sociale.

Dans les années 1950, ces convictions humanistes et ces traditions méthodologiques de l'anthropologie appliquée se sont cristallisées sur un mode radical dans l'œuvre de Sol Tax, figure rebelle de l'anthropologie américaine, dont le travail, qui cherchait à combler le fossé entre savoirs et pratiques du développement, mérite une attention bien plus soutenue (et éventuellement critique) que celle que lui ont accordée les anthropologues contemporains. Dans la terminologie de Jean-Pierre Olivier de Sardan (2004b), on pourrait décrire Sol Tax comme un précurseur dans la quête du « chaînon manquant » entre recherche et action[11]. Sol Tax dont les origines biographiques s'ancrent dans le populisme du Middle West, et qui pendant ses études avait travaillé avec Ruth Benedict sur son étude des Mescaleros Apaches et Robert Redfield au Mexique, a très tôt élaboré une distinction entre science « pure » et science « thérapeutique », cette dernière touchant à la production de savoirs sur les problèmes de la vie réelle et les fondements du quotidien comme pré-condition à une pratique progressiste (Bennett 1996 : 34ff.). L'idée centrale de Tax était celle d'une identité entre travail de terrain et développement communautaire. La tâche du travailleur de terrain est de faire prendre conscience par le biais de la recherche et d'une meilleure communication de ce qu'on pourrait appeler en langage actuel les notions populaires du développement, du bien-être social et de la bonne vie, et d'aider ces dernières à atteindre ces objectifs. Les idées de Tax ont été mises en œuvre non seulement dans le cadre du fameux projet Fox dans une réserve indienne de l'Iowa, mais aussi dans toutes sortes d'activités destinées aux Indiens d'Amérique, ainsi que dans un programme communautaire de logement et de développement dans un quartier urbain situé juste au nord de l'Université de Chicago, où il enseignait. En d'autres termes, Tax a dés-exotisé et dé-racialisé les Amérindiens. Il les voyait, à l'instar des habitants urbains blancs, comme de simples américains avec « leurs craintes, leurs espoirs et leurs besoins ». Nous pouvons ainsi dire qu'il y a cinquante ans, Sol Tax prônait déjà ce qu'Arjun Appadurai (2007) a récemment baptisé l'anthropologie du futur, même si Sol Tax s'intéressait davantage aux savoirs qu'aux pratiques, et très peu, voire pas du tout, au potentiel théorique de la recherche orientée vers l'action[12].

L'injection d'une dimension anthropologique dans le champ du développement à la fin des années 1960 et au début des années 1970 aux USA peut être considérée comme un rejeton tardif mais impressionnant de

[11] Sur le « chaînon manquant », voir aussi les contributions récentes de Bako Arifari (2007), Lavigne Delville (2007) et Le Meur (2007).

[12] Les liens potentiels entre ce programme et l'agenda de l'APAD via Roger Bastide, sur lesquels Jean-Pierre Chauveau a attiré mon attention, restent à explorer.

cette tradition d'anthropologie appliquée spécifiquement américaine (Hoben 1982). Vers 1970, l'USAID est devenue un employeur majeur d'anthropologues américains. Cette agence a contribué à développer des « analyse socialement fondées » (*social soundness analysis*) qui, sous McNamara, ont fait leur chemin jusqu'à la Banque mondiale, atteignant ultérieurement une série d'autres agences de développement bilatérales et multilatérales. En d'autres termes, l'USAID a ouvert la voie au « tournant participatif et anthropologique » du développement avec des longueurs d'avance sur tout ce qui se passait dans ce champ en Europe à la même époque. Ainsi, lorsque le projet de l'APAD prit forme au début des années 1980, prônant une implication anthropologique plus importante dans le domaine du développement, la bataille était déjà gagnée aux USA.

Mais entre-temps, l'optimisme libéral américain s'était évanoui au cours des années 1960 et 1970. Une des causes immédiates de ce phénomène dans le champ de l'anthropologie fut l'implication des anthropologues américains dans le mouvement global de contre-insurrection, avec le projet Camelot comme partie émergée de l'iceberg. En termes d'histoire « réelle », le contexte général du déclin de l'optimisme pour l'ingénierie sociale était bien sûr celui de la Guerre du Vietnam ; en termes d'histoire intellectuelle – et probablement non sans lien avec celle-ci – le postmodernisme et ses doutes à l'endroit du projet moderniste. Néanmoins, le creusement du fossé entre anthropologie pratique et anthropologie académique était aussi favorisé par les évolutions contingentes du marché américain du travail : si dans les années 1950 de nombreux anthropologues travaillaient dans les champs de l'application, leur nombre a diminué après les années 1960, quand les anthropologues américains ont progressivement trouvé des emplois dans les universités, et ont ainsi pu échapper aux travaux appliqués. Dans le secteur du développement américain, l'essor du paradigme de la modernisation a rendu les anthropologues superflus dès les années 1960 (Hoben 1982). Après 1970, la tendance s'est inversée et le marché du travail hors université a progressivement dominé.

La dégradation générale de l'optimisme libéral américain, la crise idéologique et celle de l'emploi en anthropologie du développement ont fourni à la fin des années 1970 et au début des années 1980 la toile de fond d'où a émergé une critique radicale du développement, communément associée aux travaux d'Arturo Escobar (1995) et de James Ferguson (1990).

Les deux auteurs affirment que le développement fonctionne comme un régime de savoir/pouvoir qui vise à la domination de l'Occident sur le Tiers Monde. La « machine du développement » est essentiellement une machine à dépolitiser : en s'implantant via l'ajustement structurel, les agences de développement soumettraient progressivement les pays pauvres d'Afrique, d'Asie et d'Amérique latine à un régime disciplinaire international dans lequel les questions politiques seraient technicisées, privant les pays du Sud de toute capacité d'action. Ce régime international de pouvoir/savoir ne peut être réformé de l'intérieur mais seulement « critiqué » de l'extérieur et à cet égard, une position académique dans une université états-unienne d'élite offre un poste d'observation idéal, si ce n'est le seul.

En d'autres termes, à partir des années 1980 et plus encore dans les années 1990, la situation aux USA s'est trouvée caractérisée par une polarisation (qui perdure aujourd'hui) entre deux positions antagonistes : d'une part, une anthropologie du développement appliquée très sophistiquée au plan technique, avec une riche tradition historique, et dont l'objectif principal se limite à essayer d'être utile. Ce versant appliqué de l'anthropologie fait l'économie de toute réflexivité théorique, ou plutôt, il ne réalise pas son potentiel théorique : il s'intéresse essentiellement à la contribution possible de l'anthropologie au développement, et non à son envers : l'apport potentiel de l'étude du développement à l'anthropologie en général[13]. D'un autre côté, il existe une position radicale du « n'y-touchez-pas », évitant tout engagement empirique avec l'objet « critiqué » et s'accompagnant d'une substitution de fait des références érudites et des grands noms de la philosophie à l'analyse empirique. Nous pourrions voir dans cette polarité une résurgence du vieux débat modernisation *versus* dépendance, à la différence près que la théorie néo-dépendantiste d'Escobar et de Ferguson ne s'inspire plus de Lénine et de Rosa Luxembourg mais essentiellement de Foucault. Ces positions radicalement opposées ont un ancrage institutionnel distinct et communiquent à peine l'une avec l'autre.

[13] Dans cette perspective, le développement défie la manière dont l'anthropologie est enseignée aux étudiants : celle-ci devrait être moins théorique et plus orientée sur la pratique selon certains – cf. Cernea (1996) et Nolan (2002) –, pour transmettre en premier lieu les compétences nécessaires aux professionnels du développement.

Par comparaison, les positions européennes qui se développaient en parallèle se sont plus fortement exprimées en termes d'engagement critique dans la pratique. Elles étaient de manière significative souvent formulées par des gens qui avaient, ou avaient eu au cours de leur carrière, un pied dans les deux camps, ceux de l'intervention de développement et de l'université, et qui avaient essayé de combiner pratique du développement et réflexion théorique : à Wageningen, le groupe associé à Norman Long a su s'engager dans un débat de fond avec les collègues les plus orientés vers la pratique des départements voisins de la vulgarisation ou encore de l'irrigation ; à l'École des hautes études en sciences sociales (EHESS) de Marseille, Jean-Pierre Olivier de Sardan a régulièrement accepté des doctorants issus du monde du développement ; à l'École d'études orientales et africaines (SOAS), David Mosse et ses collègues continuent de combiner travail de développement, enseignement universitaire et recherche, pour ne citer que quelques exemples. Ce type de chevauchement semble être plus rare, si ce n'est inexistant aux États-Unis.

De toute évidence, il existe aussi d'importantes nuances entre les différentes approches européennes et il faut se garder de les sous-estimer. À côté des traditions nationales auxquelles nous avons déjà fait allusion, elles me semblent largement liées à la diversité des terrains (Amérique latine, Afrique, Inde), des trajectoires personnelles et enfin du type de public auprès duquel on recherche sa légitimité[14].

Les faiblesses de la théorie néo-dépendantiste ont souvent été dénoncées (par ex : Olivier de Sardan 2001) ; je me limiterai donc ici à une brève présentation de trois points critiques essentiels :

1. La première critique concerne la fragilité des fondements empiriques. En fait, à l'instar des théoriciens classiques de la dépendance, les néo-dépendantistes tirent moins leur autorité de

[14] Norman Long par exemple, ancien doctorant de Max Gluckman, semble surtout s'adresser à un public universitaire, et essentiellement en sociologie, comme l'indiquent les titres de ses principaux ouvrages (Long 1977, 2001), tandis que Jean-Pierre Olivier de Sardan, parallèlement à ses intérêts théoriques, vise également un impact local et pratique – en Afrique de l'Ouest où il a choisi de résider, ainsi qu'auprès des agences de développement internationales, cf. Bierschenk (2007a).

l'analyse empirique que de références érudites aux théories sociales. Il en résulte une essentialisation du « néo-libéralisme » qui fait l'économie de son analyse et une surestimation de la force du « régime de pouvoir/savoir du développement » – perspective en accord avec la position foucaldienne et qui paraît plus plausible si l'on observe le monde d'une métropole ou d'un campus américains qu'à partir disons, de l'est du Congo[15]. Si ce manque d'intérêt pour ce qui se passe réellement sur le terrain est particulièrement flagrant dans le travail d'Escobar (1995), il n'est pas absent non plus chez des néo-dépendantistes plus empiriques. Ferguson (1990) par exemple, généralise un cas unique et très particulier : un projet de la Banque mondiale, paradigmatique de la modernisation des années 1960 et 1970, qu'il présente comme typique du développement dans son ensemble, dans un livre publié dans les années 1990 et donc, longtemps après le « tournant participatif » emprunté par le développement. Une lecture attentive de son analyse révèle que si les agences de développement se sont efforcées de dépolitiser le développement et de le techniciser, l'élite politique du Lesotho est restée très consciente des implications politiques des interventions de développement et très habile à les exploiter à son avantage.

2. Cette critique ne concerne pas autant, je crois, l'œuvre d'autres théoriciens de la néo-dépendance tels que Rita Abrahamsen (2000). Celle-ci nous offre une solide étude comparative en sciences politiques sur les effets dépolitisants de la greffe de la démocratie dans quatre pays africains. L'approche d'Abrahamsen – comme celle de nombreux néo-dépendantistes – souffre toutefois d'un biais fonctionnaliste qui consiste à confondre effets et causes, d'une mauvaise compréhension de la fonction des discours de politique publique, et d'une familiarité insuffisante avec la sociologie des organisations. Les anthropologues du développement ainsi que les anthropologues et sociologues des organisations ont montré que les agences de développement, comme n'importe quelle autre organisation, ne sont coordonnées, au mieux, que de manière très lâche et qu'elles sont loin d'être simplement gouvernées d'en haut

[15] Une critique de la philosophie du pouvoir de Foucault concerne le fait qu'elle dénie la possibilité de tout lieu alternatif de pouvoir et de résistance, voir Honneth (1986).

(Quarles van Ufford et al. 1988), et que la fonction du discours politique est moins de réguler les pratiques que de les justifier pour des publics particuliers, et ce souvent *ex-post* (Mosse 2004)[16]. J'ajouterais à cela le fait que les agences de développement, qui sont des organisations tournées vers la mobilisation des moyens (*input-oriented*) plus que vers les résultats (*output-oriented*), se caractérisent par un degré particulièrement élevé de « tolérance répressive », expression empruntée à Herbert Marcuse (1969) : elles révèlent une forte capacité à intégrer les critiques (et leurs auteurs) dans leur discours politique sans pour autant changer leurs pratiques. La logique d'empilement qui imprègne les *policy papers* est un autre exemple de cette tolérance répressive : dans les trois rapports majeurs sur l'Afrique produits par la Banque mondiale depuis le début des années 1980, les paradigmes structurants et les notions clefs ne se substituent pas les uns aux autres, mais s'empilent les uns sur les autres, de sorte que ce que nous trouvons dans le rapport de 1989 (World Bank 1989) n'est pas une alternative à l'ajustement structurel qui est proposé dans le rapport Berg quelques années auparavant (World Bank 1982), mais « ajustement structurel » plus « gouvernance », tandis que dans le rapport de 2001 (Gelb 2000), nous trouvons « ajustement structurel » plus « gouvernance » plus « participation » plus « réduction de la pauvreté » (Tepe 2006). En d'autres termes, même si nous concédons que les approches des grandes (et petites) agences de développement international procèdent d'une logique visant à faire des enjeux politiques des questions techniques, cela ne signifie pas qu'elles y parviennent. En effet, l'un des arguments les plus convaincants du débat sur le développement en Afrique est que, quelles qu'aient été les approches choisies par les agences de développement, les élites africaines sont toujours parvenues à les politiser à leur propre avantage (van de Walle 2001). Il semble par conséquent tout à fait plausible d'avancer que les politiques et approches sectorielles actuelles du développement sont l'objet des même stratégies locales de détournement, de démembrement et d'appropriation sélective que

[16] Une perspective similaire, largement inspirée de Luhmann (1981) est adoptée par Stefanie Hanke (1996) dans sa courte mais excellente étude de la Banque mondiale.

celles mises en lumière, il y a longtemps déjà, par les anthropologues du développement, pour des approches-projets plus classiques du développement (Bierschenk 1988 ; Bierschenk & Elwert 1988 ; Lentz 1988 ; Olivier de Sardan 1988).

3. Troisièmement, la théorie de la néo-dépendance n'a pas été capable de formuler une alternative réaliste aux pratiques critiquées. De temps à autre, nous trouvons une idéalisation des mouvements sociaux ou une vague allusion au « post-développement » (Rahnema & Bawtree 1997), mais il est principalement conseillé de rester à l'écart – une position évidemment plus facile à tenir pour un anthropologue qui dispose d'une chaire de titulaire à l'université que pour ses étudiants, dont un grand nombre travaillera dans le champ du développement.

Ceci étant dit, je ne pense pas qu'il faille jeter le bébé avec l'eau du bain ou traiter de la théorie de la néo-dépendance sur le mode du « n'y-touchez-pas » qu'elle-même applique au développement. Les contributions de la théorie de la néo-dépendance ne sont pas négligeables et il faut les traiter comme des défis pour l'anthropologie empirique du développement dont l'APAD s'est faite l'avocate. À cet égard, cinq points sont à relever :

- Tout d'abord, la théorie de la néo-dépendance ne souffre pas du biais culturaliste que l'anthropologie du développement a longtemps combattu. Elle insiste au contraire sur la centralité du pouvoir dans le développement. L'anthropologie du développement empirique centrée sur les acteurs a parfois tendance à négliger le pouvoir en tant que dimension structurante primordiale de la relation de développement (*development encounter*) ; il faudrait en fait plutôt parler de « situation de développement », par analogie avec la notion de « situation coloniale » forgée par Balandier (1951) qui met l'accent sur le fort différentiel de pouvoir qui structure cette relation.
- Deuxièmement, si l'anthropologie de développement classique était selon toutes probabilités à son mieux dans la déconstruction des projets de développement (voir les contributions dans Bierschenk & Elwert 1988) et des interventions planifiées par projets (Long 1989), la théorie néo-dépendantiste a déplacé la focale vers des formes plus récentes d'intervention de

développement, à savoir les politiques de développement et les approches sectorielles.

- Troisièmement, l'approche néo-dépendantiste propose d'étudier les politiques de développement tant du côté de leur production (c'est-à-dire des organismes de développement) que du côté de leur point d'impact et des « bénéficiaires » – même si comme nous allons le voir, les ethnographies des organismes de développement restent très rares à ce jour.
- Quatrièmement, la théorie de la néo-dépendance nous incite à repenser les effets combinés des interventions de développement, effets qui vont au-delà de ceux qu'impliquent une politique ou un projet individuel, et qui sont par conséquent « hors-champ » pour une approche empirique qui tend à se focaliser sur un projet particulier. La dépolitisation et la traduction techniciste ont été identifiées comme deux effets potentiels combinés générés par la somme de nombreuses interventions de développement individuelles ; « l'amnésie structurelle » pourrait en être un troisième (Bierschenk & Elwert 1991 ; Bierschenk, Elwert & Kohnert 1993 ; Chauveau 1994).
- Enfin, la néo-dépendance indique la bonne direction lorsqu'elle tente de relier le « développement » à d'autres pratiques de « production du monde », et dans sa volonté de mettre en relation données empiriques relatives à des micro-événements – pour laquelle une anthropologie du développement centrée sur les acteurs est particulièrement bien équipée – avec des processus de plus grande envergure – qui sont plus difficiles à saisir avec l'outillage méthodologique classique de l'anthropologie. Une grande partie de l'anthropologie du développement, celle, plus ancienne, centrée sur les projets, n'a pas réussi à enchâsser ses micro-histoires dans des récits plus larges et à faire le lien entre analyse locale et tendances globales.

Je pense que nous devrions prendre ces défis très au sérieux, mais aussi donner un tour plus empirique aux ambitions théoriques néo-dépendantistes. L'APAD n'est pas seule bien entendu dans ce champ, et nombreux sont ceux qui, ailleurs, sont occupés à produire ce que j'appellerais une nouvelle anthropologie du développement. Si l'on revient à l'une de mes typologies initiales distinguant les approches centrées sur les acteurs, les institutions et les discours, il apparaît que cette anthropologie du développement d'un nouveau genre revêt essentiellement deux formes :

- Il existe des auteurs qui se revendiquent d'une approche discursive. À y regarder de plus près, on tombe souvent sur une simple analyse de documents, et cette approche souffre des faiblesses déjà énumérées : le discours est confondu avec la pratique et les effets annoncés avec la réalité. Dans ce type d'analyse, la « machine développementiste » est une boîte noire, puisque nous n'apprenons pas comment et par qui le discours est produit, et encore moins comment il est reçu et peut-être déconstruit. En fait, ce type d'analyse essentialiste du discours s'apparente dans la plupart des cas à un retour à une anthropologie en chambre[17].
- Par contraste, certains des meilleurs travaux empiriques ont été consacrés aux nouvelles politiques de développement (même s'ils présentent une tendance à taire les voix locales). Dans une étude récente et fascinante, Tania Murray Li (2006, 2007) retrace par exemple l'émergence des stratégies néolibérales de la Banque mondiale en Indonésie, et montre comment ces politiques ont été mises en œuvre, non par la force mais par des tentatives de « réformer le sujet » avec l'aide de centaines d'anthropologues locaux. Dans son étude d'un projet sur l'eau de la Banque de développement allemande (KfW), Rottenburg dissèque le discours « doublement contraint » du développement (Rottenburg 2002) : transcrire des différentiels de pouvoir structurels dans une rhétorique de partenariat et nier le caractère politique de l'aide, une double contrainte qui concerne sur le mode collusoire tous les acteurs impliqués.

Ces études et d'autres, également récentes, sont des réussites majeures de l'anthropologie du développement, en partie basée sur des terrains non-

[17] L'étude d'Anders (2005) par exemple, malgré son titre prometteur, ne contient pas un seul élément d'information basé sur un travail de terrain ; elle aurait pu être entièrement effectuée à partir d'un bureau quelconque, à des lieues du Malawi.

africains. Il est par ailleurs surprenant de constater combien les ethnographies institutionnelles et professionnelles sont restées rares dans le champ du développement, en dépit de prétentions contraires (Watts 2001). Il existe certes quelques intéressantes analyses internes de la Banque mondiale, dont la plupart sont produites par des membres du personnel, partis du fait de désaccords politiques (voir par exemple, les rapports fascinants de Wade 1996, 1997, 2001, 2002) ; on n'a que quelques ethnographies très partielles de la Banque mondiale réalisées par des anthropologues professionnels, mais elles tendent plus vers l'ethnographie des politiques publiques plutôt que vers celle de l'institution en tant que telle (Fox 2000 ; Goldman 2001 ; Griffiths 2003). Et concernant les autres agences multi- et bilatérales, même ces ethnographies partielles semblent absentes. Nous disposons néanmoins de quelques ethnographies de professionnels du développement (Spies 2003, 2006).

Pour conclure, quelles leçons pouvons-nous tirer de ce rapide aperçu de la littérature ? Je perçois deux champs d'investigation pour l'anthropologie du développement à vocation empirique de l'APAD : l'étude empirique des États et des bureaucraties des pays du Sud et l'ethnographie des organismes de développement.*

1. *États et bureaucraties des pays du Sud :* de récents articles et les colloques de l'APAD – dont le présent – indiquent que l'anthropologie du développement apadienne classique, centrée sur les projets, est en rapide mutation vers une anthropologie de la délivrance des services publics, des politiques publiques (qui dans la « situation de développement » sont habituellement coproduites par l'État et des acteurs étrangers), des bureaucraties publiques et de l'État, au niveau tant national que local (Blundo 2001, 2006 ; Blundo et al. 2006 ; Le Meur 2006 ; Olivier de Sardan 2004a, 2005b)[18]. Dans le même temps, cette anthropologie du développement d'un nouveau genre se différencie progressivement en sous-domaines : anthropologie de la santé (Jaffré & Olivier de Sardan 2003), de l'éducation (Bierschenk 2007b ; Hartmann 2007), du droit (moderne) et du

[18] Pour un exemple antérieur mexicain, voir Arce (1993), pour un cas indonésien, voir Li (1999).

système judiciaire (Bierschenk 2004 ; Tidjani Alou 2001, 2006)[19].

2. *Ethnographies des organismes et des agents de développement* : ce qui fait résolument défaut, et dont le besoin est peut-être le plus pressant, ce sont des ethnographies des organismes de développement. Une question importante et non résolue ici est celle de l'accès, un problème moins aigu si l'objet n'est pas tant l'institution que ses agents. De telles ethnographies aideraient à faire de l'anthropologie du développement un élément constitutif de l'anthropologie de la globalisation : considérer le Développement avec un « D » majuscule comme l'un des nombreux projets de globalisation, comme un ensemble de « pratiques de production du monde »[20] peut être une manière d'enchâsser les récits localisés des anthropologues du développement dans des dynamiques englobantes.

À cette fin, nous avons urgemment besoin d'une posture comparative plus explicite. L'anthropologie apadienne du développement doit regarder plus attentivement « sur sa droite et sur sa gauche » : elle doit tenter plus activement de s'approprier les enseignements des études menées en Inde, en Amérique latine, en Asie du Sud-est, etc. Ma dernière expérience d'enseignement m'a appris combien il était dénué de sens de donner un cours d'anthropologie du développement exclusivement ciblé sur l'Afrique. Comme nous l'avons vu, certains des meilleurs travaux en anthropologie du développement ont été réalisés sur la base de cas non-africains, et il est bien sûr primordial de tenir compte de ces travaux, d'autant plus si notre ambition est de mettre l'Afrique en perspective[21].

Je souhaite conclure sur quatre réflexions d'ordre général. La première concerne les effets combinés du développement, qui ne sont pas

[19] Les bureaucraties publiques d'Afrique font l'objet d'un programme de recherche en cours (financé par la Fondation Volkswagen) sous le titre « Le travail de l'État : services publics et fonctionnaires au Bénin, au Ghana, au Mali et au Niger », et dans lequel plusieurs chercheurs de l'APAD sont actuellement impliqués.

[20] Richard Rottenburg, communication personnelle.

[21] Nous pourrions aussi ajouter le desideratum suivant : que les Apadiens publient davantage en anglais…

immédiatement déductibles de l'observation des pratiques locales. Même les projets de développement individuels réussis et des politiques publiques particulières peuvent avoir des conséquences inattendues moins positives à un niveau plus global : la dépendance institutionnalisée vis-à-vis de l'aide dans de nombreux pays d'Afrique, la généralisation et l'institutionnalisation, favorisées par l'entreprise de développement, d'un double discours de la part des élites africaines et d'un « État rusé » (Randeria 2004), la fragmentation de politiques nationales cohérentes via la création d'enclaves néolibérales comme résultat d'interventions de développement de longue durée, la création d'un système d'irresponsabilité généralisée à travers le Développement, etc. L'anthropologie du développement, quelle que soit la pertinence de son approche locale, doit être au fait des défis colossaux du développement auxquels l'Afrique est confrontée et de l'échec du Développement (avec un D majuscule) à générer du développement. Il ne s'agit pas simplement du fait que cinquante années de développement n'ont pas su relever ces défis : il se pourrait que le Développement et ses conséquences inattendues fassent eux-mêmes partie du problème (Collier & Gunning 1999 ; Ricupero 2001).

En second lieu, nous devons réfléchir à la signification du « tournant participatif » du développement alors que même la Banque mondiale emploie aujourd'hui des centaines d'anthropologues dans un projet « néolibéral » (Li 2006). Une première conclusion à tirer de cela est que l'anthropologie du développement se doit de devenir plus réflexive. Cette proposition ne doit pas être exclusivement comprise dans le sens épistémologique que les postmodernes avec leur intérêt pour le pouvoir de représentation, lui ont, à juste titre, donné. Cette proposition peut être interprétée dans un sens très pratique : ce dont nous avons besoin, ce sont des ethnographies des rôles, pratiques et fonctions des anthropologues du développement.

Troisième point, l'anthropologie du développement reprend une antienne avec laquelle les sciences sociales bataillent depuis les origines : comment combiner analyse sociale, pratique politique et responsabilité morale. L'anthropologie du développement ne peut rester en dehors de la question des valeurs morales et politiques, au nom de la rigueur méthodologique – elle doit la traiter –, ce que nos étudiants nous rappellent constamment, au cas où nous l'oublierions. Aborder la question des valeurs ne conduit pas nécessairement à la position néo-dépendantiste du « n'y-touchez-pas » (par exemple, le Développement) pour des raisons morales. Une telle position néglige le fait fondamental qu'il n'existe aucune différence de principe entre les problèmes éthiques de l'engagement pratique et de la représentation ethnographique. Interroger pour une question de principe l'éthique d'intervention de l'anthropologue du développement, comme les théoriciens de la néo-dépendance le font, c'est questionner l'entreprise ethnographique en tant que telle. Cette position est bien sûr légitime, mais elle met l'anthropologue devant un dilemme évident. Selon moi, il n'existe pas de solutions théoriques *a priori* à ce dilemme ; il n'y a que des manières pratiques et *ad hoc* de les traiter. Dans la mesure où les anthropologues du développement ne sont pas seulement des chercheurs mais aussi des enseignants, un autre élément entre en ligne de compte : celui de la responsabilité envers nos étudiants. La plupart ne demeureront pas dans le monde universitaire et devenir activiste à plein-temps d'Attac ne constitue pas non plus l'option la plus probable pour eux. Par conséquent, une posture de type « n'y-touchez-pas » vis-à-vis du développement, typique de certains courants d'une anthropologie autoproclamée « critique », est aussi irresponsable que l'enseignement non réflexif des techniques d'intervention que proposent certains programmes en « études de développement ». Comme pour d'autres champs de la pratique, c'est l'engagement critique envers le développement et la recherche de la distance optimale par rapport à ses pratiques qui me semblent être le chemin à suivre – un chemin difficile mais qui s'avère le plus ajusté aux objectifs de la recherche et de l'enseignement universitaires.

Enfin, qu'en est-il de la revendication initiale des premières années de l'APAD, selon laquelle anthropologie et développement peuvent s'enrichir mutuellement ?[22] Quel est le bilan de cette double ambition aujourd'hui ? Sa première partie est très claire : la bataille de la reconnaissance par les praticiens du développement du bien-fondé de l'anthropologie a largement été remportée. Tous s'entendent largement à l'heure actuelle sur la nécessité de fonder les projets et les politiques de développement sur des connaissances détaillées des dynamiques sociales dans lesquelles s'ancrent

[22] Cette dernière section du texte ne figurait pas dans le texte initial de la conférence, elle inclut certains éléments du débat qui a suivi l'exposé.

les interventions de développement ; et souvent, pour les pays du Sud, seule l'anthropologie peut fournir ce type de connaissances. Et depuis le tournant participatif du développement, il est généralement reconnu que projets et interventions doivent se baser sur une approche « participative » qui en retour favorise l'implication des anthropologues.

Le second objectif a-t-il été atteint ? C'est moins net. En quoi l'anthropologie du développement contribue-t-elle à l'anthropologie générale ? Leur intérêt pour le monde moderne a éloigné, il y a une cinquantaine d'années, les différentes variantes de l'anthropologie pratique du courant central de l'anthropologie. Cette tendance est révolue, à une heure où bien peu d'anthropologues continuent de soutenir que la discipline devrait se limiter aux phénomènes sociaux « traditionnels », presque tous plaidant pour une « anthropologie de la (post)-modernité ». La contribution de l'anthropologie du développement – au moins dans sa version empirique – à l'anthropologie générale s'exprime principalement dans deux champs, selon moi. Il s'agit en premier lieu du champ méthodologique : les anthropologues du développement et « appliqués » travaillant pour des institutions autres qu'universitaires ont toujours eu à rendre compte de leurs méthodes – et ils se vivaient d'ailleurs comme responsables à cet égard –, bien plus que les anthropologues académiques ; ils ont par conséquent développé un arsenal bien plus articulé et réfléchi de méthodes quantitatives et qualitatives, associant à la classique observation participante des approches sociologiques et historiques ; ils se sont aussi montrés bien plus ouverts à l'interdisciplinarité que la plupart de leurs collègues universitaires (Bennett 1996). Il est révélateur que les perspectives historiques – i.e. différentes des spéculations historiques de la plupart des évolutionnistes et diffusionnistes – aient été les premières introduites en anthropologie dans le contexte appliqué de l'Institut Rhodes-Livingstone et de l'École de Manchester (Evens & Handelman 2006) qui ont également vu l'invention de l'analyse de réseau (Mitchell 1969), l'unique méthode quantitative jamais développée en anthropologie (Schweitzer 1988). L'anthropologie du développement n'a de fait jamais été prisonnière de la seule et unique approche de l'observation participante à la Malinowski – que des générations ultérieures d'anthropologues invoquent plutôt qu'ils ne la pratiquent. De façon paradoxale, ni cette ouverture méthodologique, ni l'engagement de l'anthropologie du développement envers ses disciplines voisines n'ont bénéficié à sa légitimité au sein de l'anthropologie générale (qui voit, de façon ironique, des collègues plus connus pour leurs contributions théoriques qu'empiriques ou méthodologiques à la discipline se présenter comme les plus fervents avocats de « l'observation participante »).

La seconde contribution de l'anthropologie du développement à l'anthropologie générale tient à son rappel implicite des réalités. Le développement n'est pas simplement un projet hégémonique imposé au « Sud » par « l'Occident » (comme ça peut sembler le cas lorsque le « Sud » est observé de loin) ; il s'agit d'un métarécit auquel contribuent de nombreuses voix. Depuis les dernières phases de la colonisation (en particulier en Afrique), c'est une idée qui mobilise une foule d'acteurs, des paysans africains aux élites nationales, en passant par les agences internationales (Cooper & Packard 1997). Cette idée n'a pas perdu de sa capacité de mobilisation de nos jours et s'inscrit dans les constitutions nationales, ainsi que dans l'imaginaire populaire (pour un argument identique, voir (pour une argumentation similaire, voir Edelman & Haugerud 2004). Quel que soit le sujet de recherche des anthropologues débarquant sur leurs terrains africains, ils seront bien peu à ne pas tomber sur la centralité du « développement » (ou son absence) dans les discours locaux et les pratiques locales. En d'autres termes, les anthropologues qui dédaignent ou « critiquent » le développement, sans tenter d'en appréhender les significations locales, passent tout simplement à côté d'un part essentielle des réalités. Cela vaut pour l'Afrique et au-delà.

Bibliographie

Abrahamsen, R. 2000. *Disciplining Democracy: Development discourse and good governance in Africa*. London: Zed.

Anders, G. 2005. Good governance as technology: Toward an ethnography of the Bretton Woods Institutions. In *The Aid Effect: Giving and Governing in International Development* (eds) D. Lewis & D. Mosse. London: Pluto Press.

Anderson, L. 2003. The global reach of American social science. *Chronicle of Higher Education* (26.9.2003), B7-B9.

Appadurai, A. 2007. The anthropology of the future. Public lecture, New School for Social Research, 17 October 2007.

Arce, A. 1993. *Negotiating Agricultural Development: Entanglements of bureaucrats and rural producers in Western Mexico*. Wageningen Studies in Sociology. 34. Wageningen: Wageningen Agricultural University.

Asad, T. (ed.) 1973. *Anthropology and the Colonial Encounter*. London: Ithaca Press.

Barth, F., A. Gingrich, R. Parkin & S. Silverman. 2005. *One Discipline, Four Ways. British, German, French and American Anthropology*. Chicago, Ill.: Chicago University Press.

Bennett, J.W. 1996. Applied and action anthropology: Ideological and conceptual aspects. *Current Anthropology* 37 (1), 23-53.

Bierschenk, T. 1988. Development projects as arena of negotiation of strategic groups: A case study from Benin. *Sociologia Ruralis* 28 (2-3), 146-60.

—. 2004. Die Informalisierung und Privatisierung von Konfliktregelung in der Beniner Justiz. In *Anthropologie der Konflikte. Georg Elwerts konflikttheoretische Thesen in der Diskussion* (ed.) J. Eckert. Bielefeld.

—. 2007a. Enchevêtrement des logiques sociales. Jean-Pierre Olivier de Sardan en anthropologue du développement. In *Une anthropologie entr rigueur et engagement: Essais autour de l'œuvre de Jean-Pierre Olivier de Sardan*, éd. T. Bierschenk, G. Blundo, Y. Jaffré & M. Tidjani Alou. Paris: APAd-Karthala: 29-49.

—. 2007b. L'éducation de base en Afrique de l'Ouest francophone. Bien privé, bien public, bien global. In: *Une anthropologie entre rigueur et engagement. Essais autour de l'œuvre de Jean-Pierre Olivier de Sardan* (eds) T. Bierschenk, G. Blundo, Y. Jaffré & M. Tidjani Alou. Paris: APAD-Karthala.

Bierschenk, T. & G. Elwert (eds) 1988. "Aid and development". *Sociologia Ruralis* 28 (2-3). Assen: Van Borcum.

Bierschenk, T. & G. Elwert (eds) 1991. *Entwicklungshilfe und ihre Folgen: Ergebnisse empirischer Untersuchungen im ländlichen Afrika*. Frankfurt: Campus.

Bierschenk, T. G. Elwert & D. Kohnert 1993. The long-term effects of development aid: Empirical studies in rural West Africa. *Economics (Tübingen)* 47 (1), 83 - 111.

Blundo, Giorgio. 2001. Négocier l'État au quotidien: Intermédiaires, courtiers et rabatteurs dans les interstices de l'administration sénégalaise. *Autrepart* 20, 75-90.

—. 2006. Dealing with the local state: The informal privatization of street-level bureaucracies in Senegal. *Development and Change* 37 (4), 799-819.

Blundo, G., J.-P. Olivier de Sardan with N. Bako-Arifari & M. Tidjani Alou 2006. *Everyday Corruption and the State: Citizens and public officials in Africa*. London: Zed.

Cernea, M. 1995. Social Organization and Development Anthropology. The 1995 Malinowski award lecture. *Human Organization* 54 (3), 340-352.

Chauveau, J.-P. 1985. Mise en valeur coloniale et développement. In *Paysans, experts et chercheurs en Afrique noire: sciences sociales et développement rural* (eds) P. Boiral, J.-F. Lanteri & J.-P. Olivier de Sardan. Paris: CIFACE-Karthala.

—. 1994. Participation paysanne et populisme bureaucratique: Essai d'histoire et de sociologie de la culture du développement. In *Les associations paysannes en Afrique: organisation et dynamiques* (eds) J.-P. Jacob & P. Lavigne Delville. Paris: Karthala.

Collier, P. & J.W. Gunning 1999. Explaining African Economic Performance. *Journal of Economic Literature* 37 (1), 64-111.

Cooper, F. & R. Packard 1997. International development and the social sciences: Introduction. In *International Development and the Social Sciences. Essays on the history and politics of knowledge* (eds) F. Cooper & R. Packard. Berkeley, Ca.: University of California Press.

Delafosse, M. 1941. *Les Noirs de l'Afrique*. Paris: Payot.

Delavignette, R. 1931. *Les paysans noirs*. Paris: Stroek.

Dozon, J.-P. 1978. Logiques des développeurs/réalité des développés: Bilan d'une expérience rizicole en Côte d'Ivoire. *Mondes en Développement* 24.

Edelman, M. & A. Haugerud. 2004. Introduction: The anthropology of development and globalisation. In *The Anthropology of Development and Globalization: From Classical Political Economy to Contemporary Neoliberalism: A Reader* (eds) M. Edelman & A. Haugerud. London: Blackwell.

Escobar, A. 1995. *Encountering Development. The making and unmaking of the Third World*. Princeton, NJ: Princeton University Press.

Evans-Pritchard, E. E. 1946. Applied anthropology. *Africa* 16 (2), 92-98.

Evens, T.M.S. & D. Handelman. 2006. *The Manchester School: Practice and Ethnographic Praxis in Anthropology*. Oxford: Berghahn.

Ferguson, J. 1990. *The Anti-Politics Machine: 'Development', depoliticization and bureaucratic power in Lesotho*. Cambridge: Cambridge University Press.

Ferguson, J. 1997. The Anthropology and its Evil Twin: 'Development' in the Constitution of a Discipline. In *International Development and the Social Sciences: Essays on the History and Politics of Knowledge* (eds) F. Cooper & R. Packard. Berkeley: University of California Press.

Firth, R. 1981. Engagement and detachment: Reflections on applying social anthropology to social affairs (Malinowski Award Address). *Human Organization* 30 (3), 193-201.

Fox, J. 2000. The World Bank Inspection Panel. *Global Governance* 6 (3), 279-318.

Gardner, K. & D. Lewis 1996. *Anthropology, Development and the Post-modern Challenge*. London: Pluto Press.

Gelb, A.H. 2000. *Can Africa Claim the 21st Century?* Washington, DC: World Bank.

Gingrich, A. 2005. The German-speaking countries: Ruptures, schools and non-traditions: Reassessing the history of sociocultural anthropology in German. In *One Discipline, Four Ways: British, German, French and American anthropology* (eds) F. Barth, R. Parkin, A. Gingrich & S. Silverman. Chicago, Ill.: Chicago University Press.

Goldman, M. 2001. The Birth of a Discipline: Producing Authoritative Green Knowledge, World Bank-Style. *Ethnography* 2 (2), 191-217.

Gow, D.D. 1993. Doubly damned: Dealing with power and praxis in development anthropology. *Human Organization* 52 (4), 380-397.

Griaule, M. 1975. *Dieu d'eau. Entretiens avec Ogotemmêli.* Paris: Fayard.

Griffiths, P. 2003. *The Economist's Tale. A consultant encounters hunger and the World Bank.* New York: Zed.

Hartmann, S. 2007. The informal market of education in Egypt: Private tutoring and its implication. Contribution à AEGIS European Conference on African Studies, 11-14 July 2007, Leiden.

Hauschild, T. (ed.) 1995. *Lebenslust und Fremdenfurcht. Ethnologie im Dritten Reich, Suhrkamp-Taschenbuch Wissenschaft* 1189. Frankfurt/Main: Suhrkamp.

Herskovits, M.J. 1936. Applied Anthropology and the American Anthropologists. *Science, New Series* 83 (2149), 215-222.

Hobart, M. (ed.) 1993. *An Anthropological Critique of Development: The Growth of Ignorance*. London: Routledge.

Hoben, A. 1982. Anthropologists and development. *Annual Review of Anthropology* 11, 349-375.

Honneth, A. 1986. *Kritik der Macht. Reflexionsstufen einer kritischen Gesellschaftstheorie*. Frankfurt/Main: Suhrkamp.

Jaffré, Y. & J.-P. Olivier de Sardan (eds) 2003. *Une médecine inhospitalière : les difficiles relations entre soignants et soignés dans cinq capitales d'Afrique de l'Ouest*. Paris: Karthala.

Lavigne Delville, P. 2007. À la recherche du chaînon manquant: construire des articulations entre recherche en sciences sociales et pratique du développement. In *Une anthropologie entre rigueur et engagement: Essais autour de l'œuvre de Jean-Pierre Olivier de Sardan* (eds) T. Bierschenk, G. Blundo, Y. Jaffré & M. Tidjani Alou. Paris: Karthala.

Le Meur, P.-Y. 2006. State Making and the Politics of the Frontier in Central Benin. *Development and Change* 37 (4), 871-900.

—. 2007. Anthropologie et développement. Une relation à plaisanterie? In *Une anthropologie entre rigueur et engagement. Essais autour de l'œuvre de Jean-Pierre Olivier de Sardan* (eds) T. Bierschenk, G. Blundo, Y. Jaffré & M. Tidjani Alou. Paris: Karthala.

Leiris, M. 1999. *L'Afrique fantôme*. Paris: Gallimard.

Lentz, C. 1988. Why the most incompetent are on the Village Council: Development projects in an Indian Village in Ecuador. *Sociologia Ruralis* 28 (2-3), 199-215.

Lewis, D. & D. Mosse (eds) 2005. *The Aid Effect: Giving and Governing in International Development*. London: Pluto.

—. (eds) 2006. *Development Brokers and Translators: The ethnography of aid and agencies*. Bloomfield, Ct.: Kumarian.

Li, T.M. 1999. Compromising power: Development, culture and rule in Indonesia. *Cultural Anthropology* 14 (3), 295-322.

—. 2006. *Neo-Liberal Strategies of Government through Community: The social development program of the World Bank in Indonesia*. International Law and Justice Working Papers, Global Administrative Law Series 2006/2. New York: New York University School of Law.

—. 2007. *The Will to Improve: Governmentality, development, and the practice of politics*. Durham, NC: Duke University Press.

Long, N. 1977. *Introduction to the Sociology of Rural Development*. London: Tavistock Publications.

—. 2001. *Development Sociology: Actor perspectives*. London: Routledge.

—. (ed.) 1989. *Encounters at the Interface: A Perspective on Social Discontinuities in Rural Development*. Wageningen: Wageningen Agricultural University.

Long, N. & A. Long (eds) 1992. *Battlefields of Knowledge: The Interlocking of Theory and Practice in Social Research and Development*. London: Routledge.

Luhmann, N. 1981. Organisation und Entscheidung. In *Soziologische Aufklärung 3: Soziales Systems, Gesellschaft, Organisation* (ed.) N. Luhmann. Opladen: Westdeutscher Verlag.

Malinowski, B. 1929. Practical anthropology. *Africa* 2, 22-38.

—. 1984. *Argonauts of the Western Pacific*. Illinois: Waveland Press.

Marcuse, H. 1969. *Versuch über die Befreiung*. Frankfurt a. Main: Suhrkamp.

Mead, M. 1977. Applied anthropology: The state of the art. In *Perspectives on Anthropology* (ed.) A. F. C. Wallace. Washington, DC: American Anthropological Association.

Mitchell, J.C. (ed.) 1969. *Social Networks in Urban Situations: Analyses of Personal Relationships in Central African Towns*. Manchester: Manchester University Press.

Mosse, D. 2004. Is good policy unimplementable? Reflections on the ethnography of aid policy and practice. *Development and Change* 35 (4), 639-671.

Nolan, R.W. 2002. *Development Anthropology: Encounters in the Real World*. Boulder, Co.: Westview.

Olivier de Sardan, J.-P. 1983. Les paysans africains face au développement. In *Introductions à la coopération en Afrique noire* (eds) A. Bouillon & F. Devalière. Paris: Karthala.

—. 1985. Sciences sociales africanistes et faits de développement. In *Paysans, experts et chercheurs en Afrique noire: sciences sociales et développement rural* (ed.) P. Boiral, J.-F. Lanteri & J.-P. Olivier de Sardan. Paris: Karthala.

—. 1988. Peasant logics and development project logics. *Sociologia Ruralis* 28 (2-3), 216-226.

—. 1995. *Anthropologie et développement: Essai en socio-anthropologie du changement social*. Paris: Karthala.

—. 2001. Les trois approches en anthropologie du développement. *Revue Tiers Monde* 42 (168), 729-754.

—. 2004a. État, bureaucratie et gouvernance en Afrique de l'Ouest francophone: Un diagnostic empirique, une approche historique. *Politique africaine* (96), 139-162.

—. 2004b. Le chaînon manquant. *Le Courrier de la Planète* 74, 36-40.

—. 2005a. *Anthropology and Development: Understanding contemporary social change*. London: Zed.

—. 2005b. Classic ethnology and the socio-anthropology of public spaces in Africa. *Africa Spectrum* (3), 485-497.

Quarles van Ufford, P. 1993. Knowledge and ignorance in the practices of development policy. In *An anthropological critique of development: The growth of ignorance* (ed.) M. Hobart. London & New York: Routledge.
Quarles van Ufford, P., P. Dirk Kruyt & T. Downing (eds) 1988. *The Hidden Crisis in development: Development Bureaucracies.* Amsterdam: Free University Press.
Radcliff-Brown, A.R. 1980 [orig. 1930]. Applied anthropology. *Research in Economic Anthropology* 3, 123-134.
Rahnema, M. & V. Bawtree (eds) 1997. *The Post-Development Reader.* London: Zed.
Randeria, S. 2004. The State of globalization, legal plurality, overlapping sovereignties and ambiguous alliances between civil society and the cunning state in India. *Theory, Culture & Society* 24 (1), 1-33.
Ricupero, R, (ed.). 2001. African Economic Development in a Comparative Perspective. *Cambridge Journal of Economics* 25 (3), May 2001. London: Cambridge University Press.
Rottenburg, R. 2002. *Weit hergeholte Fakten: Eine Parabel der Entwicklungshilfe.* Stuttgart: Lucius & Lucius.
Schönhuth, M. & F. Bliss (eds) 2004. *Culture for Development-Cultures of Development: 20 Years of Development Anthropology in Germany/Kultur für Entwicklung-Kulturen der Entwicklung: 20 Jahre Entwicklungsethnologie in Deutschland, Entwicklungsethnologie. Jg. 13, Heft 1 & 2.* Saarbrücken: Breitenbach.
Schweitzer, T. (ed.) 1988. *Netzwerkanalyse.* Berlin: Dietrich Reimer Verlag.
Sibeud, E. 2002. *Une science impériale pour l'Afrique ? La construction des savoirs africanistes en France (1870-1930).* Paris: Editions de l'Ecole des Hautes Etudes en Sciences Sociales.
Silverman, S. 2005. The United States. In *One Discipline, Four Ways: British, German, French, and American Anthropology (Halle Lectures)* (eds) F. Barth, A. Gingrich, R. Parkin & S. Silverman. Chicago, Ill.: Chicago University Press.
Spies, E. 2003. Interkulturelle Kontakte im Rahmen der Entwicklungszusammenarbeit in Zinder (Niger). *Afrika Spectrum* 38 (3), 347-373.
—. 2006. Das Dogma partizipativer Entwicklung. Interkulturelle Kontakte im Kontext der Entwicklungszusammenarbeit in Zinder (Republik Niger). Dissertation, Institut für Ethnologie und Afrikastudien, Johannes Gutenberg-Universität, Mainz.
Spittler, G. 1994. Gibt es eine Entwicklungsethnologie? In *Völkerkunde-Tagung München 1991, Bd. 1* (eds) M.S. Laubscher & B. Turner. München.

Streck, Bernhard (ed.). 2000. *Ethnologie und Nationalsozialismus*. Gehren: Escher.

Tepe, I. 2006. Entwicklungsstrategien für Subsahara-Afrika von Strukturanpassung bis *good governance*: Eine kritische Auseinandersetzung mit Berichten der Weltbank. Magisterarbeit, Institut für Ethnologie und Afrikastudien, Johannes Gutenberg-Universität, Mainz.

Tidjani Alou, M. 2001. La justice au plus offrant: Les infortunes du système judiciaire en Afrique (autour du cas du Niger). *Politique Africaine* (83), 59-78.

—. 2006. Corruption in the legal system. In *Everyday corruption and the State: Citizens and public officials in Africa* (eds) G. Blundo & J.-P. Olivier de Sardan. London: Zed.

van de Walle, N. 2001. *African Economies and the Politics of Permanent Crisis, 1979 - 1999*. Cambridge: Cambridge University Press.

Wade, R. 1996. Japan, the World Bank, and the Art of Paradigm Maintenance: The East Asian Miracle in Political Perspective. *New Left Review* (217), 3-36.

—. 1997. Greening the Bank. In *The World Bank* (eds) R. Kanbur, J. Lewis & R. K. Webb. Washington, DC: Brookings.

—. 2001. Showdown at the World Bank. *New Left Review* 7 (January-February 2001).

Wade, R.H. 2002. US hegemony and the World Bank the fight over people and ideas. *Review of International Political Economy* 9 (2), 201-229.

Watts, M. 2001. Development ethnographies. *Ethnography* 2 (2), 283-300.

World Bank 1982. *Accelerated Development in Sub-Saharan Africa: An Agenda for Action*. Washington, DC: World Bank.

—. 1989. *Sub-Saharan Africa: From Crisis to Sustainable Growth*. Washington, DC: World Bank.

Annexes / Appendices

List of contributors / Liste des auteurs

Gunilla Andrae, Department of Human Geography at Stockholm University, Sweden
E-mail : Gunilla.Andrae@humangeo.su.se

Thomas Bierschenk, Department of Anthropology and African Studies at Johannes Gutenberg University in Mainz, Germany
E-mail : biersche@mail.uni-mainz.de

Sten Hagberg, Department of Cultural Anthropology and Ethnology at Uppsala University, Sweden
E-mail : Sten.Hagberg@antro.uu.se

Gabriella Körling, Department of Cultural Anthropology and Ethnology at Uppsala University, Sweden
E-mail : gabriella.korling@antro.uu.se

Abdoulaye Mohamadou, Faculté d'Agronomie, Université Abdou Moumouni de Niamey ; Laboratoire d'Etudes et de Recherche sur les Dynamiques Sociales et le Développement Local (LASDEL), Niamey, Niger
E-mail : azawagh@yahoo.fr

Lars Rudebeck, Centre for Sustainable Development at Uppsala University:
E-mail : Lars.Rudebeck@csd.uppsala.uu.se

Le Bureau de l'APAD par le 1.1.2008 / APAD Board as of 1 January 2008

Sten Hagberg	President	sten.hagberg@antro.uu.se
Mirjam de Bruijn	General Secretary	bruijnM@ascleiden.nl
Abdoulaye Mohamadou	Deputy General Secretary	azawagh@yahoo.fr
Mayke Kaag	Treasurer, APAD-Bulletin	kaag@ascleiden.nl
Jacky Bouju	Mise en ligne re-vues.org	bouju@mmsh.univ-aix.fr
Ann Cassiman	Public Relations, layout	Ann.Cassiman@soc.kuleuven.be
Laurence Boutinot		boutinot@cirad.fr
Marion Fresia		Marion.fresia@unine.ch
Mathieu Hilgers	APAD-Bulletin	mhilgers@ulb.ac.be
Félicien Kabamba		fellykabamba@yahoo.fr
Gabriella Körling	Website	gabriella.korling@antro.uu.se
Fatoumata Ouattara	Organisation APAD Ouaga 2010	fatou.ouattara@ird.bf
Mohamadou Sall		sallmoham@yahoo.fr
Maud Saint-Lary		msaintlary@yahoo.com
Josiane Tantchou		yakamjosiane@yahoo.fr

Adhérer à l'APAD – *Join the APAD*

Bulletin d'adhésion (ou de ré-adhésion) / *Registration form*

Cotisation annuelle / *Annual Subscription:*
www.association-apad.org

L'adhésion de l'APAD doit être payée au secrétariat général (adresse ci-dessous).

Fees should be paid annually directly to APAD's general secretariat (see address below).

Salariés avec un salaire mensuel plus de 800 € 39 € (ou 25 000 FCFA)
Salariés avec un salaire mensuel moins de 800 € 19 € (ou 12 000 FCFA)
For those earning more than €800/month € 39 (or FCFA 25 000)
For those earning less than €800/month € 19 (or FCFA 12 000)

Règlement / Payment
Prière de ne pas payer par chèque, mais seulement par virement bancaire. Numéro de compte en banque : 48 29 57 352 sous le nom de Afrika-Studiecentrum (APAD), B.P. 9555, 2300 RB Leiden, Pays-Bas, code BIC : ABNANL2A, code IBAN : NL97ABNA0482957352.

By bank transfer only please. Bank account no. 48 29 57 352 in the name of African Studies Centre (APAD), P.O. Box 9555, 2300 RB Leiden, The Netherlands, code BIC : ABNANL2A,
code IBAN : NL97ABNA0482957352. Specify year.

Nom / *Surname*..
Prénom / *First name*...
Institutes de rattachement / *Organization*...
Fonction / *Position*..
Adresse professionelle / *Work Address*...
Tel. ....
E-mail..
Expertise geographiques et thematiques / *Geographic and thematic expertise*
....

Sommaire des numéros précédents

BULLETIN N°1 - JUIN 1991 - épuisé

La préhistoire de l'APAD, par J.-P. Olivier de Sardan - Pourquoi l'APAD? - L'anthropologie du changement social et du développement comme ambition théorique?, par J.-P. Olivier de Sardan. -Les projets et les politiques de développement sont-ils des préoccupations légitimes de l'anthropologie?, par Th. Bierschenk. -Le dilemme connaissance/action: le développement comme champ politique, par J.-P. Dozon. - Administrateurs, développeurs et ethnologues en France: une mise en perspective historique, par J.-L. Amselle. -Existe-t-il des demandes nouvelles émanant du secteur du développement à l'adresse des sciences anthropologiques?, par J.-P. Chauveau. - Qu'attendent les bailleurs de fonds des anthropologues? par C. Freud... et les rubriques: Vie de l'APAD (rapport des groupes de travail, programme des actions prioritaires de l'APAD pour 1991-1992), Euro-Afrique (Anthropologie et Développement dans quelques pays d'Europe et d'Afrique: Burkina Faso, Sénégal, Belgique, Allemagne), Agenda, Lu et à lire, Point de vue (La question du "statut du chercheur africain" comme discours stratégique, par L-M. Sehoueto?

BULLETIN N°2 - DÉCEMBRE 1991 - épuisé

Réseau et langue de bois, par J.-P. Olivier de Sardan -Les Sciences et Techniques appliquées au Développement et l'Anthropologie, par J. Schmitz -L'expertise internationale en Afrique: le cas de l'expertise juridique sur les questions foncières, par E. Le Roy -Le projet APAD et le projet du peuple, par M. Singleton... et les rubriques: Vie de l'APAD, Journées de l'APAD (22-23-24 octobre 1992) Programme général. - Initiatives locales: Réunions APAD à Bamako, Abidjan et Dakar -Groupes de travail: Anthropologie et sciences appliquées au développement -Euro-Afrique Anthropologie et Développement dans quelques pays d'Europe et d'Afrique: Mali (F. Koné), Burkina Faso (Y. Jaffré), Pays-Bas (G. Diemer) -Agenda, Lu et à lire, Point de vue (Le développement un et indivisible? en (re)lisant Latouche, par M. Singleton).

BULLETIN N°3 - OCTOBRE 1992 - épuisé

L'APAD au milieu du gué, par J.-P. Chauveau -Light, Rapid Rural Appraisal: des méthodes brillantes et légères, par A.S. Fall et A. Lericollais -Quelques réflexions sur la multiplicité des intervenants externes et la multiplication des organisations paysannes au Burkina Faso, par J.-P. Jacob -Le "modèle participatif" de développement rural est-il alternatif? par J.-P. Chauveau -Participation paysanne, discours et pratiques. Quelques réflexions sur le texte de J.-P. Chauveau, par Ph. Lavigne Delville -Les organisations paysannes: émergence et devenir, par D. Thiéba... et les rubriques: Vie de l'APAD, Journées de l'APAD (22-23-24 octobre 1992), Nouvelles des réseaux nationaux de l'APAD: Sénégal, Burundi, Bénin -Euro-Afrique: Requiem pour l'ISH ou la fin de l'approche pluridisciplinaire institutionnelle au Cameroun, par F. Tchala-Abina - Éducation pour la santé et pratiques sociales, par Y. Jaffré -L'anthropologie et auto-promotion communautaire dans la région d'Itombwe, par Kaza Rutereza -Agenda - Bibliographie thématique: les organisations paysannes -Les "Apadiens ont publié..."- Courrier.

BULLETIN N°4 - DÉCEMBRE 1992 - épuisé
Où en est l'APAD? par J.-P. Olivier de Sardan -Journées de l'APAD, octobre 1992 "socio-anthropologie des organisations et associations paysannes": Du populisme bureaucratique dans l'histoire institutionnelle du développement rural en Afrique de l'Ouest, par J.-P. Chauveau -Le conflit dans l'"Entente". Coopération et compétition dans les associations paysannes de Koungheul (Sénégal), par G. Blundo -Les organisations populaires du Rwanda: leur émergence, leur nature et leur évolution, par J. Nzisabira -Les organisations rurales au coeur de la transformation des campagnes africaines?, par J.-C. Devèze -synthèses des groupes de travail: Capital culturel, innovation sociale et gestion de l'innovation technique animé par M. Singleton, par H. Pagezy -Microsociologie des organisations: légitimité, participation, leadership; discours développementiste et pratiques des organisations, animé par R. Mongbo, par Ph. Lavigne Delville -Interactions entre groupements et organismes d'appui: stratégies, négociations, confrontations, manipulations et alliances, animé par J.-P. Jacob -Désengagement de l'État et montée de la société civile, animé par J.-C. Devèze, par Y. Guillermou -Nouvelles des groupes de travail de l'APAD -Appel à la création du groupe thématique sur la santé et l'anthropologie de la santé, par Y. Jaffré -Nouvelles des réseaux nationaux de l'APAD - Le modèle de la coopération suisse, par A. Tonti -Lu et à lire - Point de vue - Annonces de publications -Le bêtisier -Courrier: Pour une sociologie du développement, par C. Girard.

BULLETIN N°5 - JUIN 1993 - épuisé
Éditorial, par J. Faye -Journées de l'APAD, octobre 1992 "socio-anthropologie des organisations et associations paysannes" (suite et fin): Interactions entre groupement et organisme d'appui: stratégies, négociations, confrontation, manipulation et alliances: cas du projet de développement du village de Madina Kouroulamini dans le cercle de Bougouni au Mali, Par Y. Touré -Le groupement villageois: un cadre de participation communautaire au développement ou un instrument de réalisation d'intérêts individuels et conflictuels, par R. Cocou Tossou -Journées de l'APAD 1994 (Bamako, Mali): Colloque sur le thème: "Les sciences sociales et l'expertise en développement" -Appel à contributions -Table ronde bailleurs de fonds-chercheurs-opérateurs de développement - Nouvelles des réseaux nationaux de l'APAD (Congo) -La conception du développement de la France coloniale en Afrique Noire: quelques réflexions à propos de l'APAD, par U. Schuerkens -Relations à distance des migrants et réseaux d'insertion à Dakar, par A.S. Fall -Les courtiers locaux du développement, par J.-P. Olivier de Sardan et Th. Bierschenk -Annonces -Point de vue -Courrier: L'APAD et les sciences économiques, par P.-Y. Le Meur -Enquête: Les activités d'expertise en sciences sociales auprès des membres de l'APAD -Questionnaire en vue de la réalisation d'un nouvel annuaire de l'APAD -Formulaire de pré-inscription au colloque de Bamako.

BULLETIN N°6 - DÉCEMBRE 1993 - épuisé
Éditorial, par M. Singleton -Le développement comme champ politique local, par J.-P. Olivier de Sardan -Un "mâle" nécessaire pour le programme de la Fédération Wend-Yam (Burkina Faso), par P.-J. Laurent -Quelques réflexions sur la recherche méthodologique liée aux opérations de développement, par P. Lefèvre -Colonisation, développement et sciences sociales: éléments pour une sociologie de la constitution du champ des "arts et sciences du développement" dans les sciences sociales francophones belges, par M.

Poncelet -Évaluation des enjeux sociaux lors de l'implantation d'une coopérative d'épargne et de crédit au Mali, par Cl. Rossi -Recherches qualitatives et quantitatives dans une thèse de démographie camerounaise, par S.D. Yana -Programme du Colloque "Les sciences sociales et l'expertise en développement" -Annonces -Lus pour vous -Courrier: Prémices à une anthropologie du développement, vu du côté du Sud et vécu au quotidien, par Th. Maï Manga Keita.

BULLETIN N°7 - JUILLET 1994 - épuisé

Les sciences sociales et l'expertise en développement

Éditorial, par G. Diemer et E. Crowley -Les sciences sociales et l'expertise en développement. Communications présentées aux 3èmes journées APAD à Bamako (14-17 février 1994) -Première partie -Du paradigme perdu au paradigme ... retrouvé ? Pour une sociologie du développement orientée vers les acteurs, par N. Long -ECRIS: Enquête Collective Rapide d'Identification des conflits et des groupes Stratégiques..., par J.-P. Olivier de Sardan & Th. Bierschenk -L'expertise en sciences sociales dans les projets d'aménagement hydro-agricoles, par I. Dia -Chercheur à la croisée des demandes, par C. Quiminal -Anthropologie et foresterie sociale: une exploration théorique, par H. van den Breemer, R. Bergh et M.J. Vermeij -Le marché de l'expertise et la place du socio-anthropologue: le chercheur en sciences sociales en Afrique, par M. -Akam -L'expertise socio-anthropologique et la coopération technique, par R. Foster -Vie de l'APAD: Appel à communications du réseau "Cultures et identités culturelles" -P. Titi Nwel et M. Singleton -Compte-rendu du séminaire "Politique économique? Vous avez dit politique économique?" -N. Bako-Arifari, K. Fghoul, N. Perrot -Euro-Afrique: Que se passe-t-il en Allemagne? Le groupe de travail sur l'anthropologie du développement, par B. Kannen -Ateliers, colloques, appels d'offre -Revues et réseaux -Annonces -Lu et à lire -Compte-rendu de lectures.

BULLETIN N°8 - DÉCEMBRE 1994 - épuisé

Les sciences sociales et l'expertise en développement (deuxième partie)

Éditorial, par A.S. Fall et D. Koné -Les sciences sociales et l'expertise en développement. Communications présentées au colloque -Deuxième partie Bamako (Mali), 14-17 février 1994 -Faut-il des professionnels de l'expertise distincts des chercheurs? par Jean N. Engono - Le développement comme arène: implications pour l'évaluation des projets, par P. Lefèvre et P. Kolsteren -L'expertise à l'oeuvre: le cas de la coopération européenne en Bolivie, par A. Le Naëlou -Recherche sociale, solidarité et rapports de genre: réflexion à propos d'une étude sur les migrantes seerer à Dakar, par P. Simard, Y. Pelchat, K. Tall Thiam -Appliquer l'anthropologie au domaine de la santé. Entre recherche et expertise, par M-É. Gruénais -Socio-anthropologie d'une expertise: cas d'une évaluation externe d'un projet au Niger, par M. Sani Sanda -Local management of common property. Theory and practice of the common pastures in Marocco, par B. Venema -L'anthropologie, la recherche et l'intervention sur le Sida: enjeux méthodologiques d'une rencontre, par L. Vidal -Le diagnostic institutionnel et la méthodologie du développement institutionnel: l'expérience du projet d'appui aux ONG/USAID au Sénégal, par A. Paye Guèye et M. Dieng -Vie de l'APAD; Nouvelles des groupes de travail -Euro-Afrique; Au forum des ONG, les femmes se mobilisent pour l'égalité, le développement et la paix, par

C. Cécilia -Annonces -Lu et à lire -Thèses; Résumés des thèses soutenues en anthropologie du développement.

BULLETIN N°9 - JUILLET 1995 - épuisé
Éditorial, par J.-P. Olivier de Sardan -Appel à contribution aux journées de l'APAD (Stuttgart 1996) -Competition over juridictions and political manoeuvers in Niger, par C. Lund -Pratiques de la médiation dans le secteur informel à Dakar, par A.S. Fall & A. Mboup -Pour la construction d'un champ du développement rural, par D. Pesche -Petite histoire d'un grand mariage entre le néolibéralisme et le culturalisme, par P. Labazée -Ex-père, expertise toi-même, par M. Singleton -Anthropologie parallèles: description d'une procédure d'Enquête Anthropologique Rapide, par J. Bouju -Vie de l'APAD; APAD Niger, APAD Bénin; APAD Côte d'Ivoire, APAD Congo, APAD Sénégal -Annonces -Lu et à lire- Thèses - Courrier.

BULLETIN N°10 - DÉCEMBRE 1995 - épuisé
Éditorial, par G. Lachenmann - Appel à contribution aux journées APAD (Stuttgart 1996) -Boundaries, cohesion and seitching. On we-groups in ethnic national and religious forms, par G. Elwert -Les Peuls, les Sénoufo et l'État au nord de la Côte d'Ivoire. Problèmes fonciers et gestion du pastoralisme, par Y. Diallo -Développement local, stabilité politique et décentralisation. L'exemple du Burkina Faso, par P.-J. Laurent -La recherche en sciences sociales au Dahomey et au Bénin: l'hégémonie du paradigme développementiste, par Th. Bierschenk et R. Mongbo -Les sciences sociales sont-elles utiles pour un projet de recherche-développement? Un opérateur de développement (le projet piscicole du Centre-Ouest, Côte d'Ivoire) face aux diagnostics accessibles, par M. Oswald et F. Sanchez -Rapport sur le forum des ONG à Huairou du 30 août au 8 août 1995 -à l'occasion de la Conférence Mondiale sur les femmes à Pékin, par G. Lachenmann -Vie de l'APAD; APAD Cameroun, APAD Côte d'Ivoire, APAD Mali, APAD Niger -Annonces; Cours en sociologie de développement et en anthropologie sociale -Lu et à Lire -Thèses.

BULLETIN N°11 - MAI 1996 - 8 € (adhérents) 13 € (non adhérents).
Le développement négocié : courtiers, savoirs, technologies
Éditorial, par Ph. Lavigne Delville -Colloque International de l'APAD (Stuttgart Juin 1996); Objectifs et programme du colloque -Thème 1: La négociation des dispositifs techniques: Agrarian technologies as socio-technical hybrids. Food crop improvement and management of land and water in sub-Saharan Africa par P. Richards & G. Diemer -How should the bunds be built?. Negotiating technologies for soil and water conservation in semi-arid South India par B. Adolph -The genus Oryza: sources and uses of genetic variability by S. & L. farmers in Sierra Leone par M. S. Jusu -Thème 2: Les courtiers locaux du développement: Des courtiers ruraux pour le développement au Bénin par R.L. Mongbo -The role of local brokers in the development system. Experiences with "self-help projects" in East Africa par D. Neubert -Seu Néné, leader paysan à Massaroca (Bahia, Brésil): une trajectoire nordestine par E. Sabourin, J.-Ph. Tonneau & P. Caron -Leaders paysans et autorités religieuses comme courtiers du développement en milieu rural sénégalais par M. Salzbrunn -Mélanges: Per-diem et topping-up. Quelques enjeux de pouvoirs et stratégies dans un projet de santé au Mali, par T. Berche; Conférence

internationale de Pékin..., Ôtez-moi d'un doute! par M. Mathieu; L'élaboration de la politique de décentralisation au Mali: des logiques plurielles, par J. Félix -Vie de l'APAD; APAD Mali -Annonces -Lu et à Lire -Thèses.

BULLETIN N°12 - DECEMBRE 1996 - épuisé

Le développement négocié : courtiers, savoirs, technologies. ***Negociated Development: Brokers, Knowledge, Technologies***

Editorial, by Th. Bierschenk -Colloque International de l'APAD (Stuttgart Juin 1996) Le développement négocié: courtiers, savoirs, technologies »Les courtiers locaux du développement» (1ère partie). De la gloire à la déchéance: histoire d'un courtier local en Côte d'Ivoire, par M. Koné- Le développement négocié: cas de Codebriwak à Talamanca, Costa Rica, par M. Laforge- Trajectoires d'une reconversion du militantisme associatif au courtage en développement: le cas de Timidria au Niger, par M. Tidjani Alou- Beyond 'Negotiation', challenges of participatory projects for the anthropology of development, by J. Gould- The rural concillor as development agent: an uneasy connection: a report from Senegal, by B. Venema- Les courtiers locaux du développement: Synthèse, par P.-Y. Le Meur- Chronique scientifique, Colloques, Réseaux et Annonces- Lu et à Lire- Vie de l'APAD- Vers les Journées de l'APAD 1998 à Cotonou: Décentralisation, pouvoirs locaux et réseaux sociaux: 1ères réflexions sur le thème des Journées de l'APAD 1998- Développement local, stabilité politique et décentralisation: exemple du Burkina Faso, par P.-J. Laurent.

BULLETIN N°13 - MAI 1997 - épuisé

La négociation sociale des dispositifs techniques pour le développement. ***The social negotiations of technologies for development***

Editorial, by G. Diemer -Colloque International de l'APAD (Stuttgart Juin 1996) Le développement négocié: courtiers, savoirs, technologies "Technologies négociées" (2ème partie). Discours d'ouverture de la conférence de Stuttgart, par P. Hountoundji -Local knowledge and participatory technology development: Beekeeping in Ouélességougou, Mali, by A. Gnägi -Le plan d'aménagement de la lagune Aby-Tendo-Ehy, jeux et enjeux d'un développement négocié, par G. Kponhassia -Une production négociée de technologies de gestion de la fertilité des sols, une recherche-action au Bas-Bénin, par A. Floquet -Femmes rurales et innovations techniques: cas du projet Moulin au Mali, par B. Béridogo -An ethnography of the social and cultural content of new methods of public sector crop improvement research aimed at resource poor farming: cowpea for african farmers, by S. Squires -Du changement sous contrôle: les recompositions de la filière élevage en Nouvelle-Calédonie, par M. Djama -Agritechnology and anthropology: smallholder sprinkler systems in Zimbabwe, by G. Diemer -La fabrique sociale du poisson au sud du Mali, par B. Kassibo -Mélanges: Développement, connaissance, idéologie, par P.-Y. Le Meur -Soil, water, fisch and forest, by G. Diemer -Chronique scientifique, Colloques, Réseaux et Annonces -Lu et à Lire -Vie de l'APAD -Vers les Journées de l'APAD 1998 à Cotonou: Décentralisation, pouvoirs locaux et réseaux sociaux: Appel à contribution; Invitation sur ce thème à la rencontre de Louvain-la-Neuve du 20 au 22 novembre 1997; La décentralisation au Bénin: aperçu sur la réforme et les recherches, par N. Bako Arifari.

BULLETIN N°14 - DECEMBRE 1997 - épuisé

La décentralisation au Mali : état des lieux

Editorial "La décentralisation au Mali: Etat des lieux", par B. Kassibo -Processus de décentralisation au Mali et couches sociales marginalisées, par B. Béridogo -Des dynamiques villageoises au service d'une "démocratie décentralisée". Le cas de Mali-sud, par J. Coll -Les micro-communes: expression de logiques locales, par Y. F. Koné -La décentralisation face à l'ordre ancien, par S. Koné -Mélanges: À quoi servent les sciences sociales dans les projets de développement rural? Points de vue d'un "Agent double", par Ph. Lavigne Delville -Chronique scientifique, Colloques, Réseaux et Annonces -Lu et à Lire -Vie de l'APAD -Vers les Journées de l'APAD 1998 à Cotonou: Décentralisation, pouvoirs locaux et réseaux sociaux: Compte-rendu de la rencontre de Louvain-la-Neuve du 20 au 22 novembre 1997, sur le thème "Pouvoirs locaux et décentralisation", par P.-Y. Le Meur.

BULLETIN N°15 - MAI 1998 - épuisé

Les dimensions sociales et économiques du développement local et la décentralisation en Afrique au Sud du Sahara. ***Social and Economie Dimensions of Local Development and Decentralization in Sub-Saharan Africa***

Editorial "La décentralisation comme ambition multiple", par N. Bako-Arifari et P.-J. Laurent -"Les dimensions socio-économiques du développement local en Afrique au sud du Sahara: quelles stratégies pour quels acteurs?", par P.-J. Laurent et J.-P. Peemans -"Logiques de gestion publique dans la décentralisation sénégalaise: participation factionnelle et ubiquité réticulaire", par G. Blundo -"Décentralisation par le bas et participation clientéliste au Bénin", par P.-Y. Le Meur -"Chefs et projets au village (Niger)", par J.-P. Olivier de Sardan -"La décentralisation en Haïti", par V. Dorner -"La décentralisation et le destin des délégués de quartier à Dakar", par S. M. Tall -"L'enlisement des réformes de l'administration locale en milieu rural africain. La difficile négociation de la décision de décentraliser par les États et les intervenants externes", par J.-P. Jacob -Chronique scientifique, Colloques, Réseaux et Annonces -Lu et à Lire.

BULLETIN N°16 – DECEMBRE 1998 - 8 € (adhérents) 13 € (non adhérents).

Décentralisation, pouvoirs sociaux et réseaux sociaux. ***Decentralization, local-level politics, and social networks***

Editorial, par G.Blundo & R. Mongo –Programme Journées APAD Cotonou 25-28 novembre 1998 –"La face cachée de la décentralisation", par R. Lemarchand –"L'Etat est-il soluble dans la société civile?", par P-Y. Le Meur, T. Bierschenk & A. Floquet – "Décentralisation de la gestion foncière et "petits reçus"", par M. Koné & J-P. Chauveau –"Organisations professionnelles agricoles et décentralisation", par M. Bouy, J. Dasnière & F. Loua –"Pratiques et perceptions d'un appareil étatique en voie de décentralisation", par C. Anthoine –"Compétition des acteurs sociaux pour le contrôle du pouvoir et des ressources dans la commune rurale de Zégoua", par B. Béridogo –"Décentralisation et enjeux politiques", par Hassane Dramé –"Décentralisation, réseaux sociaux et privatisation de la violence", par D. de Lame –"Décentralisation et rapport global-local", par N: Bako-Arifari –"Décentralisation et pouvoirs locaux", par G. Blundo – "Décentralisation, services de développement agricoles ruraux et affaires sociales", par P-J. Laurent –"Décentralisation, migrations et identités", par R. Mongbo –"Quelques réflexions autour de la décentralisation comme objet de recherche", par J-P. O. de Sardan.

-Vie de L'APAD: Rapport moral, par T. Bierschenk – Rapport financier, par N: Bako.Arifari –Compte-rendu de l'assemblée générale, par P-Y. Le Meur -Vers les prochaines journées de l'APAD: Appel à contribution pour le séminaire de Dakar (janvier 2000).

BULLETIN N°17 – JUIN 1999 - épuisé

Anthropologie de la santé. ***Medical Anthropology***

Éditorial, Par Jean-Pierre Olivier de Sardan ; -Les services de santé "pour de vrai". Politiques sanitaires et interactions quotidiennes dans quelques centres de santé (Bamako, Dakar, Niamey), par Yannick Jaffré -Le sida en Afrique, un objet politique?, par Marc-Eric Gruénais, Karine Delaunay, Fred Eboko, Eric Gauvry; -Projets de santé et prévention en milieu dogon du Mali, par Sidiki Tinta -Pharmacies des villes, pharmacies"par terre", par Yannick Jaffré; -"L'accouchement c'est la guerre" - De quelques problèmes liés à l'accouchement en milieu rural nigérien, par Jean-Pierre Olivier de Sardan, Adamou Moumouni, Aboubacar Souley; -Aperçu sur un système de soins - Le cas de Mbandjock, par Nicolas Monteillet; -Décentralisation et développement local, par Jean-Pierre Olivier de Sardan; - Jean-Pierre Jacob: entre a priori et tentation autoritaire, par Dominique Gentil; -L'empirisme idéologique de Dominique Gentil, par Jean-Pierre Jacob; -Décentralisation et développement local. Espace public, légitimité et contrôle des ressources, par Pierre-Yves Le Meur; Chronique scientifique / Scientific diary - Lu et à lire / Reviews of publications; -vie de l'apad / apad in action -Corruption, gouvernance et développement en Afrique. Proposition pour la création d'un nouveau réseau au sein de l'APAD, par Michel Ahohounkpanzon -A socio-anthropology of corruption in Africa: comparative perspectives: Panel to be held at the 42nd meeting of the African Studies Association, Philadelphia, November 99, 11-14th. Call for paper by Thomas Bierschenk & Jean-Pierre Olivier de Sardan.

BULLETIN N°18 – DECEMBRE 1999 - 8 € (adhérents) 13 € (non adhérents).

Itinéraires de "déflatés" au Cameroun. ***Trajectories of Cameroonian Laid-off Civil Servants***

Éditorial Par Cornelius Bayie Kamanda - Cameroon : The retrenched Workers of te Civil Service and Parastatals. Assessing the Needs for the forms, par Cornelius Bayie Kamanda - "Les "déflatés" du développement. De la tradition de dépendance à l'autogestion, par Edjenguèlè Mbonji - Les déflatés de la fonction public au Cameroun : du rêve de la réussite sociale au désenchantement. Étude de cas sur l'itinéraire des "déflatés" du Minrest, par Jean Nzhie Engono - Rethinking the Role of Integrity at Public-Private Sector Interface : Coherence or Confusion. Mapping a New Vision for Africa at the Dawn of a New Millennium, par John W. Forje - Building a Vibrant State-Civil Society in Cameroon; Facing the Changes of the New Millennium, par John W. Forje – Chronique Scientifique / Scientific Diary – Lu et à Lire / Reviews of Publication – Vie de L'APAD / APAD in Action : Rapport moral, par Thomas Bierschenk; Rapport Financier, par Nassirou Bako Arifari; Compte rendu de l'Assemblée Générale, par Pierre-Yves Lemeur; Compte rendu du Bureau, par Giorgio Blundo.

BULLETIN N°19 – JUIN 2000 - 8 € (adhérents) 13 € (non adhérents).

Les intéractions rural-urbain : circulation et mobilisation des ressources. ***Rural-urban interactions : resources circulation and mobilisation***

Éditorial, par Abdou Salam Fall, Cheikh Guèye, Ibrahima Dia – Les interactions rurales – urbaines en Afrique de l'Ouest et Centrale, par Paul Pélissier – Transactions foncières marchandes dans l'ouest du Burkina Faso : vulnérabilité, conflits, sécurisation, insécurisation, par Mahamadou Zongo, Paul Mathieu – Le paradoxe Touba : une ville produite par des ruraux, par Cheikh Guèye – Manipulations foncières sur les zones dans les villes africaines, par Alphonse Yapi-Diahou – Circulation des biens et approvisionnement des villes, le raccourci par l'agriculture péri-urbaine et les rôles des femmes, par Cheikh Ba – Les commerçants et les transporteurs dans l'approvisionnement vivrier et la distribution à Douala, parHatcheu Emil Tchawe - Women and agro-processing in Africa : a case study of the state of women in fish smoking in the central region of Ghana, par E.L. Okorley, J.A. Kwarten – Dynamique des pouvoirs locaux liés à la gestion du Marché Central de Parakou, par Abou-Bakari Imourou – La personalisation de l'impersonnel. Réflexion autour du commerce de l'igname à Cotonou, Bénin, par Jean Adanguidi – Intégration horticulture – élevage dans les systèmes agricoles urbains de la zone des Niayes (Sénégal), par Safiétou Touré Fall, Abdou Salam Fall, Ibrahima Cissé, Aminata Badiane, Cheikh Alassane Fall, Maty Ba Diao.

BULLETIN N°20 – DECEMBRE 2000 - 8 € (adhérents) 13 € (non adhérents).
Genre et développement. ***Gender and development***
Etudes de genre et developpement, de l'archétype à la polynomie, par Danielle de Lame – Structure par genre de l'enchâssement trans-local de l'économie. Exemples d'Afrique de l'Ouest, par Gudrun Lacheman – Groupements de femme rurale au Sénégal. Espaces de liberté ou plates-formes pour le changement ? , par Joëlle Piraux – Le beurre et l'argent du beurre. Intérêt e tlimites du concept "genre« dans les études préalables aux projets de développement, par Laurence Boutinot – Gender and Power in the Use and Management of Coastal Space and Resources in Saasani Village, Tanzania, par Rosemarie R.N. Mwaipopo – Enduring passions : The fallacies of "gender-focused« development in Kenya, par Stella Nyacham-Okemwa- Genre et développement : bibliographie sélective, par Danielle de Lame – Chronique Scientifique/*Scientific diary* – Lu et à Lire/*Reviews of publications* – Vers les journées de l'APAD 2002/*Towards the APAD congress 2002 in Leiden*

BULLETIN N°21– JUIN 2001 - 8 € (adhérents) 13 € (non adhérents).
Un système de santé en mutation : le cas du Cameroun. ***Changing a Health System : the Cameroon case***
Editorial, par Marc-Eric Gruénais – Cameroun : de la réorientation des soins de santé primaires au plan national de développement sanitaire., par Raphaël Okalla, Alain Le Vigouroux – Décentralisation du système de santé publique et ressources humaines au Cameroun, par Jean-François Médard – L'organisation de la lutte contre le sida au Cameroun : de la verticalité à la dispersion, par Fred Eboko – La difficile mise en place des districts sanitaires urbains, par Eric Gauvrit, Raphaël Okalla – Le district de santé d'Akonolinga, par Raphaël Okalla – L'État à la conquête de son territoire national. L'exemple de la réforme du système de santé dans la province de l'extrême nord du Cameroun – par Marc-Eric Gruénais – La prise en charge de la santé par les associations du quartier de Biyem Assi (Yaoundé), par Séverin Cécile Abega, Noël Solange Ngo Yebga – Infirmiers privés, tradipraticiens, accoucheuses traditionnelles à la campagne et à la ville, par Eliwo Mandjale Akoto, Paulette Béat Songue, Samson Lamlenn, Jacques

Pokam Wadja Kemajou, Marc-Eric Gruénais - Chronique Scientifique/*Scientific diary* - Lu et à Lire/*Reviews of publications.*

BULLETIN N°22– DECEMBRE 2001 - 8 € (adhérents) 13 € (non adhérents).

Gouvernance foncière au quotidien en Afrique. ***Everyday governance of land in Africa***

Editorial, par Pierre-Yves Le Meur et Christian Lund – Contested boundaries : decentralisation and land conflicts in northwestern Ghana., par Carola Lentz – La gestion décentralisée des ressources forestières au Sénégal : transfert de compétences et transfert de pouvoir, par Laurence Boutinot – How to transfer an manage a public pesource, par Wiebe Nauta – Pouvoir local et coopération au développement à Ross-Betho : gestionsélective de l'offre de services fonciers et exclusion, par Aïssatou Faye – Nouvelles transactions et formalisation des transaction foncières dans l'ouest du Burkina Faso : le cas d'un village de la province du Houët, par Sita Zougouri, Paul Mathieu – Rules which pay are going to stay : Indigenous institutions, sustainable resource use and land tenure among the Oulddeme a Paltha, Mandara Montains, Northern Cameroon – par Tobias Haller - Chronique Scientifique/Scientific diary - Lu et à Lire/Reviews of publications.

BULLETIN N°23-24– JUIN 2002 - 8 € (adhérents) 13 € (non adhérents).

La gouvernance au quotidien en Afrique. Les services publics et collectifs et leurs usagers

Editorial, par Giorgio Blundo – Programme des journées l'APAD de Leiden (Pays-Bas) 22 et 25 mai 2002 – Les poissons ne peuvent pas voter un budget pour l'achat des hameçons. Espace public, corruption et constitution de l'Afrique comme objet scientifique, par Mamadou Diouf – Like chameleons. Civil servants and corruption in Malawi, par Gerhard Anders – La chefferie coutumière face au projet de décentralisation dans une localité de l'Ouest nigérien, par Eric Hahonou – Le service public de l'eau dans la Commune de Kanel : appropriation forcée et stratégies d'acteurs, par Amadou Amath Dia – Gouvernance quotidiennes au coeur des professionnels de santé (exemple pris à Orodara et à Banfora au Burkina Faso, par Fatoumata Ouattara – Aide humanitaire et production de services publics et collectifs en Afrique de l'Ouest : le cas de la gestion des populations mauritaniennes réfugiées au Sénégal, par Marion Frésia – Getting ot of the shit : toilets and the daily faillure of governance in Ghana, par Van der Sjaak Geest and Nelson Obirih-Opareh – Ateliers : "Urban Public Services" reporter Han Van Dijk – "santé" rapporteur Marc Eric Gruénais – "Décentralization and Local Politics" reporter Thomas Bierschenk – "Foncier et gestion des ressources naturelles" rapporteur Pierre Yves Le Meur – "Violence, Security and Justice" reporter Stephen Ellis – "Corruption et bureaucratie" rapporteur Giorgio Blundo – "Migrations et réfugiés" rapporteur Danielle de Lame – Vie de l'APAD : Rapport moral, par Abdou Salam Fall – Rapport financier, par Marilou Mathieu – Compte rendu de l'assemblée générale, par Giorgio Blundo – Compte rendu de la réunion du nouveau bureau, par Jacky Bouju – Vers les prochaines journées de l'APAD : Appel à contribution pour le Colloque de 2005 – Lu et à Lire/Reviews of publications.

BULLETIN N°25- JUIN 2003 - 8 € (adhérents) 13 € (non adhérents).

La Violence endémique en Afrique. ***Endemic violence in Africa***

Editorial, par Séverin Abéga - Pratique et productivité de la criminalité transfrontalière en Afrique centrale : l'exemple des Zargina, par Claude Abé - Violence et corruption : cas de l'Algérie, par Djilali Hadjadj - Devoir de soigner et droit d'exercer la violence : ethnographie des consultations de planification familiale à Niamey/Niger, par Hadiza Moussa - La production de la violence au fil des décisions dans quelques services publics de santé maternelle au Mali, par Aïssa Diarra - Violence et funérailles au Congo-Brazzaville, par Vincent Dississa - Roue libre : Mort d'un héros. Tensions politiques autour de l'enterrement de Bienvenu Roland Faigmond à Brazzaville, par Marc Eric Gruénais - An article that doesn't sway is not going to stay, par Jean-Pierre Jacob - Lu et à lire : à lire /Reviews of publications.

BULLETIN N°26- DECEMBRE 2003 - 8 € (adhérents) 13 € (non adhérents).

Gestion des ressources naturelles : Participations et méditations. ***Natural Ressources Management : Participation & Intermediation.***

Le double "je"des ONG environnementalistes d'Afrique centrale ; le cas de l'ANZAS au Congo-Brazzaville, par Henri Boukoulou – Gouvernance des aires protégées : l'importance des "normes pratiques" de régulation de la gestion locale pour la faisabilité des réformes dans le Bassin du Congo, par Jean-Claude Nguinguiri – Société civile et nouvelle gouvernance au Bénin. Quelques réflexions illustrées à partir de l'analyse du nouveau secteur ONG à Cotonou, par Gautier Pirotte et Marc Poncelet – La décentralisation de la gestion des ressources forestières au Sénégal ; un processus contraint par le marché?, par Laurence Boutinot – Exploring the context of service provision in Senegal : Social dynamics and decentralisation in the Senegalese countryside, par Mayke Kaag – Lu et à Lire/Reviews of publications – Compte rendu du Comité consultatif de déontologie et d'éthique, par Fatoumata Ouattara – Compte rendu de la recherche agronomique au Niger: pratiques et dynamiques, par Jean-Pierre Chauveau – Compte rendu des Violences ordinaires, par Sylvie Ayimpam – Appel à contribution pour un numéro spécial du Bulletin de l'APAD

BULLETIN N° 27/28- DECEMBRE 2005 - 10 € (adhérents) 15 € (non adhérents).

Violences Sociales & Exclusions: Le développement social de l'Afrique en question. ***Social violence & exclusion. Questioning Africa's social development.***

Editorial : Violences structurelles et violences systémiques. La violence ordinaire des rapports sociaux en Afrique, par Jacky Bouju & Mirjam de Bruijn – Les fils textuels des violences familiales au Mali, par Sébastien Le Potvin – Violence sociale, anomie et discordance normative. La trajectoire migrante des '52' de la région de Djenné (Mali), par Jacky Bouju – Violences sociales et exclusions réciproques en milieu urbain africain. Les grossesses hors mariage et ruptures du lien social au Burkina Faso, par Fatoumata Ouattara & Katerini Storeng – Surviving structural violence in Zimbabwe : The case study of a family coping with violence, par Otrude N. Moyo – La violence quotidienne des enfants de la rue : Bourreaux et victimes à Lubumbashi, par Olivier Kahola Tabu – La 'belle famille' et 'la famille élargie' : Acteurs des violences conjugales et domestiques dans les foyers Camerounais, par Yves Alexandre Chouala – Changing life worlds and contested space : Seclusion practices among the Iraqw of Northern Tanzania, par Jonathan Baker and Hege Wallevik – Lu et à lire/Review of publication – Compte rendu Violences urbaines au Sud du Sahara, par Sylvie Ayimpam – Appel à communications pour le Colloque international de l'APAD à Louvain et Louvain-la-Neuve en décembre 2007

BULLETIN N° 29/30- Juin 2009 - 10 € (adhérents) 15 € (non adhérents).

Entrepreneurs et entreprises en quête de normes/Entrepreneurs and Enterprises in Search of Norms

Éditorial : Séverin Abéga, Kalliopi Ango Ela et Marc-Eric Gruénais & Maud Saint-Lary – Hommage à Sévérin Cécile Abéga : la pédagogie par le vécu, par Noël Solange Ngo Yebga, Estelle Kouokam Magne & Odile Christiane Ossanga – Introduction : des entrepreneurs entre rhétorique et action sur le monde, par Maud Saint-Lary – L'Eglise Universelle du Royaume de Dieu du Cap-Vert : croissance urbaine, pauvreté et mouvement néo-pentecôtiste, par Pierre-Joseph Laurent, Claudio Furtado et Charlotte Plaideau – L'éducation comme entreprise : légitimations marchance, civique et culturelle de l'école bilingue au Burkina Faso, par Géraldine André – Le métier d'entrepreneur culturel au Burkina Faso : itinéraire et conditions de réussite d'un professionnel du spectacle vivant, par Sarah Andrieu – La malédiction, l'honneur et la spéculation : principes historiques de la propriété foncière en Afrique de l'Ouest, par Jacky Bouju – le « Centre commercial de Chinguetti », à Nouakchott (Mauritanie) : promotion féminine ou égards promotionnels ?, par Céline Lesourd – Les nouvelles figures de l'entrepreneuriat au Cameroun : les acteurs de la traite des enfants entre accumulation et déconstruction, par Claude Abé - Lu et à lire/Review of publication – Compte rendu Territoires, mondialisation et développement, par Sylvie Ayimpam